I0494391

Photographer's Guide to the Nikon Coolpix P500

Photographer's Guide to the Nikon Coolpix P500

Getting the Most from Nikon's Superzoom Digital Camera

Alexander S. White

White Knight Press
Henrico, Virginia

Copyright © 2011 by Alexander S. White. All rights reserved.
No part of this publication may be reproduced, stored in a
retrieval system or transmitted in any form or by any means,
electronic, mechanical, photocopying, recording or otherwise, without the prior written permission of the copyright
holder, except for brief quotations used in a review.

Published by
White Knight Press
9704 Old Club Trace
Henrico, Virginia 23238

ISBN: 978-0-9649875-7-9

Printed in the United States of America

This book is dedicated to my wife, Clenise.

Contents

Acknowledgments

For this entry in the "Photographer's Guide" series of books about advanced compact digital cameras, I chose the Nikon Coolpix P500 from a field of several strong candidates. Because this is my first book about a Nikon camera, I sought help in figuring out the unfamiliar aspects of this model from the contributors to the "Nikon Talk" forum at dpreview.com, a premier web site for discussions about digital photography. As has been the case for the earlier books, the response from forum members was very helpful. I am particularly grateful to Bernie DeBot, Rick Greenawalt, John Mentzer, Per Mortensen, and Achilles Zafiris for their assistance in scouring a draft of the book for errors or points that needed better discussion. Any remaining errors or problems are solely my responsibility.

Finally, as with my earlier books, the greatest support in every possible way, from joining me on trips to take photographs for this book to editing and proofreading the final text, has come from my wife, Clenise.

Introduction

This book is a guide to using the features and controls of the Nikon Coolpix P500 digital camera, a compact model that has most of the major capabilities shared by other cameras in its class, but that, at this writing at least, outshines just about all of them in one particular attribute—the extent of its zoom range. As a reader of this book, chances are you already are convinced that the P500 is one of the best choices available today for a compact digital camera that does not use interchangeable lenses. Cameras that can use different lenses, like DSLR (digital single-lens reflex) cameras, give you great quality, but at considerable expense, and with the bulk and complications that come with changing lenses on a camera body that is heavy enough even with no lens.

You could opt instead for a truly "compact" camera, like the Panasonic Lumix LX5, the Canon PowerShot S95, or the Nikon Coolpix P300, among others. Such cameras can fit in a pocket and offer a great variety of features, but, because of the need to keep their size to a minimum, their built-in lenses cannot offer the powerful image-magnifying performance of a DSLR's zoom (or non-zoom telephoto) lens.

The Coolpix P500 fits into a niche between the powerful DSLR and the pocketable compact. A camera in this class is often labeled a "bridge" camera—that is, a camera that has several of the attributes of a more robust DSLR model, but, because it is smaller and has a non-interchangeable lens, is considered a "bridge" between the bulky but highly capable DSLR and the more compact "point-and-shoot" type of camera. When you choose this sort of camera you are, of course, giving up the ability to slip it into a pocket or purse and forget about it until a photo opportunity arises, as you can with a true compact. On the positive side, though, you gain some attributes not shared by smaller models. For one thing, you get a camera with a solid construction that lets you get a good, firm grip, almost like holding a DSLR. You also are likely to get a strong array of features, such as continuous shooting, various scene modes, and options for things like setting ISO and white balance, and correcting difficult lighting situations. Perhaps most importantly, especially with the P500, you get a virtually unmatched range of focal lengths with the camera's "superzoom" lens, which offers an array of focal lengths all the way from the very wide 22.5mm to the amazing telephoto extent of 810mm.

Besides its superiority in zoom range, the P500 brings with it a full order of sophisticated features. The camera offers complete manual control of focus and exposure, several advanced modes of rapid continuous shooting, exposure bracketing, excellent low-light performance, and numerous special features, including a variety of ways to manipulate colors, a built-in HDR (High Dynamic Range) shooting mode, high-speed video shooting, and time-lapse photography. And, as would be expected of a modern camera in this class, the P500 provides HD (high-definition) video shooting. In addition, it has an electronic viewfinder, which provides a clear view of your image even in bright sunlight, when the LCD screen would be washed out by the glare. And speaking of the LCD screen, that display has very high resolution, with 920,000 pixels, providing fine detail when viewing your images. Moreover, the screen swivels to positions that allow you to take low-level shots near ground level and to hold the camera over your head to overcome crowds of people or other obstacles.

The P500 is not the perfect camera, of course; no camera can serve as the ideal tool for all situations. In this case, one drawback often cited is that the camera lacks an accessory shoe, which could be used to attach items such as an optical viewfinder or an external flash unit. (There are other ways to use external flash units with the P500, as discussed in Appendix A.) In addition, the camera does not offer the very useful RAW quality for its images, although it does provide a wide array of high-quality JPEG formats.

This discussion of the camera's features is, of course, not complete, but it serves to illustrate that this camera has a solid set of capabilities that should be attractive to serious amateur photographers—those who want a camera that gives them numerous options for creative control of their images and that is light enough to be carried around at all times, so they will have a substantial photographic apparatus with them when a good picture-taking opportunity pops up. The P500 should be of particular interest to those photographers who have an interest in capturing images of birds and other wildlife, in situations that call for the use of a powerful telephoto lens for long-distance shots.

My goal with this guide is to provide a thorough introduction to the camera's features, explaining how they work and when you might want to use them. The book is aimed largely at beginning and intermediate photographers who are not satisfied with the technical documentation that comes with the camera and who need a more user-friendly explanation of the camera's many controls and menus. For those who are seeking more advanced information, I provide some discussion of topics that go beyond the basics, and I include in the appendices information to help you uncover additional resources.

One note on the scope of this guide; I live in the United States, and I bought my camera in the U.S. market. I am not familiar with the variations for cameras sold in Europe, the United Kingdom, or elsewhere, such as different batteries or chargers.

The photographic functions are not different, though, so this guide should be useful to photographers in all locations, apart from that narrow range of issues. I have stated measurements of distance and weight in both the English and metric systems for the benefit of readers in various countries around the world.

All photographs in this book that illustrate the capabilities of the Coolpix P500 are ones that I took with that camera. The menu illustrations are screen captures taken from the P500 using the EyeTV 250 Plus video receiver and capture device by Elgato Systems. The photographs of the P500 and accessories used with it are ones that I took using a Sony DSLR-A850 camera with a Sony f/2.8 50mm macro lens.

Chapter 1: Preliminary Setup

Setting Up the Camera

I will assume your Nikon Coolpix P500 has just arrived at your home or office, perhaps purchased from an internet site or a retail store. The box should contain the camera itself, battery, battery terminal cover, battery charging adapter, neck strap, USB cable, audio-video cable, lens cap with cord for attaching it to the camera, software and user's manual on two CDs, and the brief "Quick Start Guide" instruction pamphlet. There should also be a warranty card and one or two other items, such as an advertising sheet or safety notice.

It is a very good idea to attach the neck strap to the camera right away, and in the same procedure to attach the lens cap to its cord. In this process, you loop the other end of the lens cap cord over the neck strap before it is attached to the camera. When you're finished, the lens cap should be tethered by its cord to the strap. The lens cap cord should be attached to the neck strap where it joins the camera, on the left side as you hold the camera.

Charging and Inserting the Battery

The Nikon battery for the Coolpix P500 is the EN-EL5. With this camera, the standard procedure is to charge the battery while it's inside the camera, by connecting the supplied AC adapter charger to the Nikon USB adapter or to the USB port on a computer or other device. There are pluses and minuses to this approach to battery-charging. On the positive side, you don't need an external charger and the camera can charge automatically when it's connected to your computer. The main drawbacks are that you cannot use the camera while the battery is charging, and you cannot charge another battery outside the camera. The solution to this situation is to purchase extra batteries and a device that will charge those batteries outside the camera. I'll discuss batteries and other accessories in Appendix A.

For now, let's get the battery charged by inserting it into the camera and connecting the charger. You first need to open the battery compartment door on the bottom of the camera and put in the battery. You can only insert it fully into the camera one way; look for the set of three goldish-colored metal contact strips on the battery, then look for the corresponding set of three contacts inside the battery compartment, and insert the battery so the two sets of contacts will meet up.

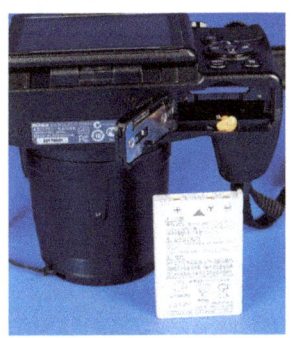 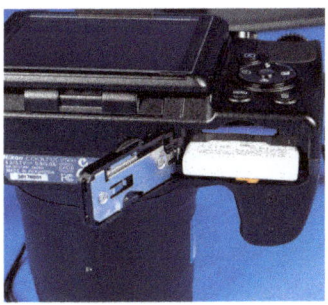

If the battery will not go all the way down into the compartment, don't force it; reverse its orientation and insert it the other way. You may have to push the small orange plastic retaining clip to one side to allow the battery to slip all the way into its slot; the clip will then fasten the battery in place.

With the battery inserted into the camera, plug the small end of the USB cable into the small USB port under the door marked HDMI on the left side of the camera, and plug the other end of the USB cable into the AC adapter that ships with the camera.

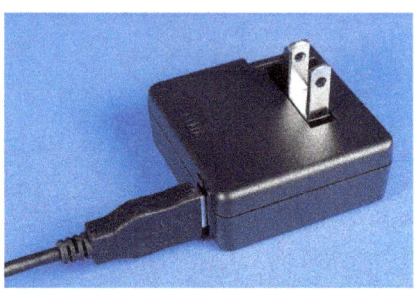

Then plug that AC adapter into a standard electrical outlet or surge protector. The orange light on the camera's on-off switch will blink slowly to indicate that the battery is charging. When the light goes off, the battery is fully charged and ready to use. It can take almost five hours to charge a fully depleted battery. (This length of time is another factor that makes it practically a necessity to obtain other batteries and an external charger, as discussed in Appendix A.)

You can also charge the battery in the camera by connecting the USB cable to a compatible USB port on a computer, if that option is selected in the camera's menu system. I'll discuss that process in Chapter 7.

Inserting the Memory Card

The Coolpix P500 does not ship with any memory card included. With this camera, unlike some others, this is not a fatal omission, because the camera has some built-in memory that will let you take a few photographs even with no memory card inserted. The amount of built-in memory is not great—102 megabytes (MB)—which is pretty minuscule compared to the capacity of modern storage cards that can hold up to 128 gigabytes (GB), more than a thousand times more. But if you're in a situation where you need to take a picture and don't have an available card, 102 MB might be enough. The internal memory can hold about 17 still photos at the largest size of 4000 x 3000 pixels at Fine quality, and 940 photos at the lowest quality of 640 x 480 pixels, with proportional figures for intermediate levels of image size and quality. (You can't save any video to the internal memory, though—only still photos.)

If you have no card inserted in the camera, the letters IN will display in the lower right corner of the display, indicating that internal memory is being used, next to the number of remaining images.

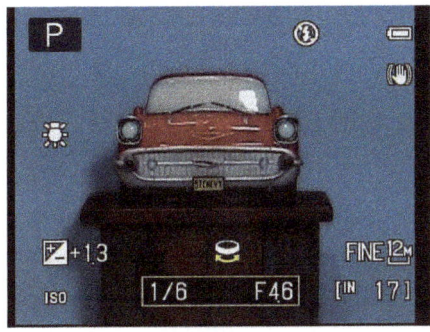

If a card is inserted, the letters IN are not displayed; only the number of remaining images is shown inside the brackets. If you fill up the internal memory, you will be greeted with the message Out of Memory on the camera's display, and your shooting will come to a halt unless you delete some images from the internal memory or insert an SD card that has some free space on it.

Because of its limited capacity, you don't want to rely on the built-in memory if you don't have to, so you need to insert a separate memory card. The P500 uses SD cards, which are quite small, about the size of a large postage stamp. They come in several varieties. The standard card, called simply SD, comes in capacities from 8 MB to 2 GB. The next higher-capacity card, SDHC, comes in sizes from 4 GB to 32 GB. The newest, and highest-capacity card, SDXC (for extended capacity) comes in sizes of 48 GB, 64 GB, and up; this version of the card can have a capacity up to 2 terabytes (TB), theoretically, and SDXC cards have faster transfer speeds than the smaller-capacity cards. Note that the P500 cannot use another type of memory card called a MultiMediaCard (MMC), even though those cards are the same size as SD cards.

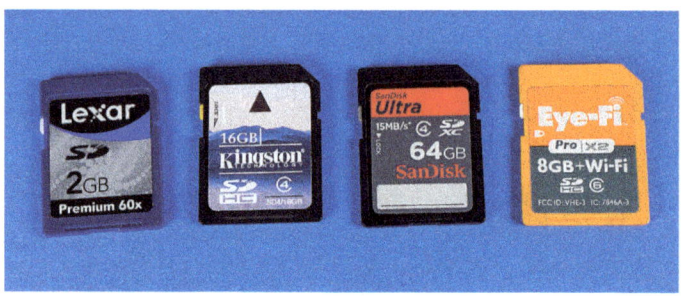

What card and size should you use? It depends on your needs and intentions. If you're planning to record a good deal of high-definition (HD) video or large numbers of high-resolution still photos, you should get the biggest card you can afford. There are several variables to take into account in computing how many images or videos you can store on a particular size of card, such as which aspect ratio you're using (16:9, 4:3, 3:2, or 1:1), picture size, and quality. To cut through the complications, here are a few samples of what can be stored on a 4 GB SDHC card: At the largest size of 4000 x 3000 pixels and with Fine quality, a 4 GB card can hold 650 still photos; at the next-lower size of 3264 x 2448 pixels and with Normal quality, the same card can hold 1,910 images.

If you're interested in video, here are some guidelines. You can fit about 35 minutes of the highest-quality 1080p high-definition (HD) video on a 4 GB card. The same size card will hold about 55 minutes of lesser-quality HD 720p video or about 2 hours and 30 minutes of video at the lowest quality, VGA, or 640 X 480 pixels. In any of these formats, though, you can record only about 29 minutes of video in any one scene.

One other consideration is the speed of the card. If you plan to record video, you should get a card that is rated as Class 6 or higher for its speed.

Finally, you need to realize if you have an older computer with a built-in card reader, or just an older external card reader, there is a chance it will not read the newer SDHC cards. In that case, you would have to either get a new reader that is compatible with SDHC cards, or download images from the camera to your computer using the USB cable.

Using the newest variety of card, SDXC, can be even more problematic; at this writing there are compatibility issues with some cards and some computers. For example, I tried to use a Lexar 64 GB SDXC card in my Coolpix P500, and the camera displayed the message, "This card cannot be used." No amount of formatting the card, even with a special program downloaded from sdcard.org, improved the situation. Upgrading the camera's firmware to version 1.1 did not help, either. (See Chapter 7 for a discussion of upgrading the firmware.) A check of Nikon's list of approved cards at page 214 of the Nikon user's manual shows that the Lexar SDXC cards are not approved; those on the approved list are cards by SanDisk, Toshiba, and Panasonic. When I tried a SanDisk Ultra 64 GB SDXC card (shown on the previous page), it worked fine.

In addition to compatibility problems with some brands of SDXC card, some computers with older operating systems cannot read any SDXC cards, even if you obtain a new card reader that can read the cards. However, over the past year or two, the situation with SDXC cards has improved. If you are using a computer with a relatively new version of the operating system, it will be able to read SDXC cards, provided you are using a compatible card reader (and one of the approved brands of card). Specifically, the cards can be read by Windows 7; by Windows Vista with Service Pack 1 or 2; and by

Windows XP with a software patch for reading the exFAT file system. That patch is available at http://www.microsoft.com/downloads. For Macintosh computers, you need to have Max OS X version 10.6.6 or later; otherwise, you need a patch such as one I found at www.sonnettech.com, which allowed my MacBook Pro to read SDXC cards through a compatible card reader before the operating system was updated.

As I write this, SDXC cards are quite expensive, though prices are dropping. You may want to wait until the prices come down some more, unless you absolutely need the 48 GB, 64 GB, or greater storage capacity, and can deal with the compatibility issues.

Finally, if you will have access to a wireless (Wi-Fi) network where you use your camera, you may want to consider getting an Eye-Fi card. This special type of storage device looks very much like an ordinary SDHC card, but it includes a tiny transmitter that lets it connect to a wireless network and send your images to your computer over that network as soon as the images have been recorded by the camera.

I have tested an 8 GB Eye-Fi card, the Pro X2 model, with the P500, and it works well. Within a few seconds after I snap a picture with this card installed in the camera, a little thumbnail image appears in the upper right corner of my computer's screen showing the progress of the upload. When all images are uploaded, they are available in the Pictures/Eye-Fi folder on my computer. The Pro X2 model can handle RAW files and video files as well as the smaller JPEG files. At this writing, the Pro X2 is the only variety of Eye-Fi card that can handle RAW files. Of course, this capability does not matter with the P500, which does not use the RAW format, but you may want to use your Eye-Fi card with other cameras that do shoot in RAW someday, and the Pro X2 card will serve you well in both cases. An Eye-Fi card is not a necessity, but I enjoy the convenience of having my images sent straight to my computer without having to put the card into a card reader or to connect the camera to the computer with a USB cable.

In summary, you have quite a few options for choosing a memory card. Personally, I like to use a high-speed 16 GB or 32 GB SDHC card, just to have extra capacity and speed in case they are needed. I like the convenience of the Eye-Fi card also, but, unless you do a lot of photography within range of a wireless network so the images can be uploaded quickly, it may not be worth your while to get that type of card.

Once you have selected your card, open the same little door on the bottom of the camera that covers the battery compartment, and slide the card into the card slot until it catches, with the label facing the back of the camera. To remove the card, you push down on it until it releases and springs up so you can grab it. Once the card has been pushed down until it catches, close the compartment door and push the latch back to the locking position.

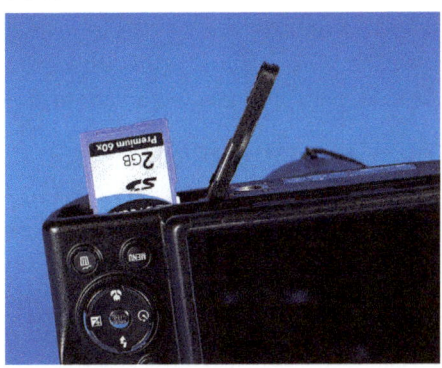

One note for when you're shooting continuous pictures with the P500: When the camera is writing its image data to the memory card, the indicator showing the number of remaining images, in the lower right of the display, blinks. When that indicator is blinking, it's important not to turn off the camera or otherwise interrupt its functioning, such as by taking out the battery or disconnecting an AC power adapter. You need to let the card complete its recording process in peace.

Setting the Language, Date, and Time

You need to make sure the date and time are set correctly before you start taking pictures, because the camera records that information (sometimes known as "metadata," meaning data beyond the information in the picture itself) invisibly with each image, and displays it later if you want. Someday you may be very glad to have the date (and even the time of day) correctly recorded with your archives of digital images. If you purchase the camera brand new, it will prompt you to set the date and time when you first power it on.

If you later need to set the time and date, here is the process to follow. Remove the lens cap and press down on the camera's power switch, marked On/Off, on top of the camera, to turn the camera on. Then press the Menu button at the lower right of the camera's back. Press the left side of the large round control pad on the back of the camera, known as the multi selector. That spot is marked with a clock (timer) icon. When you press on that spot, the yellow selection block will move to the far left of the screen, to the list of icons, with P at the top.

Then use the bottom of the multi selector, marked with a flower (tulip), to move the selection block down to highlight the wrench icon that represents the Setup menu. Press the right side of the multi selector, marked with a plus and minus sign, to move the highlight back to the right, where it becomes a yellow rectangle highlighting a menu item. Then use the up and down parts of the multi selector to move the yellow selection bar to the Time Zone and Date line on the menu, and press the center button in the multi selector, marked OK, to activate the date and time settings. Move left and right through the date, year, and time settings, and change the settings with up and down movements of the cursor. When everything is set correctly, press the center OK button to confirm and press the Menu button to exit the menu system.

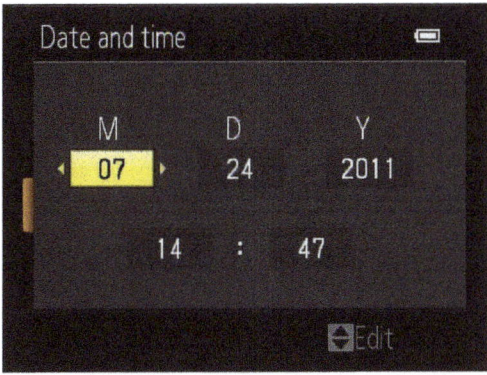

If you need to change the language that the camera uses for the menus and other messages, navigate on the Setup menu to the line that says Language, and press the OK button or the right cursor button (right edge of multi selector) to select the Language menu item. Then navigate with the up and down cursor buttons (the top and bottom edges of the multi selector) to the language of your choice, and press the OK button to select it. Then press the Menu button to exit from the menu system.

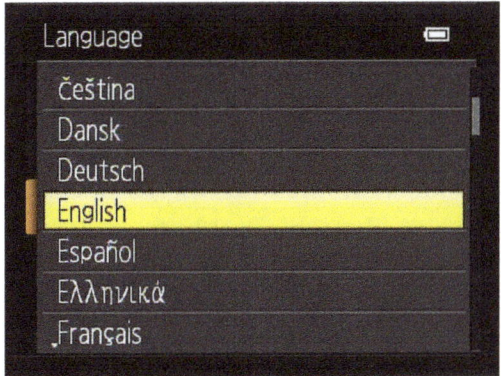

Chapter 2: Basic Operations

Taking Pictures

Now that the Coolpix P500 has the correct time and date set and has a fully charged battery inserted along with a memory card, let's explore some scenarios for basic picture-taking. For now, I won't get into discussions of what the various options are and why you might choose one over another. I'll just lay out a reasonable set of steps that will get you and your camera into action and will deposit a decent image on your memory card.

Fully Automatic—Auto Mode

Here's the drill if you want to set the camera to its most automatic mode and let it make (almost) all of the decisions for you. This is a good way to go if you're in a hurry and need to grab a quick shot without fiddling with settings, or if you're new at this and would rather let the camera do its magic without having to provide much input.

1. Remove the lens cap from the lens and let it dangle by its cord. (It's important to do this first; if you don't, and turn the camera on with the lens cap in place, you will see an error message and will have to turn the camera off and on again before proceeding further.)

2. Turn on the power by pressing the On/Off button. The LCD screen will illuminate to show that the camera has turned on.

3. Find the mode dial on top of the camera to the right of the viewfinder, and turn the dial until the green camera icon is next to the small white indicator line. The camera is now set to Auto shooting mode.

4. Press the Menu button at the bottom of the control area on the back of the camera. Use the direction buttons to navigate to the entry for Image Quality, select that line with the OK button or the right direction button, highlight the Fine setting, and press OK. Then navigate down to the Image Size setting, select it, and choose 4000 x 3000 pixels. (Of course, you can choose other settings for both of these options if you wish, but the ones I have mentioned provide the highest quality.)

5. If you want to compose your image on the LCD screen on the back of the camera, no action should be needed. If you want to use the electronic viewfinder instead, find the small button to the left of the viewfinder with an icon that looks like a TV screen between two vertical lines. Press that button, and the display will switch to the viewfinder, blacking out the LCD. You can then look inside the viewfinder to compose the shot and view the camera's settings. You can adjust the view for your eyesight by turning the diopter adjustment dial on the left side of the viewfinder's housing. Toggle between the LCD and the viewfinder whenever you want, using the viewfinder selection button.

6. If you are indoors or otherwise in conditions that might call for the use of flash, press the button on the left side of the camera's built-in flash unit, marked with a lightning bolt, to pop up the flash.

7. If you have popped up the flash, press the up direction button on the large round control pad, marked with a light-

ning bolt, to bring up the Flash menu. Make sure the Auto setting, at the top of this menu, is highlighted. (Later, in Chapter 9, I'll discuss the other flash options.)

8. Aim the camera toward the subject and look at the LCD screen (or into the viewfinder window, depending on your choice in Step 5) to compose the image as you want it. Locate the zoom lever on the ring that surrounds the shutter button on the top right at the front of the camera. Push that lever to the left, moving its indicator toward the letter W, to get a wider-angle shot (including more of the scene in the picture), or to the right, moving the indicator toward the letter T, to get a telephoto, zoomed-in shot. Or, if you prefer, use the equivalent zoom switch on the left side of the lens, and move it up for telephoto or down for wide-angle.

9. Once the picture is composed as you want it, push the shutter button halfway down. You should hear a little beep and see the brackets in the center of the image turn green, indicating that the picture will be in focus. If the brackets turn red, that means the camera is having difficulty achieving focus. In that case, try moving the camera to a different angle before pressing the shutter button halfway down again.

10. Push the shutter button all the way down to take the picture.

Basic Variations from Fully Automatic

At this point I won't go into a discussion of all of the various still-picture shooting modes, except to name them. Besides Auto, which I just discussed, there are Program, Shutter Priority, Aperture Priority, Manual, User Setting, Scene, Night Landscape, Night Portrait, Backlighting, and Smart Portrait. I'll discuss all of those shooting modes in Chapter 3, and motion-picture shooting in Chapter 8. For now, I'm going to discuss the various functions and features of the Coolpix P500 that you can adjust to suit whatever picture-taking situation you may be faced with. Not all of the settings can be adjusted in Auto mode, so we'll set the camera down to a lower level of automation, to Program mode. In that mode, you'll be able to control most of the camera's functions for taking still pictures.

I'm not going to repeat the preliminary steps for taking a picture, because those are pretty basic. If you need a refresher on those items, see the list in the above discussion of Auto mode.

We'll start by setting the mode dial on top of the camera to P, for Program.

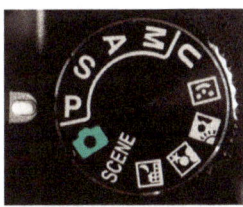

You will immediately see some different indications on the LCD screen, to show that some of the Auto mode settings have changed. More dramatically, if you press the Menu button you will see that a great many more options are now available for you to set on the Shooting menu—instead of the two menu lines available in Auto mode, you are presented with two full screens containing 14 settings that you can adjust, including, white balance, ISO, metering mode, exposure bracketing, and others. In the Program shooting mode, the camera will determine the proper exposure, both the aperture (size of opening to let in light) and the shutter speed (how long the shutter is open to let in light). In this mode you won't be making any decisions about those settings; you can have more control over your settings in other modes, which we'll discuss later. That still leaves lots of decisions you can make, though, so let's talk about the various settings you can adjust in Program mode.

Focus

Now that the camera is no longer set to Auto mode, you have more control over focus. Your first choice is between manual focus and autofocus. In other words, you now have the option of setting the camera to the MF setting, for manual focus, which is not available in Auto mode. You also have the ability to select which of several types of autofocus operation you want the camera to use, if you opt for autofocus instead.

I'll discuss the various autofocus modes in Chapter 4 in some detail. For now, let's just make sure a standard autofocus mode is selected. First, press the down direction button on the multi selector (marked by a flower icon). This action puts a block with four options on the display. From top to bottom, they are the letters AF, for normal autofocus; the flower icon, for macro (close-up) focus; a mountain icon, for focus on infinity; and the letters MF, for manual focus.

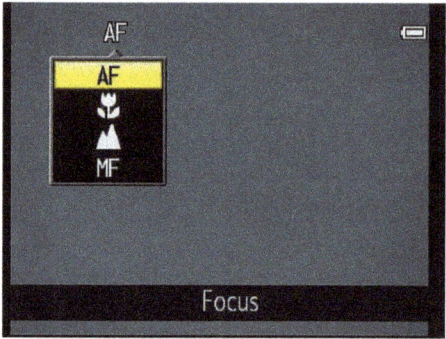

For now, use the direction buttons to select the top icon, for normal autofocus. (You have to be quick; the four choices disappear within a few seconds.) Press the OK button to select and confirm your choice. The letters or icon for your choice will appear at the upper left of the display, unless the choice is AF; those letters will appear for a few seconds and then disappear, because that is the default setting.

There are several other focus-related options you can set, but for now, let's just use one of them. Press the Menu button at the lower right of the camera's back, then press the left direction button to highlight the P icon at the top of the left column. That icon represents the shooting menu. Move the selection block back into the list of menu items using the right direction button, and scroll with the up and down direction buttons until the yellow selection rectangle highlights the line for AF Area Mode, at the top of the second screen of the menu. Press OK to select that item, then use the up and down direction buttons to change the value for this item to Center, which means the autofocus system will place a focus frame in the center of the screen and will focus on that area. Press OK to confirm, and press the Menu button again to exit the menu system.

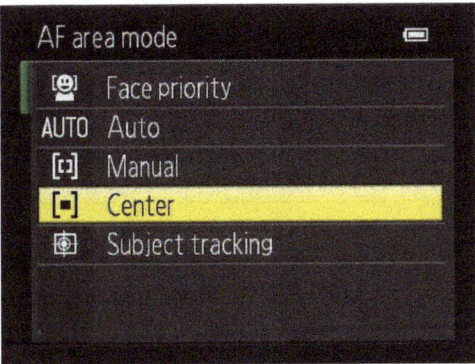

Now, when you aim the camera at a subject, center the most important subject between the white focus brackets. Press the shutter button halfway down so the camera will evaluate the exposure and the focus. You should hear a beep and the focus brackets should turn green to confirm the focus. If everything looks okay to you, go ahead and press the shutter button all the way down to take the picture.

Suppose you want to take a picture in which your main subject is not in the center of the screen. Maybe your shot is set up so that a person is standing off to the right of center, and there is some attractive scenery to the left in the scene. Place the focus frame over the part of the picture that needs to be in focus; in our example, the person to the right. Then press the shutter button halfway down until the camera focuses and beeps. Keep the button pressed halfway to lock in the focus (and exposure) while you move the camera back to create your desired composition, with the person off to the right. Then take the picture, and the area you originally focused on will be in focus.

There is another way to handle this sort of situation, by setting AF Area Mode to Manual, a feature that lets you move the focus area around the display so it covers an off-center subject; I'll discuss that option in Chapter 4.

Manual Focus

There are other autofocus modes, but I won't discuss those at this point. Let's talk instead about manual focus, the other major option for focusing. Why would you want to use manual focus when the camera will focus for you automatically? Many experienced photographers like the amount of control that comes from being able to set the focus exactly how they want it. And, in some situations, such as focusing in dark areas or areas behind glass, taking extreme close-ups, or cases where there are objects at various distances from the camera, it may be useful for you to be able to control exactly where the point of sharpest focus lies.

For example, when I first got my P500, I went into the back yard to experiment with using the superzoom lens to capture images of birds in our small fountain. It was a cloudy day, and the autofocus mechanism was having problems settling on a sharp focus. I finally decided to switch to manual focus, and the results improved. Of course, manual focus was useful on that occasion partly because I was sitting in one place, the birds tended to stay in one place to take a bath, and the fountain wasn't going anywhere; with a moving subject, manual focus is not going to be as useful.

To activate manual focus, press the down direction button, with the flower icon; on the menu that pops up on the display, navigate to and select the MF icon. At that point, all you need to do to adjust the focus is to press the up and down direction buttons.

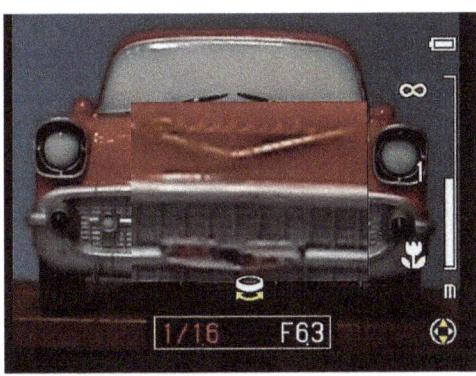

Press the up button to focus farther from the camera, and press the down button to bring the focus closer. As you move the focus point, you will see a white bar go up and down inside a scale on the right side of the display, indicating the approximate focusing distance. You also will see an enlarged area in the center of the screen, to help you focus on details in the subject. Continue adjusting until the focus is as sharp as you can get it, and then take the picture.

Exposure

Next, we'll consider some possibilities for controlling exposure, beyond just letting the camera make the decisions. The Coolpix P500's Auto mode is very good at choosing the right exposure, and so is the Program mode. But there are going to be some situations in which you want to override the camera's automation.

Exposure Compensation

First, let's take a look at the control for adjusting exposure to account for an unusual, or non-optimal, lighting situation.

Suppose you want to take a picture showing the details in the bark of a large tree with the camera set for Program mode. Let's suppose further that it's a bright, sunny day, but that the bark of the tree, naturally enough, is in fairly deep shade from the branches and leaves of the tree. The camera will do a good job of averaging the amount of light coming into the lens, and will expose the picture accordingly. The problem is, the bright scenery beyond the tree will likely "fool" the camera into closing down the aperture, because the overall picture will seem quite bright. But your subject, the bark of the tree, will seem too dark in the picture, because the camera will take into account the very bright light beyond the tree.

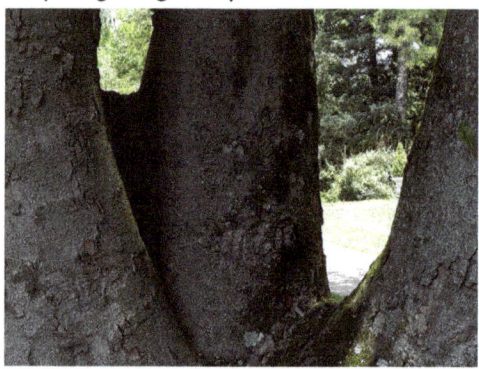

One solution here, which the Coolpix P500 makes very easy to carry out, is the exposure compensation control. Look closely at the right direction button on the multi selector. That button is labeled with a little plus and minus sign, with the plus on a black background and the minus on white. This control activates the exposure compensation system, which will override the automatic exposure as much as you tell it to, within limits.

Select Program mode and aim at your subject. Press the right button, and a vertical scale will appear up on the left side of the display, with a plus sign at the top and a minus sign at the bottom. (If the camera is in manual focus mode, you have to press the OK button first, before you can use the right direction button; otherwise, that button will adjust the focus position.)

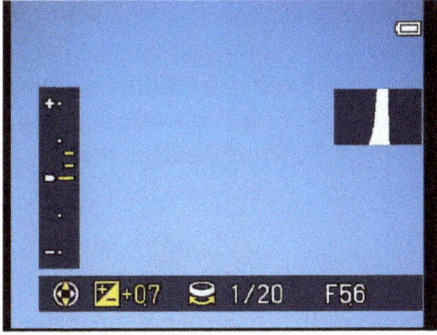

Once the exposure compensation scale has appeared (as shown above on a plain screen), press the up and down direction buttons on the multi selector to move the values higher and lower, as indicated by yellow tick marks that appear on the scale to show the value that is being set. If you use the buttons to extend the yellow marks all the way to the bottom of the scale, the picture will be considerably darker than the automatic exposure would produce. If you move the yellow tick marks to the top, the picture will be noticeably brighter. The camera's screen brightens and darkens to show you how the exposure is changing, before you take the picture. The camera also displays a histogram—a chart showing peaks and valleys of brightness values—on the right side of the screen. In this case, you would adjust the exposure to be brighter, so the camera will expose the bark of the tree properly, and let the background be washed out in brightness.

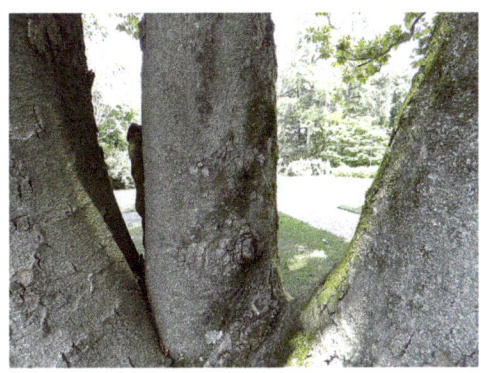

37

I'll discuss the meaning of the histogram in more detail in Chapter 6. For now, you should know that brighter values in your image skew the chart to the right, and darker ones skew it to the left. As you adjust exposure compensation, you should generally try to keep the white peaks of the chart in the center of the histogram.

After taking the picture, you should reset the exposure compensation back to zero, in the middle of the scale, so you don't unintentionally affect the pictures you take later. You need to be careful about this, because the camera will retain any exposure compensation value you set, even when it's turned off and then on again.

There is one aspect of setting exposure compensation that can be a bit tricky, so here is some further explanation. When you first press the exposure compensation button and the scale appears on the left of the display, you will also see on the display a small circular icon that represents the multi selector. (See the image at the top of the previous page.) That icon contains four small triangles, standing for the four buttons on the multi selector. Once exposure compensation has been activated, this icon appears next to an exposure compensation icon with a plus and minus sign. The top and bottom triangles on the circular icon appear in yellow, indicating that pressing the up and down buttons on the multi selector will adjust exposure compensation. Even after the exposure compensation scale disappears from the display, these icons remain, meaning that all you have to do is press the up or down button to adjust exposure compensation again.

To the right of these two icons you will see an icon looking like a dial with a two-headed arrow beneath it, next to the shutter speed value (such as 1/100 second). That icon and arrow mean that you can adjust the shutter speed by turning the command dial—the ridged dial on the back of the camera, just below the on/off switch. In other words, look for the icons with yellow markings; the yellow markings indicate what settings can be made using the controls indicated by the yellow icons.

Flash

Later on, I'll discuss several other topics dealing with exposure, such as Manual, Aperture Priority and Shutter Priority modes, exposure bracketing, and others. For now I'm going to discuss the basics of using the Coolpix P500's built-in flash unit, because that is something you may need to do on a regular basis. In Chapter 9 I'll discuss other options for using the flash, such as controlling its output and preventing "red-eye," and, in Appendix A, I'll discuss using other flash units.

The built-in flash on the P500 is not especially powerful, but it can provide enough illumination to let you take pictures in dark areas and to brighten up areas that would otherwise be lost in shadows, even outdoors on a sunny day. Here is one fundamental point that you need to be aware of: The built-in flash will not pop up by itself. If you are in a situation in which you think flash may be needed or desirable, you need to take the first step of popping up the flash unit. To do so, find the small, round button on the left side of the flash unit, marked by a lightning bolt. Press in on this button, and the flash springs up into place. (Later, when you're done with the flash, just push down on the unit until it catches again.)

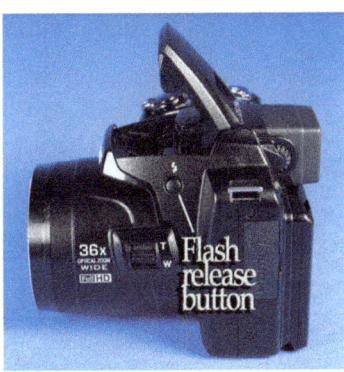

Even though you have popped up the flash unit, in some shooting situations it will never fire. In the situations in which you're likely to want it to, though, it will be ready and willing to illuminate your subject as well as it can.

Let's explore a common scenario to see how the flash works. Make sure the camera is turned on and the flash unit has been popped up by pressing the round flash release button. Now turn the mode dial on top of the camera to select the Night Landscape shooting mode, represented by the white icon just below the Scene mode icon.

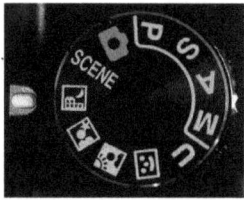

Go ahead and press the up direction (Flash mode) button, with the lightning bolt icon on it. Nothing will happen. You will see the universal negative symbol—a circle with a line through it—over a lightning bolt, indicating that the flash is turned off. (If you don't see this symbol, press the Display button to switch to the more detailed shooting screen.) In this situation, because you have chosen a shooting mode that will not use flash under any circumstances, you cannot turn the flash on.

Next, with the flash unit still popped up, try setting the mode dial to P, for Program mode, and then press the Flash button on the multi selector. You will see a menu on the screen with six options available: Auto, Auto with Red-eye Reduction, Off, Fill Flash, Slow Sync, and Rear-curtain Sync. You can move through this list by pressing the up and down buttons or by turning the command dial. Later on, in Chapter 9, I'll talk more about the various flash options, such as Slow Sync, and how they work. For now, you know how to choose them, and you know that they will not all be available at all times.

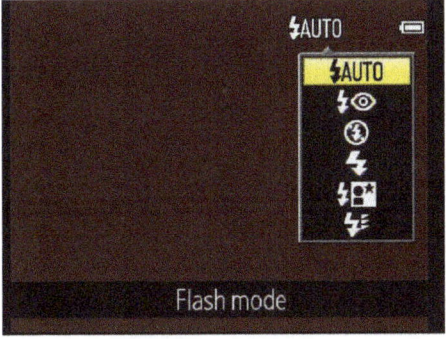

Motion Picture Recording

Let's take a look at recording a short video sequence with the Coolpix P500. In Chapter 8, I'll discuss other options for video recording, but for now, let's stick to the basics. First, make sure the flash unit is pressed down in the off position, because it will be of no use. Then, once the camera is turned on, locate the small Movie mode switch, surrounding the red Movie button at the top right of the camera's back, just below the mode dial. Turn that switch so its little white indicator points to the letters HD, for high definition. (The other choice, HS, is for high speed video, which I'll discuss in Chapter 8.)

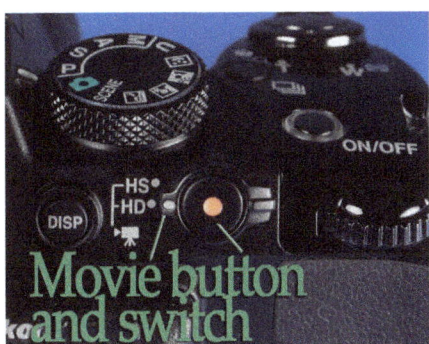

That is really all the preparation you need at this point. Now compose the shot the way you want it, and when you're ready, press the red Movie button once. You don't need to hold the button down; just press and release. The camera's display will

41

blank out briefly, then will show a flashing red REC indicator, and the camera will keep recording until it reaches a recording limit, or until you press the red button again to stop the recording. Don't be concerned about the level of the sound that is being recorded, because you have no control over the audio volume while recording.

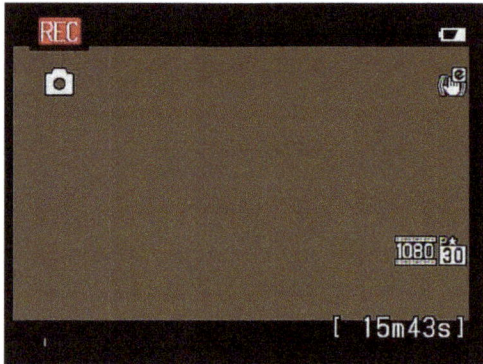

The camera will automatically adjust the exposure as lighting conditions change.

One other point that's not specific to the Coolpix P500: Unless you have a good reason to do otherwise, try to hold the camera as steady as possible (use a tripod if possible), and don't zoom unnecessarily or move the camera except in very smooth, slow motions, such as a pan (side-to-side motion) to take in a wide scene gradually. Video from a jerkily moving camera can be very disconcerting to the viewer.

Viewing Pictures

Before I delve into more advanced settings for taking still pictures and movies, as well as other matters of interest, I need to discuss the basics of viewing your images in the camera.

Review While in Shooting Mode

First, every time you take a still picture, the recorded image will show up on the screen for a brief amount of time, if you have the Setup menu's Monitor Settings option set to turn on the Image Review function. I'll discuss the details of that setting in Chapter 7. By default, your image will stay on the screen for about two seconds after you take a new picture.

Reviewing Images in Playback Mode

If you are reviewing images that were taken previously, you enter Playback mode by pressing the Playback button, marked with a small triangle, to the right side of the LCD screen. You can then scroll through the recorded images using the left and right or up and down direction buttons on the multi selector or by turning the command dial. You can enlarge any image using the zoom lever on top of the camera, and you can scroll around in the enlarged image using the direction buttons. If you have used the continuous-shooting features of the camera, you may see some images labeled with an OK followed by a colon and a triangle at the bottom center.

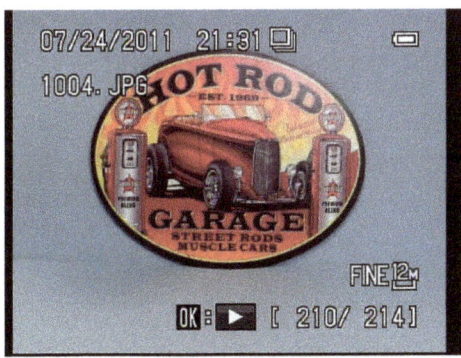

In those cases, you can press the center OK button to "open" a series of continuous shots, and then use the direction buttons to move among the various individual shots in that series. To exit back to the main viewing screen so you can see other images and series of images, press the up direction button. (I'll discuss playback options in more detail in Chapter 6.)

Playing Movies

To play back motion pictures, move through the recorded images by the methods described above until you find an image for which there is a movie options icon at the right of the screen, showing a movie format such as 1080p.

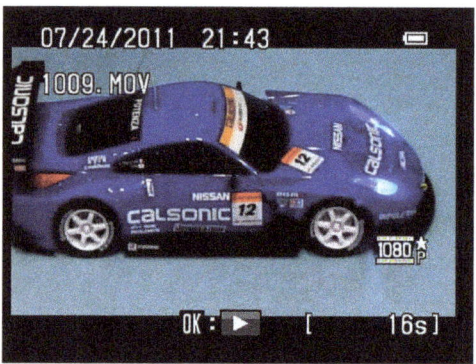

While the still frame from the motion picture is displayed on the screen, press the OK button (the button in the center of the multi selector) and the movie will start playing on the LCD, or in the electronic viewfinder if that display option is active instead of the LCD.

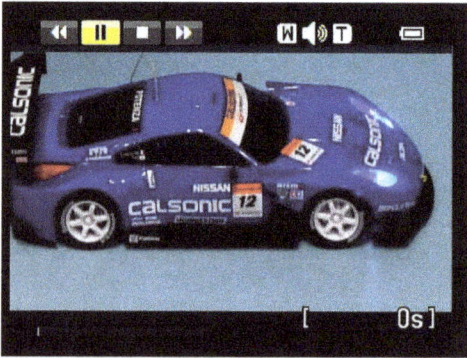

At the top of the display there will be a menu of VCR-like controls. Scroll through the line of controls using the direction buttons on the multi selector, and press the OK button to activate one. You also can turn the command dial to the right to fast-forward or to the left to rewind. You can raise or lower the volume of the audio by turning the zoom lever (surrounding the shutter button) towards the T position (louder) or the W position (softer). You will see a little set of volume "waves" increase or decrease next to a speaker icon at the top of the screen when you adjust the sound in this way.

If you want to play the movies on a computer or edit them with video-editing software, they will import nicely into software such as iMovie for the Macintosh, or any other program for Mac or Windows that can deal with video files with the extension .mov. This is the extension for Apple Computer's QuickTime video playback software; QuickTime itself can be downloaded from Apple's web site. For some Windows-based video editing software, you may need to convert the P500's movie files to the .avi format before importing them into the software. You can do so with a program such as mp4cam2avi, which is easily found through an internet search.

I will discuss more of your options for playing movies and editing them in the camera in Chapter 8.

Chapter 3: The Shooting Modes

U p until now I have discussed the basics of how to set up the camera for quick shots, relying heavily on features such as Auto mode, for taking pictures whose settings are controlled mostly by the camera's automation. As with others of the more sophisticated digital cameras, though, with the Coolpix P500 there is a large and potentially bewildering range of options available for setting the camera, particularly for recording still images. One of the main goals of this book is to remove the "bewildering" factor from the camera's aura while extracting the essential usefulness from the broad range of features available. To do this, we need to turn our attention to two subjects; shooting modes and the Shooting menu options. First, I'll discuss the shooting modes.

Whenever you set out to record still images, you need to select one of the available shooting modes: Auto, Program, Shutter Priority, Aperture Priority, Manual, User Setting, Smart Portrait, Backlighting, Night Portrait, Night Landscape, or Scene. (The only other shooting mode available is for movies.) So far, we have worked with the Auto and Program modes. Now we will look at the others, after some review of the first two.

Auto Mode

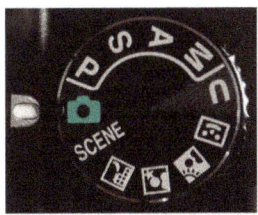

I've already talked about the Auto shooting mode. This is the one you'll want if you just need to have the camera ready for a quick shot, maybe in an environment with fast-paced events when you won't have much time to fuss with settings.

To set this mode, turn the mode dial, on top of the camera to the right of the viewfinder, to the green camera icon. When you select this mode, the camera makes quite a few decisions for you and limits your options in several ways. For example, you can't set ISO or white balance to any value other than Auto, and you can't choose the metering method, use exposure bracketing, or select an autofocus mode. In addition, you will find that the button on top of the camera for selecting continuous shooting is inactive; you can press it all you want but nothing will happen.

There are still a few settings you can make, however. For instance, you can choose any of the options for Image Size and Image Quality, you can use exposure compensation, and you can select any of the six available modes for the built-in flash (if you have raised the flash unit). You also can select macro (close-up) focus or infinity focus (but not manual focus), and you can use the self-timer.

Program Mode

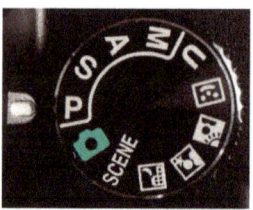

Choose this option by turning the mode dial to the P slot. The Program shooting mode lets you control many of the settings available with the camera, apart from shutter speed and aperture. However, even though you can't directly set those two values, you still can override the camera's automatic exposure to a fair extent by using exposure compensation, the Flexible Program feature, and exposure bracketing.

I discussed exposure compensation in Chapter 2, and I'll explain exposure bracketing in Chapter 4. Flexible Program is the name Nikon uses for what is often called "Program Shift" for other cameras. This option lets you adjust the values the camera selects in Program mode for shutter speed and aperture. For example, if the camera selects, say, 1/80 second at f/3.4, the Flexible Program feature will find equivalent combinations that result in the same exposure, such as 1/60 second at f/3.5, 1/50 second at f/4.0, or 1/40 second at 4.5. To use this feature, when the camera is in Program mode, aim at your subject and just turn the command dial to find an equivalent pair of shutter speed and aperture.

When the camera is using one of these equivalent match-ups of settings rather than the originally chosen setting, it displays an icon to the lower right of the P that signifies Program mode in the upper left of the display. That icon, which represents Flexible Program, looks like an X with a vertical line down through its center.

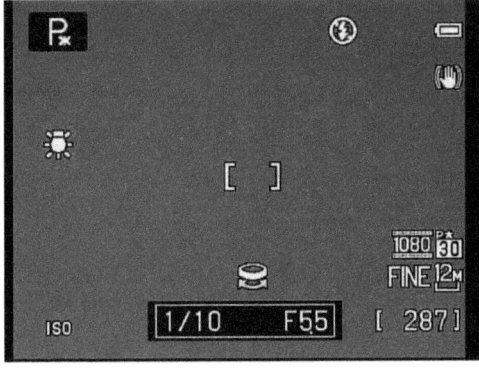

Why would you use the Flexible Program option? Does it make sense to let the camera make its best calculation of the proper exposure and then override it? Well, yes, it may, in some cases. For example, you may want to see what the "proper" exposure is, and then see if you can use a wider aperture to achieve a blurred background, or a faster shutter speed to stop the action or prevent blur from camera motion. And, when you're experimenting with the camera to see what it is capable of, it can be very helpful to try various combinations of aperture and shutter speed to find out which combination gives you the best results in different situations. With a digital camera, there's no added cost for trying these different approaches, and Flexible Program is a useful way to experiment.

One way to look at Program mode is that it greatly expands the choices available through the Shooting menu. You will be able to make choices involving image size and quality, white balance, ISO sensitivity, metering method, autofocus mode, tand others. I won't discuss all of those choices here; if you want to explore that topic, go to the discussion of the Shooting menu in Chapter 4 and check out all of the different selections that are available to you.

Shutter Priority Mode

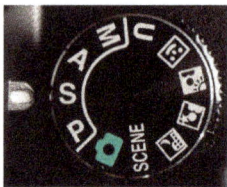

In Shutter Priority mode, you choose whatever shutter speed you want, and the camera will set the corresponding aperture in order to achieve a proper exposure of the image. In this mode, you can set the shutter to be open for a variety of intervals ranging from 2 full seconds to 1/1500 of a second. (If the ISO is set to 3200, the slowest shutter speed available is ½ second.) If you are photographing fast action, such as a baseball swing or a hurdles event at a track meet, and you want to stop the action with a minimum of blur, you will want to select a fast shutter speed, such as 1/1000 of a second. In other cases, for creative purposes, you may want to select a slow shutter speed to achieve a certain effect, such as leaving the shutter open to capture a trail of automobiles' taillights at night.

Controlling shutter speed is a powerful tool for creative photography. Here are some of examples. First, take a look at the two photographs on the next page taken by the Coolpix P500 of a fountain on a sunny summer day. Both were taken with an aperture of f/8.0, which means the camera's opening for light was closed down as far as it could be. For the first image, I used a shutter speed of 1/500 second, one of the fastest settings available. As you can see, this fast shutter speed stopped the action of the flowing water quite well, "freezing" it so you can just about make out the individual parts of the spray.

For the second image, I used a much slower shutter speed of 1/15 second, which required the use of a tripod to avoid blur from camera shake. Because it was a bright day, I could not have selected such a slow shutter speed ordinarily; the image would have been washed out with the brightness. To use that setting, I had to place a neutral density (ND) filter over the lens to cut down the light. (I discuss how to do that in Appendix A.)

In this image, you should be able to see that the longer shutter speed captured a steady stream of the water, making it look like a continuous flow.

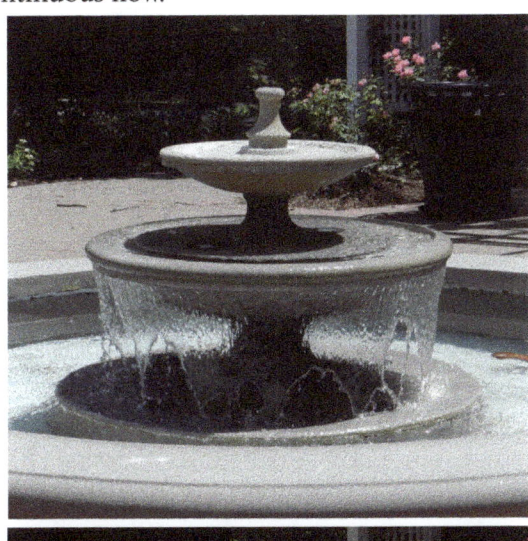

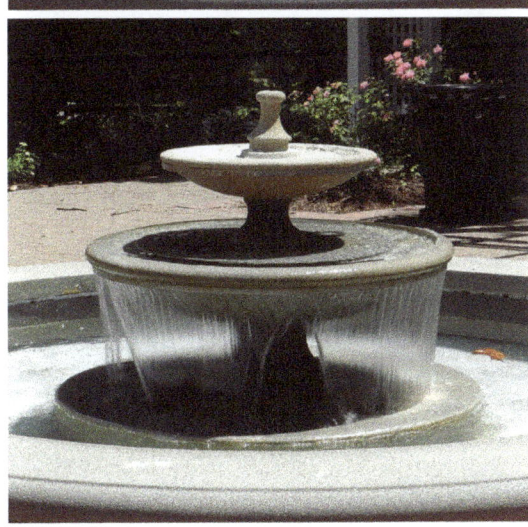

Because shutter speed can be used for great creative purposes,

I'm going to include one more set of photos as a second example. In this case, I used a working model of a Ferris Wheel, with colored, blinking lights on a bar that rotates inside the wheel. All three shots were taken indoors under artificial light at f/3.7, which was the widest aperture available at the camera's focal length of 32mm.

For the first exposure, I used a shutter speed of 1/1500 second, the fastest available, to stop the rapid motion of the wheel. In this image, the wheel is basically frozen in place; you can see the rotating light bar standing still. For the second exposure, I used a shutter speed of 1/40 second, considerably slower, but still fast enough to make the wheel look as if it's stopped, though blurred. Finally, for the last photo, I used a slow shutter speed of 0.8 second (1/1.3 as shown on the camera). For this one, I turned out the lights to allow the colored lights on the rotating bar to show up. This approach resulted in the solid, circular trails of color traced by the blinking lights as they rotated rapidly in the dark room. Using the slowest shutter speed essentially transformed the subject of the picture into a different object.

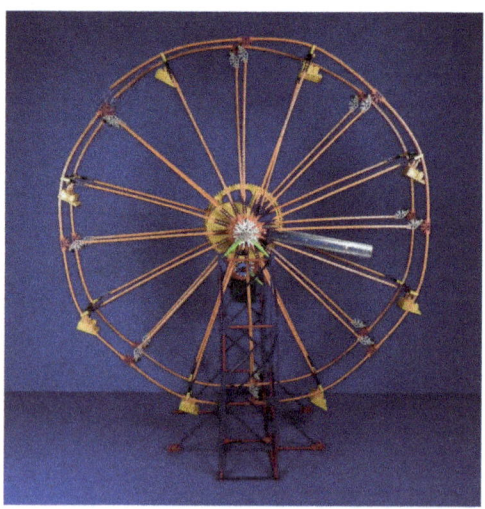

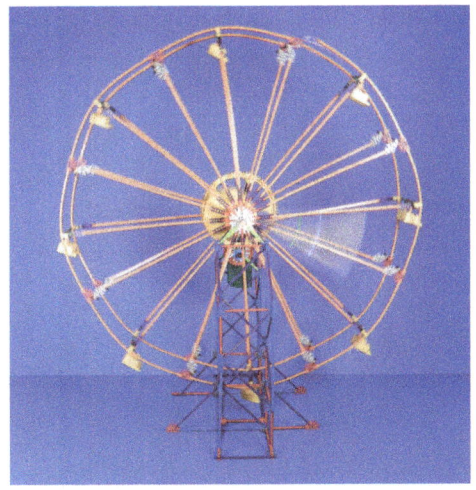

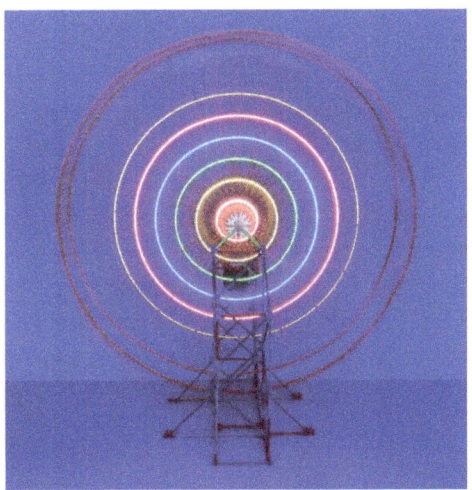

You select Shutter Priority by setting the mode dial on top of the camera to the S indicator. Then you set the shutter speed by turning the command dial—the ridged dial at the top right of the camera's back, just below the on/off switch. The LCD (or viewfinder, if selected) will display the selected shutter speed inside a yellow rectangle at the bottom center of the screen.

53

As you point the camera at scenes with varying lighting, the camera will select and display the appropriate aperture (such as f/4.5, for example) to achieve a proper exposure.

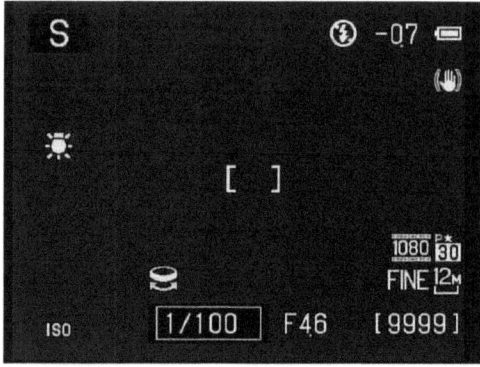

Once you've pushed the shutter button halfway down, you need to watch the shutter speed number on the screen. If that number blinks, that means that proper exposure at that shutter speed is not possible at any available aperture, according to the camera's calculations. For example, with a shutter speed of 2 seconds in a well-lighted room, the shutter speed number (which may be f/8.0, the most narrow setting) may begin to blink, indicating that proper exposure is not possible. One good thing in this situation is that the camera will still let you take the picture, despite having blinked the number to warn you. The camera is saying, in effect, "Look, maybe you shouldn't do this, but that's your business. If you want an overly bright picture for some reason, help yourself." (Note: This situation is less likely to take place when you're in Aperture Priority mode, because in that mode, there is a wide range of shutter speeds for the camera to choose from—a range from 8 seconds to 1/4000 second in some situations, depending on factors such as ISO and continuous-shooting settings.)

One other note on the shutter speed number: Any value of ¼ second or slower will appear in red. This is just the camera's warning that visual "noise" may result at such slow speeds, because of the nature of digital image processing.

When you are setting shutter speed, the fractions of a second are easy to read because they are displayed as standard fractions, such as 1/5 or 1/200. Some of the longer times are a bit harder to read; the camera displays them using quotation marks. So, for example, 2 seconds is displayed as 2", and 1.3 second is displayed as 1.3."

One feature of the shutter speed display on the Coolpix P500 is a bit confusing, at least to me. Some of the camera's shutter speeds are displayed as fractions whose denominators are decimal numbers, such as 1/1.3. I would have trouble understanding that number without doing some arithmetic, so here is a brief chart that converts these few values into terms that may be easier to comprehend:

1/2.5   0.4 or 2/5 second

1/1.6   0.625 or 5/8 second

1/1.3   0.8 (actually 0.77) or 10/13 second

Aperture Priority Mode

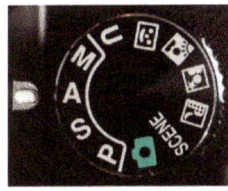

Aperture Priority mode is the inverse of Shutter Priority. You activate it by turning the mode dial to the A setting. Before discussing the settings for this mode, let's talk about aperture and why you would want to control it. The camera's aperture is a measure of the current width of its opening that lets in light to create the image. This width is measured numerically in f-stops. For the Coolpix P500, the range of f-stops is from f/3.4 (wide open) to f/8.0 (most narrow). The amount of light that is let into the camera to create an image is controlled by the combination of aperture (how wide open the lens is) and shutter speed (how long the shutter remains open to let in the light).

For some purposes, you may want to control how wide open the aperture is, but let the camera choose the corresponding shutter speed, so you can control the depth of field. Depth of field is a measure of how well a camera is able to keep multiple objects or subjects in focus at different distances (focal lengths). For example, say you have three friends lined up so you can see all of them, but they are standing at different distances—five, seven, and nine feet (1.5, 2.1, and 2.7 meters) from the camera. If the camera's depth of field is quite narrow at a particular focal length, such as five feet (1.5 meters), then, in this case, if you focus on the friend at that distance, the other two will be out of focus and blurry. But if the camera's depth of field when focused at five feet is broad, then it may be possible for all three friends to be in sharp focus in your photograph, even if the focus is set for the friend at five feet.

What does all of that have to do with aperture? One of the rules of photographic optics is that the wider the camera's aperture is, the smaller its depth of field is at a given focal length. So in our example above, if you have the camera's aperture set to its widest opening, f/3.4, the depth of field will be relatively small, and it will be possible to keep fewer items in focus at varying distances from the camera. If the aperture is set to the narrowest, f/8.0, the depth of field will be greater, and it will be possible to have more items in focus at varying distances.

It can be difficult to illustrate this effect with a camera like the Coolpix P500, for a couple of reasons. First, the image sensor, where the light is gathered to form the image, is relatively small, which results in the depth of field being quite wide. Second, the largest aperture available is f/3.4, whereas some compact cameras have lenses that open as wide as f/2.0, or even f/1.8. With such cameras it is easier to achieve a blurred background, because the depth of field can be quite narrow at such a wide aperture. With the P500, the widest aperture you can shoot with is f/3.4, and that aperture is available only when the lens is zoomed back to its extreme wide-angle setting, where depth of field is greater. If you zoom the lens in to a telephoto setting, the maximum aperture decreases steadily. At the maximum zoom range, the widest aperture available is only f/5.7, which is not far from the narrowest aperture of f/8.0.

However, by setting up a shot with fairly extreme conditions, I created the two images below to illustrate the different depths of field that are achieved with two different apertures. For both images, the camera was about 11 inches (28 cm) away from the wooden duck head, and the lucky bamboo plants were about 9 feet (2.75 m) further past the duck head. The lens was zoomed in slightly, to 46mm. I set the P500 to shoot in Aperture Priority mode. The top image was taken at f/4.2, the widest aperture available at that focal length; the bottom one was taken at f/8.0, closed all the way down. In both cases, I set the AF Area Mode to Manual and focused on the duck head by moving the focus brackets over the head.

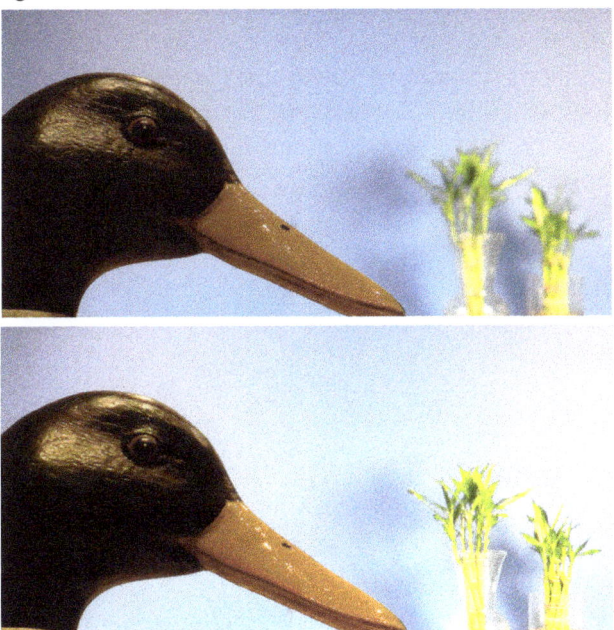

As you should be able to see, in the top image, with the wider aperture, the lucky bamboo plants appear quite blurred because the depth of field is relatively narrow at that setting. In the bottom image, on the other hand, the bamboo plants are in relatively sharp focus because the depth of field is greater at the narrower f/8.0 aperture.

If you want to have the sharpest picture possible, especially when you have subjects at varying distances from the lens and you want them to be in focus to the greatest extent possible, then you may want to control the aperture, and make sure it is set to the highest number (narrowest opening) possible.

On the other hand, there are occasions when photographers prize a narrow depth of field. This situation arises often in the case of outdoor portraits. For example, you may want to take a photo of a person standing outdoors with a background of trees and bushes, and possibly some other, more distracting objects, such as a swing set or a tool shed. If you can achieve a narrow depth of field, you can have the person's face in sharp focus, but leave the background quite blurry and indistinct. This effect is sometimes called "bokeh," a Japanese term describing an aesthetically pleasing blurriness of the background.

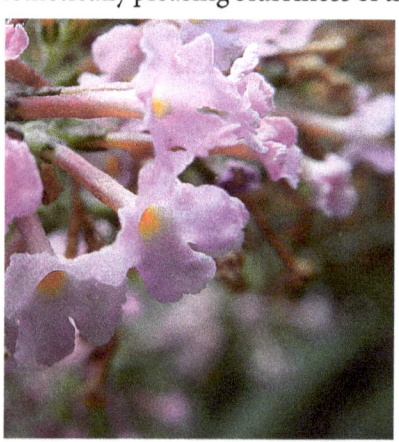

You have undoubtedly seen images using this effect. In this situation, the blurriness of the background can be a great asset, reducing the distraction factor of unwanted objects and highlighting the sharply focused portrait of your subject. The example on the previous page shows a flower on the left, in fairly sharp focus, with the background heavily defocused; this image was shot in close-up mode with the lens very close to the foreground, resulting in a very narrow depth of field.

So with our awareness of the virtues of selecting an aperture, on to the technical steps involved. Once you have moved the mode dial to the A setting, the next step is quite simple. Aim the camera at your subject, and use the command dial (the ridged wheel below the power switch) to change the aperture. The number of the f-stop will appear inside a yellow rectangle at the bottom right of the screen. The shutter speed chosen by the camera will show up also, to the left of the aperture.

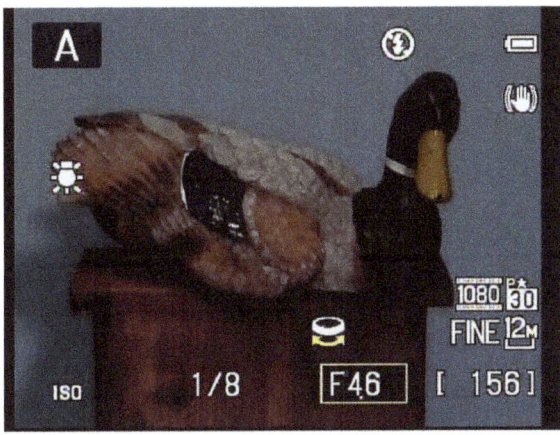

One more note on Aperture Priority mode that might not be immediately obvious and could easily lead to confusion: As I noted briefly above, not all apertures are available at all times. In particular, the widest-open aperture, f/3.4, is available only when the lens is zoomed out to its wide-angle setting (moved toward the letter W). At higher zoom levels, the widest aperture available is f/5.7. To see an illustration of this point, here is a quick test. Zoom the lens out by moving the zoom lever all the way to the left, toward the W setting. Then select Aperture Priority mode and select an aperture of 3.4 by turning the command dial all the way to the left, the direction for lower f-numbers. Now zoom the lens in by moving the zoom lever to the right, toward the T setting. If you try to set the aperture to f/3.4 after the zoom action is finished, you will see that the lowest aperture number you can set is f/5.7, because f/5.7 is the widest aperture available on the P500 at the telephoto zoom level. (The aperture will change back to f/3.4 if you move the zoom back to the wide-angle setting.)

Manual Exposure Mode

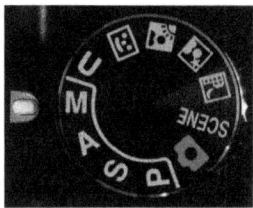

The Coolpix P500 has a fully manual mode for control of exposure, which is one of the great features of this camera. Not all compact cameras have a manual exposure mode, which is a tremendous boon for photographers who want to exert full creative control over exposure decisions.

The technique for using this mode is not too far removed from what we discussed in connection with the Aperture Priority and Shutter Priority modes. To control exposure manually, set the mode dial to the M indicator. You now have to control both shutter speed and aperture by setting them yourself. This situation presents a small problem, in that there is only one control available—the command dial—for changing both of these values. The solution to this problem is that you can toggle the function of the command dial by pressing the exposure compensation button, which is the right direction button on the multi selector. (This button is available for this purpose because you cannot control exposure compensation in Manual exposure mode.)

To set these values, first look at the camera's display and find where the shutter speed (such as 1/30) and aperture (such as F3.4) are displayed at the bottom of the screen. You will see an icon of a dial with a yellow arrow above one of these values, which will be inside a yellow rectangle; that is the value that is currently being controlled by the command dial. If you press the exposure compensation (right direction) button, you will see the dial icon and the yellow rectangle jump from one value to the other.

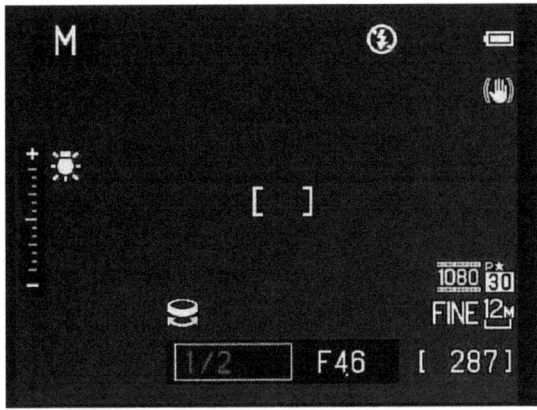

Make sure the dial icon and the yellow rectangle are located on the left value, for shutter speed, and turn the command dial until you have selected the shutter speed you want. Next, press the exposure compensation button to move the dial icon and rectangle to the right value, for aperture. Then turn the command dial to select the aperture you want.

As you adjust these values, watch the vertical scale at the left side of the screen. You will see the tick marks on the scale turn yellow, either above or below the scale's center point, as the values change. When the exposure is set the way the camera's meter judges to be accurate, there will be a lone yellow tick mark in the center of the scale. If the marks below the center turn yellow, the exposure is too dark; if they turn yellow above the center, it is too bright. If the setting becomes more extreme than the scale can indicate, the indicator turns orange.

61

Of course, you don't have to center the indicator on the scale; it is there only to give you an idea of how the camera would meter the scene. You very well may want parts of the scene (or the whole image) to be darker or lighter than the metering would indicate to be "correct." With Manual exposure mode, the settings for aperture and shutter speed are independent of each other. When you change one, the other one stays unchanged until you change it manually. The camera is leaving the creative decision about exposure entirely up to you, even if the resulting photograph would be washed out by excessive exposure or underexposed to the point of near-blackness.

One note to remember: As with Aperture Priority mode, you cannot set the aperture to f/3.4 when the lens is zoomed in.

Scene Modes

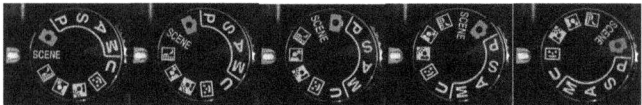

The Coolpix P500 offers several of what I will call Scene modes. The terminology can be a bit confusing, because the camera's menus and documentation use the word "scene" in several similar and overlapping contexts. First, there are several Scene modes that occupy individual slots marked by icons on the mode dial: Smart Portrait, Backlighting, Night Portrait, and Night Landscape. Next, there is another slot on the mode dial marked SCENE. When you select that setting, you can press the Menu button to the lower left of the multi selector and scroll through a list of 15 specific Scene settings: Portrait, Landscape, Sports, Party/Indoor, Beach, Snow, Sunset, Dusk/Dawn, Close-up, Food, Museum, Fireworks Show, Black and White Copy, Panorama, and Pet Portrait. Finally, there is a 16th entry on this list, which actually is the first entry at the top of the list: Scene Auto Selector. If you choose that option, the camera will analyze the scene using its digital circuitry and try to determine the most appropriate shooting mode to use from among these choices: Auto, Portrait, Landscape, Night Portrait, Night Landscape, Close-up, and Backlighting.

If the camera can identify what appears to be a scene calling for one of the listed seven settings, it displays an icon for that setting in the upper left corner of the screen. If the flash may be needed and is not popped up, the camera will display a message reminding you to raise the flash. In this mode, you can use exposure compensation and the self-timer, but you cannot switch out of the normal autofocus mode. If you press the Flash button (up direction button), you are offered only two options: auto flash or flash off.

If the camera chooses a Scene mode that you don't like, you of course have the option of using the mode dial to select another mode, such as Auto, or a specific Scene mode.

Scene modes are rather different from the other shooting modes we have discussed. These modes do not have a single defining feature, such as permitting control over one or more aspects of exposure. Instead, when you select SCENE mode, and then choose a particular Scene type within that mode, you are in effect telling the camera what type of environment the picture is being taken in, and what type of image you are looking for, and you are letting the camera make a group of decisions as to what settings to use to produce that result.

Some photographers may not like Scene modes because they take some creative decisions away from you and limit your options in some unfortunate ways. For example, you will find that your Shooting menu options are severely limited when the mode dial is turned to the SCENE setting or any of the Scene modes with slots on the mode dial, such as Night Landscape. That means that you cannot set the white balance, but must rely on the camera's Auto White Balance setting, which may not always properly evaluate the existing light source. You also cannot take advantage of features such as continuous shooting, and you can't choose your metering mode or your ISO setting.

Despite the limitations, though, I have found the various Scene settings to be quite useful in certain situations. Remember that you don't have to use the various settings only for their labeled purposes; you may find that some of them offer a group of settings that is well-suited for some shooting scenarios that you are regularly faced with. For example, you may find the Sports setting works well for shots of children at play, or that the Sunset setting, which emphasizes red hues, is great for images in a particular garden that is rich with reddish plants and flowers.

That concludes our general introduction to the Scene modes. But there are numerous choices, and you need to know something about each option to decide whether it's one you would want to select. In general, a given Scene setting carries with it a variety of values, including things like focus mode, flash status, range of shutter speeds, sensitivity to various colors, and others. Let's look at the complete list of Scene settings, so you can make informed choices.

Night Landscape

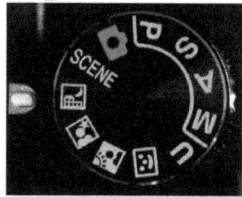

This mode, marked by an icon of a crescent moon above a building, occupies the slot on the mode dial just below the SCENE setting. It is intended for use without flash to take shots outdoors at night in areas that are not brightly lighted. When you select this shooting mode, there are two sub-options: Hand-held and Tripod. To choose, press the Menu button, then select Night Landscape, the bottom item on the brief menu list that appears. Then press the OK button or the right direction button, and choose either Hand-held or Tripod.

With Hand-held, the camera will take a continuous group of pictures and combine them in the camera into a single image, to overcome the effects of the high ISO setting the camera uses to take a good exposure in dim light without flash. A single image could be degraded from the visual "noise" that results from the use of high ISO values; by combining several images, the camera can create a single image using the best aspects of each, and can digitally smooth away the noise. You should try to hold the camera as steady as possible when shooting, but it will use a relatively fast shutter speed if at all possible to avoid blur from camera shake. When the camera senses that the scene is dark enough to need multiple images, the shooting mode icon in the upper left of the display turns green. If that icon remains white, the camera will take just a single image.

If you choose the Tripod option from the menu, then the camera will use a slower shutter speed and a lower ISO setting, so as to avoid noise. The use of the tripod will avoid the effects of camera shake. Of course, this setting is useful only if you actually attach the camera firmly to a tripod.

Night Portrait

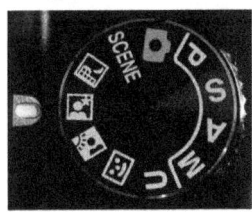

This mode is similar to Night Landscape, but, because your subject will be a person or persons in a dark outdoor setting, the camera will expect to use the built-in flash. Apart from the use of flash, this mode operates in a similar way to Night Landscape. The menu lets you select either Hand-held or Tripod. If you select Hand-held, the shooting mode icon will turn green when the camera is ready to take its multiple shots. The multiple shots will be combined into a single final image. If you choose Tripod, the camera will take a single shot at a

65

slower shutter speed.

Backlighting/HDR

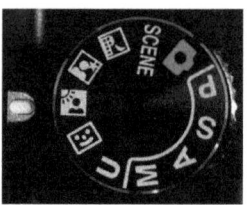

This mode, marked on the mode dial by an icon of a person with a bright light in the background to the upper left, is intended to be used in difficult lighting situations—in particular, when there is bright light present, but it is not located in a way that is helpful to the photographer. (Nikon calls this mode simply "Backlighting," but its single sub-mode is HDR, which is an important feature for modern cameras, so I have added HDR to the heading here for easier identification.)

When this mode is selected, as with the two previous modes, you have two sub-options selectable by pressing the Menu button. In this case, though, rather than Hand-held and Tripod, the two options are HDR on and HDR off.

If you choose the default value, HDR off, the camera forces the built-in flash to fire in order to overcome the shadows that are caused by your subject's being lighted from behind.

If, instead, you choose HDR on, you have a considerably different situation. With the HDR-on setting, the camera internally performs its own version of HDR, or High Dynamic Range, processing. In case you haven't encountered this phenomenon before, HDR has been a very popular photographic style for the past several years. Essentially, HDR photography involves using special techniques to deal with subjects that include areas of extreme contrast between light and dark. For example, if a building is partly lit by bright sunshine and partly hidden in deep shadow, the contrast is likely to be so great that a photograph cannot depict both parts of the building with normal exposure. Either one area of the image will be much too bright, so the highlights are blown out, or one area will be much too dark, so the details are swallowed in the shadows.

In the past, HDR was carried out in post-processing, using software such as Photoshop or special programs such as PhotoAcute or Photomatix Pro. The photographer would take multiple exposures of the scene using different exposure levels, some of them exposing the dark parts of the scene properly and some of them exposing the bright parts properly. When combined in HDR software, the images could be combined to result in a final composite image that showed all parts of the image nicely exposed. These HDR composite images often have an unnatural or surrealistic appearance, because it is obvious that a "normal" photograph could not include such a wide range of brightness values for this sort of image.

With many modern cameras, including the Coolpix P500, the manufacturer has included programming that gives the photographer the ability to take multiple photographs that are combined inside the camera to result in an HDR-like image. With the P500, I would not say that the result can match the "true" HDR that you can obtain through software, but it certainly does make a noticeable difference. Here is how it works.

When you choose the HDR-on setting on the P500, the camera turns the built-in flash unit off. Then, if the camera detects that there are sharply contrasting areas of bright and dark in the scene, the shooting mode icon in the upper left of the screen turns green, meaning the camera will take multiple shots. At this point, you should hold the camera very steady, or, ideally, place it on a tripod. After you press the shutter, you will see a yellow progress bar appear on the display and extend to the right as the camera processes the multiple images into two final ones. The first of the two final images will be an image taken with the Active D-Lighting feature turned on, to brighten shadowy areas of the image to bring out details.

The second image will be an HDR composite that contains the best-exposed parts of multiple images, thereby expanding the dynamic range of the shot.

The images below illustrate the effects of this setting, followed by an HDR image done with software. These images show a small wooden cabinet with colorful cards of yarn inside, brightly lit on one side and in shadow on the other. The first shot, immediately below, was taken with the camera in Aperture priority mode, with no special settings.

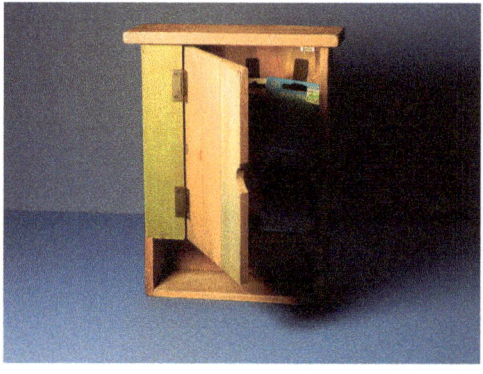

The next shot was taken in Backlighting mode, with HDR turned off. In this mode, the camera always uses flash.

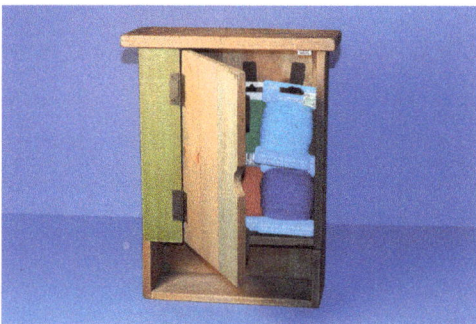

The first image on the next page was taken with the HDR setting turned on. In that situation, the camera takes multiple images, and the first one it saves is one taken with the flash off, but with Active D-Lighting (not HDR) turned on.

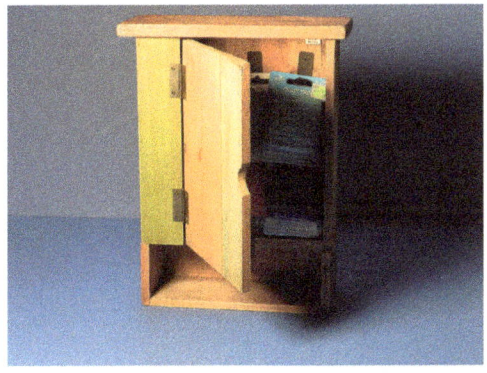

Now, below, comes the composite shot that is the result of the P500's in-camera HDR processing.

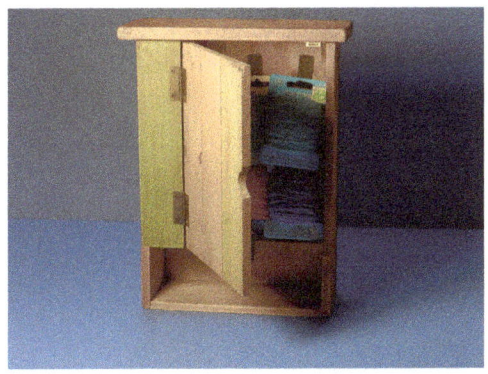

This last shot is a composite image created in Phototshop CS5.

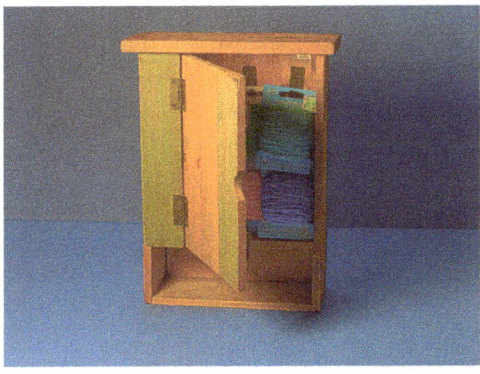

Here is one more set of examples, taken outdoors under more natural conditions. This time, the three images show, from top to bottom, normal exposure in Program mode; Backlighting mode, with in-camera HDR; and multiple exposures combined using the Merge to HDR Pro feature in Photoshop CS5.

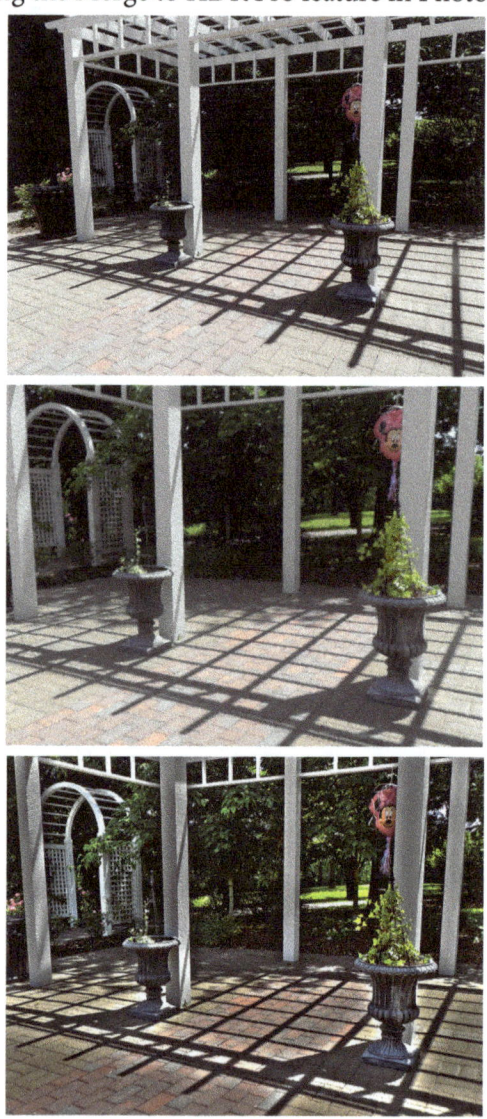

Smart Portrait

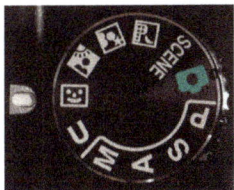

This next setting is designated by the smiling-face icon right next to the U setting on the mode dial. The word "smart" in its name signals that this mode, unlike the more ordinary Portrait mode that is available from within the Scene menu, has some additional capabilities and functions. With its default options active, the Smart Portrait mode automatically detects up to three faces, places its focus priority on faces, and applies a digital skin-softening process to your images. The image here was taken with the default settings.

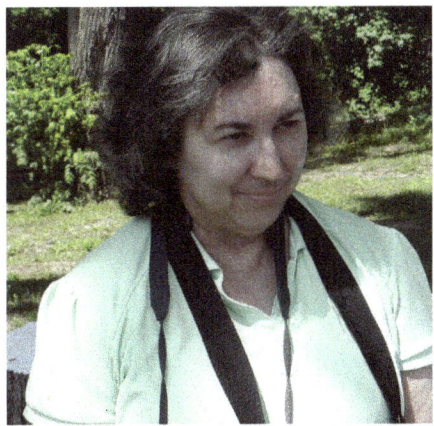

In addition, the Smart Portrait setting gives you several tools for taking photos of people automatically when they smile. All of these settings can be controlled through the menu system by pressing the Menu button when you have dialed in this shooting mode and selecting Smart Portrait from the menu that appears.

71

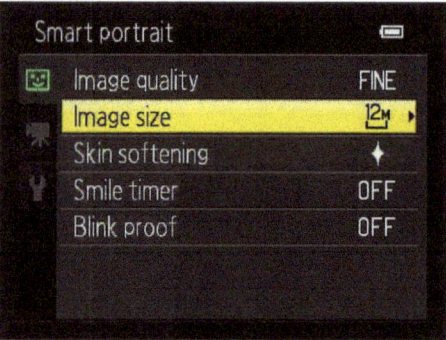

The first two options on the Smart Portrait menu, Image Quality and Image Size, work just the same as in any other shooting mode. The third option, Skin Softening, has four possible settings: High, Normal, Low, and Off, which let you select to what extent the camera should automatically apply its softening formula to make the subject's skin look smooth, somewhat along the lines of movies where the star was filmed through gauze over the lens to smooth away wrinkles and blemishes.

The next Smart Portrait menu sub-option is the Smile Timer, which fires the shutter automatically when the camera detects a smile. This feature works together with the camera's face detection system, which is always in effect in Smart Portrait mode. When this option is turned on through the menu system, whenever the camera detects faces, it focuses on the face closest to the center of the image and places a yellow double border around that face. (You can force it to focus on another face by pressing the OK button.) The shutter will be triggered if the face inside the double border smiles. When the camera sees the smile, the red-orange self-timer lamp on the front of the camera blinks, and the shutter fires five times in quick succession; the camera then processes those images internally and keeps the image that has the most smiling faces. (If the flash is popped up and fires, the shutter fires only once.)

The third and final sub-option is called Blink Proof. This option is not available if the Smile timer is turned on. With Blink

Proof activated, when you press the shutter, the camera fires five times continuously, and it then internally processes the images and selects one, if possible, in which all subjects had their eyes open. If the only images available include blinking eyes, the camera will display a message saying blinks were detected, but it will still record an image.

You may want to experiment with Smart Portrait mode to see if it is of use in certain situations. I originally thought I would never use gimmicky features such as smile timers and blink detectors, but I have found that they can be useful on some occasions, such as when you find yourself with your camera at an office function and you need to take pictures quickly while your colleagues are assembled in a corner. There may not be a lot of time for you to exercise your photographic judgment, and it may well be useful to have a camera that will fire when people are smiling, or when they are not blinking.

SCENE Mode Settings

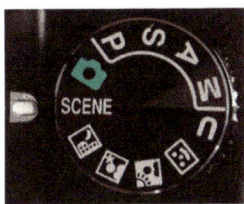

Next, I'll discuss the settings that are available with the mode dial at its SCENE position. To review, this option brings up a list of 16 choices, including Scene Auto Selector and 15 specific scene types. When the mode dial is set to SCENE, you can select any one of these choices by pressing the Menu button and selecting a scene setting from the menu list. Note, though, that when you select any of these settings, the Menu system offers few other choices; that is, when you have made a selection such as Portrait or Landscape from the SCENE setting, you cannot make any more choices using the menu system other than Image Size and Image Quality. The camera will make all other settings as it deems appropriate for the given selection.

So, these Scene settings are convenient if you are faced with a certain type of photographic situation and you want the camera to make reasonable choices for that situation, but you have very little control over the camera's settings. Following are the details about each of those types, including what sorts of settings the camera chooses for each.

Portrait

The camera automatically sets itself for face detection, which means it looks for human faces and focuses on the one closest to the camera. It also automatically applies skin softening, which smooths out wrinkles. However, you cannot control the amount of skin softening or turn it off, as you can when using the Smart Portrait setting, discussed earlier.

Landscape

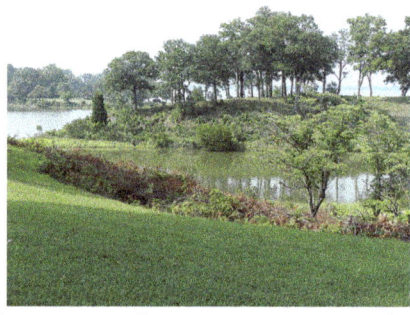

The camera focuses at infinity, so you may not be able to focus clearly on closer objects. You cannot change the focus mode or turn on the flash, but you can use exposure compensation or the self-timer.

Sports

Intended for subjects that move around unpredictably. The camera sets itself for continuous shooting and takes a rapid series of as many as five images at a rate of up to eight frames per second, depending on conditions such as image size and quality and available lighting. The flash is forced off, and focus and

74

exposure are locked when the first image is taken, to increase the speed of the sequence of shots. This mode is useful when you need to stop action in relatively bright lighting conditions.

Party/Indoor

This setting is intended for indoor photos of people. You should make sure the built-in flash unit is popped up; the flash mode is initially set to Auto with Red-eye Reduction, but you can change the flash setting if you want to. The camera will focus on the subject at the center of the frame and will attempt to use a relatively slow shutter speed in order to allow the background to be shown under the available ambient light. So, you should hold the camera very steady or place it on a tripod. (Realistically, though, you probably are not going to be setting up a tripod for candid or impromptu pictures at a party.)

Beach

With this selection, the camera optimizes its settings for the beach, where there is likely to be bright sunlight reflected from the ground. In this environment, the camera will have a tendency to underexpose the subject because the exposure meter will be measuring the brightness of the beach. Therefore, the camera will set the flash mode to Auto in order to light the subject sufficiently, and it is quite likely that the flash will fire in order to enhance the brightness of the subject so it will be clearly visible against the glare of the background.

Snow

This setting is similar to Beach, in that the camera will likely use the flash to compensate for the brightness of the snowy background. The camera processes the image somewhat differently in other respects; it appears to use a greater amount of reddish hue than the beach setting, as a balance against the bluish color temperature of a snowy scene.

Sunset

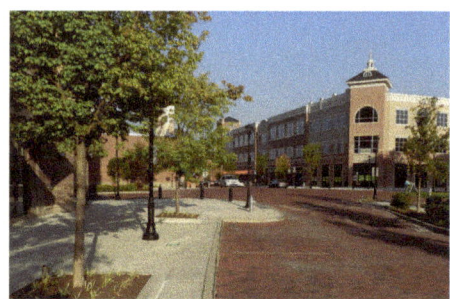

Choose this setting when you want to capture the rich, reddish hues of the setting (or rising) sun. The camera turns the flash off, though you can still make adjustments to that and other settings. The camera processes your image to emphasize the red-orange tones in the heavily slanted rays of the late afternoon or early morning sun. Of course, you don't have to limit the use of this (and other) Scene settings to sunset or sunrise; if you are photographing autumn leaves with reddish hues, red-brick buildings, or other subjects with reds you want to emphasize, consider this setting as one tool that may be of use. For example, the image above does not show a sunset, but I felt that the emphasis on reddish light was appropriate for this scene that was lit by the sun's long rays in the late afternoon.

Dusk/Dawn

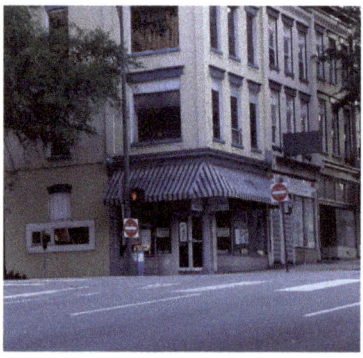

If you are taking pictures before sunrise or after sunset, this is a setting to be aware of. With the Dusk/Dawn setting activated, the camera forces the flash off and intensifies the colors in order to add interest to images that otherwise might seem flat or washed out because of the low intensity of the available light. I like to experiment with modes like this one; the image on the previous page was taken shortly after 7:00 on a July morning in Virginia, when the sun had been up for some time, but was still casting its rays with a reddish hue. I believe the Dusk/Dawn mode enhanced this downtown view.

Close-up

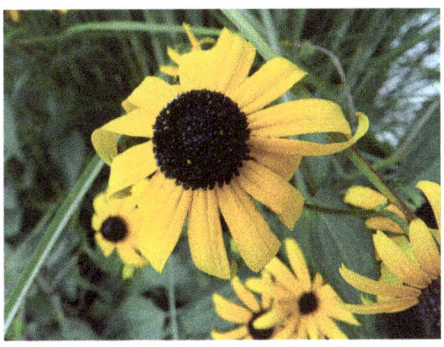

With this setting, the camera switches into macro mode so it will focus properly on items close to the lens. If the lens is zoomed in to a telephoto position, when you switch into the Close-up setting it will automatically zoom back out to a position that allows the camera to focus on the subject. The camera also switches the AF Area Mode setting to Manual. This means that you can control exactly where the focus point is placed. To do this, you press the OK button in the center of the multi selector, then press one of the four direction buttons on the multi selector to move the focus area around the screen so that it covers the point where you want the camera to focus. If you need to use one of the direction buttons for its other function (self-timer, flash, or exposure compensation), press the OK button again, and those functions will be available. Press the OK button once more if you need to move the focus area another time. Finally, the camera also uses continuous autofocus, so it continues to adjust the focus until you press the shutter button halfway down to lock in the focus.

You could, if you want, use another shooting mode, such as Program or Auto, and just select macro focusing using the focus button (down direction button). But, if you want to quickly set up the camera for close-up shooting, it can be convenient to have this Scene mode available. You need to hold the camera very steady to avoid blurring the image. Use of a tripod or monopod is the best practice, but of course that is often impractical.

Food

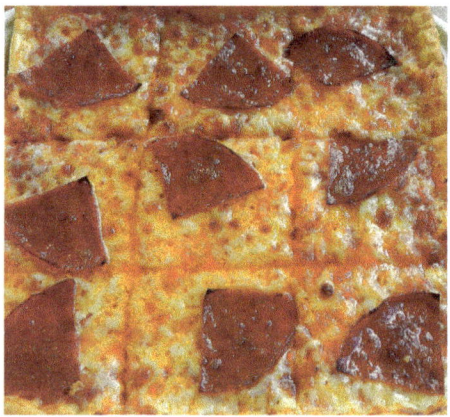

This setting is quite similar to the Close-up setting, discussed directly above. The camera switches to macro focus mode and zooms back if necessary so that it can focus on a nearby subject. It also turns on Manual for the AF Area Mode, so you can move the focus point around, and it uses continuous autofocus. The one major difference from Close-up mode is that, in Food mode, the camera places a scale of colors at the left side of the screen and allows you to adjust the hues of your images by moving the pointer up and down along the scale using the direction buttons. Move towards the top for more reddish hues, and towards the bottom for more bluish ones. This setting is suited for people who are in the habit of documenting their meals through food blogs or photographic diaries of their dining experiences. With the hue slider, you can experiment until you achieve the desired effect of emphasizing the colors of meats, vegetables, or other aspects of the meal. The image on the previous page was taken just after my pizza was served; I cranked up the red hue on the slider to its maximum level to emphasize the color of the salami.

Unless you have a reason to leave a hue adjustment permanently in place, be sure to return the hue slider to the neutral position when you're done shooting for a given session, because the adjustments you make will remain in place the next time you choose the Food setting, even if the camera has been turned off in the meantime.

Museum

The Museum setting is useful when you are taking photographs in a museum or other location where the use of flash is prohibited. The camera forces the flash off, and will not use it even if the flash unit is popped up. The camera also disables the autofocus assist lamp, which could be distracting in a museum setting. In addition, the P500 automatically activates the Best Shot Selector function. With this option, which normally is controlled with the continuous-shooting mode button near the shutter release button, the camera takes 10 shots in rapid succession while you hold down the shutter release, and automatically saves the one shot that is sharpest and has the most detail. In this way, even though you are taking pictures in dim light with no flash, you have a good chance of getting a usable image because the camera will take multiple shots and discard the ones that exhibit motion blur.

Here again, as with most of the Scene settings, don't let the name of this setting exclude it from consideration for other purposes. You might want to use it in any dimly lit area when you can't (or don't want to) use flash.

Fireworks Show

With this setting, the camera sets the focus to infinity and uses a slow shutter speed so you can capture a relatively long burst of color from a fireworks display. The flash is forced off. You should set the camera on a tripod if possible, or hold it firmly on a fence post or other solid object as an alternative.

Black and White Copy

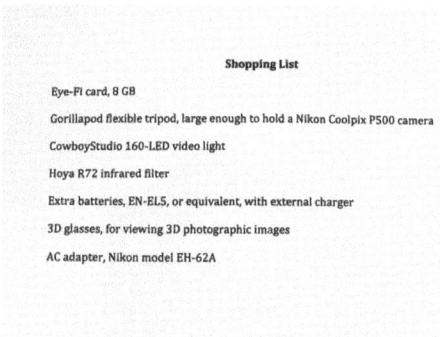

Shopping List

Eye-Fi card, 8 GB

Gorillapod flexible tripod, large enough to hold a Nikon Coolpix P500 camera

CowboyStudio 160-LED video light

Hoya R72 infrared filter

Extra batteries, EN-EL5, or equivalent, with external charger

3D glasses, for viewing 3D photographic images

AC adapter, Nikon model EH-62A

This setting lets you copy black-and-white text, like words on a blackboard or whiteboard, or perhaps on a poster. I consider it to be a handy way to capture a document you need to carry with you, such as the shopping list shown above. In effect, your P500 becomes a very portable photocopier; you can copy the item quickly and crisply, and enlarge the view on the screen.

When you choose this setting, the camera switches into a black-and-white mode and captures the image in monochrome format. The focus is initially set to normal autofocus, but you can switch into macro autofocus if you are copying something close up, such as words on a sheet of paper. Of course, this mode is of no use to you if you need to record any colors at all, such as colors of highlighting of the text, or of images that accompany the text. Again, don't let its name limit your use of this mode; you might want to try it for street photography, as discussed in Chapter 9.

Panorama

This setting gives you two sub-options for taking panoramic scenes with the P500like the one shown here.

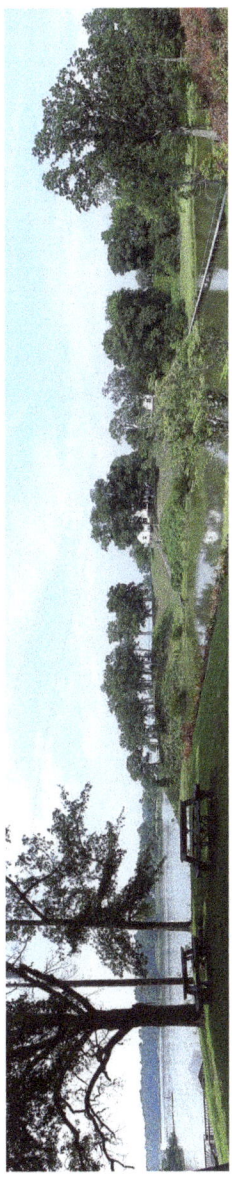

Once you have selected Panorama from the Scene menu, select either EASY or ASSIST from the sub-menu. With Easy Panorama, the camera does most of the work for you; with Panorama Assist, the camera gives you some guidance, but you have to handle more of the details yourself. The image on the previous page was taken with the Easy Panorama feature.

Easy Panorama

When you select this option, you are presented with yet another sub-menu with two more options—Normal (180°) or Wide (360°). Make your selection and then aim the camera at the first part of your panoramic scene. For example, if you are shooting a panorama of a wide mountain range, you may want to aim at the far left side of the range. Press the shutter button halfway down to lock in focus and exposure; the camera will automatically zoom back to the wide-angle position, and will not let you zoom in.

When you are satisfied with the initial view, press the shutter button and release it; you don't need to hold it down while the panorama shooting proceeds. Now hold the camera steady and level as you sweep it in the direction of your shot—in this case, from left to right—until you have covered the entire scene. The camera will detect the direction you are moving in, and it will automatically stop shooting when it detects the end point of the 180-degree shot. You should take about 15 seconds to complete this arc.

You can shoot the panorama moving either from left to right or right to left, or you can shoot it vertically, moving the camera from low to high or vice-versa. And, if you select the Wide option, you can move the camera through a complete circle to cover an entire scene. In that case, you should take about 30 seconds to complete the entire circuit.

When you are done, you can view the whole panorama on the screen by pressing the Playback button. To see the panorama scroll by on the screen, press the OK button, and it will scroll in the same direction in which it was taken.

Panorama Assist

Use this setting when you want to exercise more control over the shooting of your panorama. When you select Assist from the Panorama sub-menu, you will see a pair of yellow arrows on the display pointing either up, down, right, or left, indicating the direction in which the panorama will be shot. Press one of the direction buttons if you want to change that direction. For example, if the two yellow arrows are pointing to the right, press the left direction button, and the two arrows will point to the left, indicating that the panorama will be shot from right to left.

With the Assist setting, it is a good idea to use a tripod in order to keep the multiple shots lined up properly, because you will be taking them one at a time, rather than in a continuous stream as with the Easy setting. When you have set up the focus, zoom range, and exposure as you want them, press the shutter button to take the first shot. Within a second or two, you will see that image appear on the camera's display, with about one-third of the image appearing translucent.

Use the translucent part of the first image to line up the next shot. That is, try to superimpose the translucent area over its real-life counterpart, as viewed through the camera's lens. When you do that, the first and second images will overlap by the proper amount. Then repeat this process for as many images as you would like to include in the panorama. When you have finished shooting your images, press the OK button to end the panorama shooting.

To actually create the panorama, you need to load the individual images onto your computer and use "stitching" software to create the panorama. You can use the software supplied with the CoolPix P500, which is called Panorama Maker 5 Pro, from Arcsoft. Following the prompts in the software, load the panorama images into the program. You will find all the files for any one panorama in a folder on your memory card with a number starting with the letter "P." For example, I shot a panorama with five images, and they were saved in a folder on my SD card named 104P_004. Other sets of panorama images were in folders named 103P_003, and so on.

Once the files are all loaded into the program, look for the buttons and prompts in the software that let you select the type of panorama to create; in my case, I chose Horizontal. Then choose the "Next" prompt at the lower right corner of the screen and continue following prompts until the computer has stitched together the images into a continuous panorama. Along the way, you will have the opportunity to make various adjustments, such as changing the order of the images, cropping them, aligning them, and other matters.

The Nikon-supplied panorama software works well and has the advantage of coming with the camera, but you can also use other programs, such as Adobe Photoshop or Photoshop Elements, and there undoubtedly are others that I have not tried.

The advantage of using the Assist option rather than the Easy option for shooting panoramas with the P500 is that you have considerably more control over the creation of the panorama, including the ability to zoom, to choose a focus mode, and to choose the number of images that make up the view. You also can take your time making each shot from your tripod, rather than panning the camera within 15 seconds. Finally, you can fine-tune the panorama in your software rather than just relying on the camera's internal processing to create the final product. But, it's very nice to have the option of creating a panorama quickly with the Easy setting when you don't have time to deal with all the steps required for creating a panorama with the Assist option.

Pet Portrait

This setting is specifically designed for shooting pictures of the family dog or cat. When you choose this Scene mode, the camera sets itself for continuous shooting and activates a feature called "Pet portrait auto release." With this feature, the camera looks for the face of a dog or cat, and, if it detects one, it triggers the shutter automatically and takes three pictures in quick succession, to try to capture a good expression on the pet's face. If the camera does not display the double-bordered frame that indicates detection of a face, you can just press the shutter button to take the image when you're ready.

The default setting with this shooting option is continuous shooting, but you can switch to single-shot exposures by pressing the continuous-shooting button (on top of the camera, near the shutter button), and change the setting. You also can change the Pet portrait auto release setting, which is turned on by default. To turn it off, press the self-timer button (left direction button), and select the Off setting, rather than the icon that shows a pet's face.

User Setting Mode

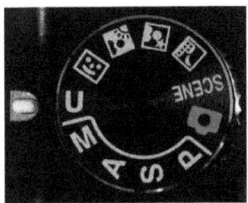

The last slot on the mode dial to be discussed is the U setting, which allows you, the user, to store a full set of your favorite or most often-needed settings for instant recall. When you turn the mode dial to the U setting, you take advantage of a very powerful and convenient feature of this camera. You can set up the camera exactly as you want it, with a shooting mode, zoom amount, white balance, ISO, and other settings, and then recall all of those settings instantly just by turning

85

the mode dial to the letter U. The only shooting modes that you can save settings for are Program, Aperture Priority, Shutter Priority, and Manual; you cannot save them for the Auto, Scene, or Movie modes.

Here is how this works. First, set up the camera with all of the settings you want to be able to recall. For example, suppose you are going to do street photography. You may want to shoot with a fast shutter speed, say 1/250 second, at ISO 1600 in black-and-white, using continuous shooting with autofocus, at the 16:9 aspect ratio with a large image size and Fine quality. Your first step is to make all of these settings. Turn the mode dial to S for Shutter Priority, and turn the command dial to set a shutter speed of 1/250 second. Then press the Menu button to summon the Shooting menu, and go to the menu item for Image Quality and choose Fine. For Image Size, select 3868 x 2232 pixels, which, as indicated to the left of those numbers, translates to a 16:9 aspect ratio with an image size of 9 megapixels. Then navigate in the menu system to the Optimize Image selection, and select the Black-and-White option. Set ISO to 1600. Next, press the continuous-shooting button on top of the camera and navigate to the second selection, for high-speed shots. You also may want to push the zoom lever all the way to the left, for wide-angle shooting.

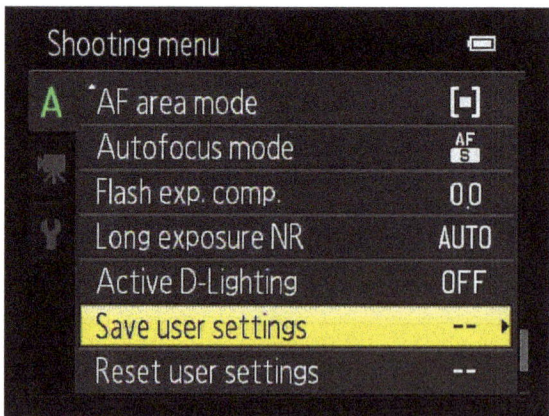

Once all these settings are made, press the Menu button to call up the Shooting menu, and scroll down (or scroll up and wrap around to the bottom) to select the Save User Settings item, and then press the OK button or the right direction button; you will see a confirming message saying Done. Be sure you have all the settings the way you want them before you press OK or the right button, because the camera does not ask you to confirm your choices; it just says "Done." I was a bit taken aback the first couple of times I used this feature, because in most other cases there's a chance to back out before you make your choices final; not here.

Now, to check how this option worked, try making some very different settings, such as Manual exposure with a shutter speed of one second, Optimize Image set to Normal, continuous shooting turned off, the zoom lever moved all the way to the right for telephoto, ISO set to Auto, and Image Size set to the maximum, 4000 x 3000 pixels. Then turn the mode dial to the U setting, and you will see that all of the custom settings you made have come back, including the zoom position, shutter speed, black-and-white shooting at ISO 1600, and everything else. This is really a wonderful feature, and more powerful than similar features on some other cameras, which can save menu settings but not settings such as shutter speed and zoom position.

The lone flaw I find with this mode is that there is only one slot for it on the mode dial, and therefore only one group of settings that can be saved at a time. But it's much better than nothing. I suggest you experiment and find one custom settings group that is the most useful to you, and save it to the U mode for instant recall. Of course, you can change the settings that are stored as often as you like. You may want to jot down in a notebook some of your favorite groups of settings for various situations, so you can program them in to the U slot when you're setting out for a particular type of shooting session.

Chapter 4: The Shooting Menu

Much of the power of the Nikon Coolpix P500 resides in the many options included in the Shooting menu, which provides the user with control over the appearance of the images and how they are captured. Depending on your own preferences, you may not have to use this menu too much. You may prefer to use the various Scene types, which choose many of the options for you, or you may prefer, at least on occasion, to use Auto mode, in which the camera makes its own choices. However, it's nice to know that you do have this degree of control available if you want it, and it is very useful to understand what types of items you can exercise control over.

The Shooting menu is quite easy to use once you have played around with it a bit. As I discussed earlier, the menu options can change depending on the setting of the mode dial on top of the camera. For example, if the mode dial is set to the green camera icon, for Auto mode, the Shooting menu options are very limited, because that mode is for a user who wants the camera to make almost all of the decisions without input. If the mode dial is set to one of the dedicated Scene types with its own slot on the dial (Night Landscape, Night Portrait, Back-lighting, or Smart Portrait), the Shooting menu is re-named after the currently active mode.

For example, if you select the Night Landscape mode from the mode dial and then press the Menu button, the menu that appears on the display is labeled Night Landscape, rather than Shooting. These menus, as in Auto mode, are abbreviated versions of the Shooting menu; they include only a few items from the normal Shooting menu, usually Image Quality and Image Size. In addition, they include a specific menu item for the mode that is in effect. In this case, there is a Night Landscape menu item, which lets you select either Hand-held or Tripod for shooting.

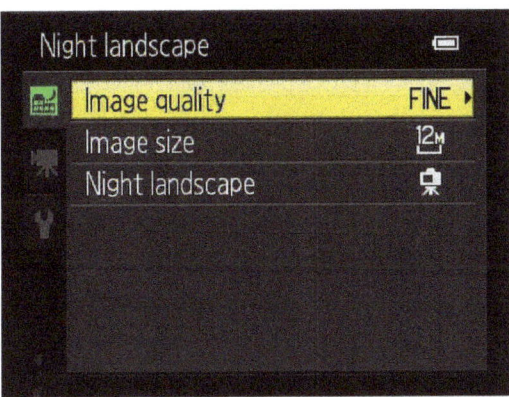

When the mode dial is turned to the SCENE setting, pressing the Menu button brings up another version of the Shooting menu, in this case called the Scene menu. This menu provides a way to select either Scene Auto Selector or any one of the 15 specific scene types (Portrait, Landscape, Sports, etc.). In addition, at the very bottom of the Scene menu, just after the entries for Panorama and Pet Portrait, the camera presents you with the options for choosing Image Quality and Image Size.

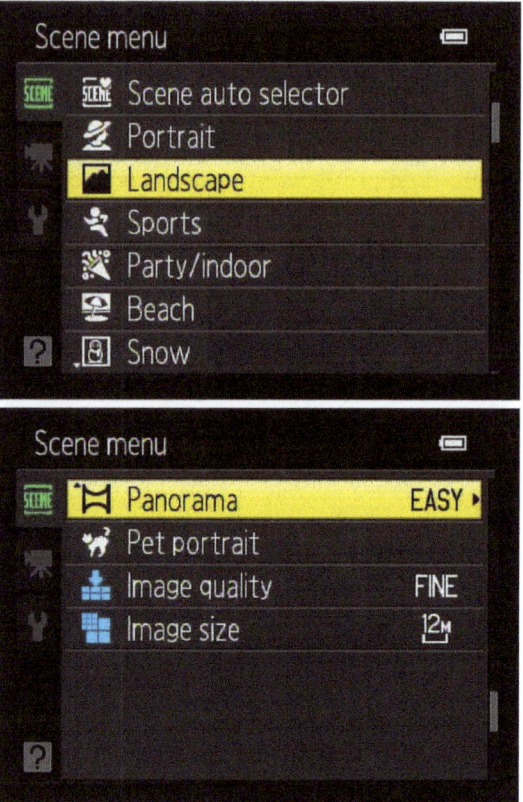

A basic point to bear in mind is that, although the Menu button presents you with some choices in all shooting modes, in the more automatic modes, including Auto and the various Scene types, there are only a few options, apart from options specific to a given mode, such as choosing a Scene type. It is only when the mode dial is set to the P, S, A, or M setting for the Program, Shutter Priority, Aperture Priority, or Manual exposure mode, that the wide variety of Shooting menu options is available.

For the following discussion, I'm assuming you have the camera set to Program mode (shooting mode dial turned to the P setting), because in that setting you have access to all of the power of the Shooting menu. (Though some menu options will be unavailable in certain situations.)

So turn the mode dial to P for Program mode, then enter the menu system by pressing the Menu button.

In the menu system, when the camera is in shooting mode, besides the Shooting menu (or Scene menu), there are the Movie menu, designated by a movie camera icon in the column at the left of the menu, and the Setup menu, marked by a wrench icon at the left of the menu. When the camera is in Playback mode the three choices are the Playback Mode, Playback, and Setup menus. For now, I will discuss only the Shooting menu, which is designated by a capital letter at the left standing for the current shooting mode: P, S, A, or M.

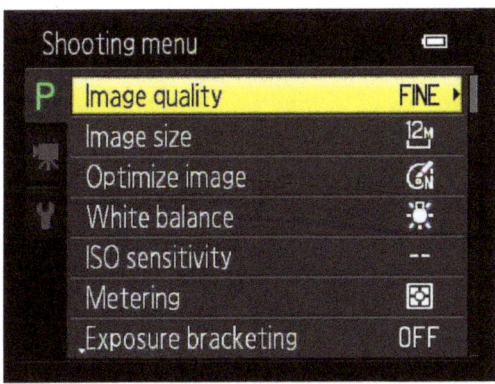

On the Shooting menu, you'll see a fairly long list of options. Each option (such as Optimize Image) occupies one line, with its name on the left and its current setting (such as the Normal icon) on the right. You have to scroll through two screens to see all of the options. If you find it tedious to scroll using the up and down direction buttons, you can turn the command dial at the top of the camera's back, which may help you speed through the menus a bit more quickly. Also, depending on the menu option, you may be able to reach it more quickly by reversing direction with the direction buttons or command dial, and wrapping around to reach the option you want. In other words, if you're on the top line of the menu, you can scroll up to reach the bottom option. Or, if the highlight is already near the bottom option, you can scroll down to go back to the options at the top of the menu.

Once you have highlighted the menu item you want, you can make any sub-selections by pressing the OK button or the right direction button, which will take you to the next screen for that menu item. To go back to a previous menu screen, press the left direction button; to exit the menu system, press the Menu button. Note that it's important to press the OK button to confirm your choice of a particular menu item selection; just highlighting it and then exiting from the menu screen will not activate that item.

On occasion you will find that you are unable to select a certain menu option. That is, although it will appear on the menu screen, you will not be able to navigate to it and select it. This situation occurs when there is an option in effect that is not compatible with the menu option you are trying to select. For example, if you have selected Multi-shot 16 by using the continuous-shooting button on top of the camera, the Image Quality setting is fixed at Normal and the Image Size setting is fixed at 5 megapixels (2560 x 1920 pixels), and neither of those settings can be changed (or even selected) in the menu system. Or, if you have selected the option to shoot in black-and-white from the Optimize Image menu setting, you will not be able to get access to the White Balance menu option.

With the mode dial set to P you should have access to just about every option on the Shooting menu. If you find that you can't select certain menu options, check to make sure you have set other options to compatible settings. For example, use the continuous-shooting button on top of the camera to select Single-shot exposures rather than a continuous setting. If you have trouble getting to some menu options and can't figure out what setting is causing the problem, you can go the Setup menu (marked at the left by the wrench icon) and scroll down (or scroll up and wrap around) to the Reset All option, the next-to-last option on the menu. Using that operation will reset all of the camera's basic shooting functions to their default values. In this way, you will undo whatever setting is causing a conflict with the setting you are trying to make.

Starting at the top line of the Shooting menu, I will discuss below each option on the menu's two screens.

Image Quality

There are two basic settings to make when you are deciding on your overall image "quality" in the broadest sense: Image Quality, discussed here, and Image Size, discussed below. The Image Quality option lets you select how much "compression" the camera applies. That is, the camera "compresses" the data by squeezing out a certain amount of information, preserving enough to recreate the image, but trimming it down so the file does not take up too much storage space. The three options are Fine, Normal, and Basic. Each option uses up about twice as much storage space as the next lower option. So, for example, if you choose Fine for your quality setting, the camera can store 650 of the largest-sized images on a 4 GB memory card. If you choose Normal, it can store 1,280 of those images. If you choose Basic, it can store 2,510 images. Of course, there is a tradeoff of quality against storage space. If you are planning to make large prints, you should choose Fine.

It is worth noting that the Coolpix P500 does not offer RAW as an option for image quality. Virtually all DSLRs and quite a few advanced compact cameras today offer the RAW format, which preserves the maximum image data and gives the photographer considerable flexibility in processing images in software. However, using RAW has its disadvantages, including very large file sizes and incompatibility with some post-processing software (at least until software updates are provided). Using a RAW format also requires that the images be

93

processed in software; you cannot use them straight from the camera. The P500 provides a great deal of flexibility in producing excellent JPEG images, and you should have no problem in using this camera to make excellent prints or other photographic products.

Image Size

The next option on the Shooting menu, Image Size, works hand-in-hand with Image Quality to determine the overall quality of your images. With the Coolpix P500, Image Size actually has two components, which can be selected separately on some other cameras: resolution and aspect ratio. On the P500, these two components are not named, but their numerical values are listed on the Image Size menu. (The aspect ratio values are listed only for the settings that deviate from the normal aspect ratio of 4:3.)

The resolution of the image is the number of pixels it contains, given in a formula that contains the horizontal pixel count followed by the vertical pixel count. For example, the largest Image Size setting available on the P500 is 4000 x 3000, meaning the image has 4000 pixels horizontally and 3000 vertically. When you multiply these two numbers together, the result is 12 million pixels, also written as 12 megapixels or 12M. So, you will see the figure 12M on the menu screen when you select this largest value for Image Size.

You can also determine the aspect ratio of the image by examining the Image Size setting. For example, the 4000 x 3000 setting results in an image that is 4 units wide for every 3 units tall, which means it has a 4:3 aspect ratio. Most of the Image Size settings for the P500 are in that ratio, which is a standard one for digital images, being the same shape as the camera's LCD display. However, if you scroll down through the second screen on the Image Size menu, you will see a few entries that note a different aspect ratio. Specifically, just below the setting for VGA on the second screen, there is the entry for 3984 x

2656 pixels. At the far left on the line for this entry, rather than the number of megapixels, which is shown for the previous entries, the menu shows the notation 3:2, meaning this Image Size is in a 3:2 aspect ratio: 3 units wide for every 2 units tall. This aspect ratio is another fairly common one, which corresponds to the standard print size in the United States of 6 by 4 inches (15 by 10 cm).

Below that entry is the one for the Image Size of 3968 x 2232 pixels, which translates to an aspect ratio of 16:9, as noted at the far left of that menu item. The following entry, 1920 x 1080, also is in the 16:9 aspect ratio, often labeled "widescreen."

Finally, the last entry on the Image size menu, 2992 x 2992 pixels, is easily seen to be in an aspect ratio of 1:1, resulting in a square image.

With the Image Size menu setting, you have two choices to make. First, you can choose your images' resolution, or number of pixels (megapixels). The larger the number of pixels, the larger you can make clean-looking enlargements on paper, and the more options you have for cropping the image to highlight particular details from the exposure. Second, although most of the choices on the menu are in the standard 4:3 aspect ratio, you have the option of selecting an aspect ratio of 3:2, 16:9, or 1:1 if you want. Of course, you should bear in mind that you can always just shoot with the maximum image size of 4000 x 3000 and then crop the image down in software later; in that way, you can create any aspect ratio you want, including those listed here or any other. But, if you want to use a 1:1 aspect ratio for creative reasons, or you are taking a landscape photo and prefer the 16:9 widescreen look, and you don't want to be bothered with a lot of editing in software, you can go ahead and select an Image Size setting that corresponds to your desired aspect ratio, so the final result will come straight out of the camera.

Optimize Image

This next menu option provides you with a list of seven options for the appearance of your images through different types of in-camera processing: Normal, Softer, Vivid, More Vivid, Portrait, Custom, and Black-and-White. With each of these options, the camera provides varying degrees of adjustment to three basic parameters: contrast, sharpening, and saturation. Following are descriptions of the individual settings, with a sample photo included, illustrating the general appearance given by the different choices:

Normal

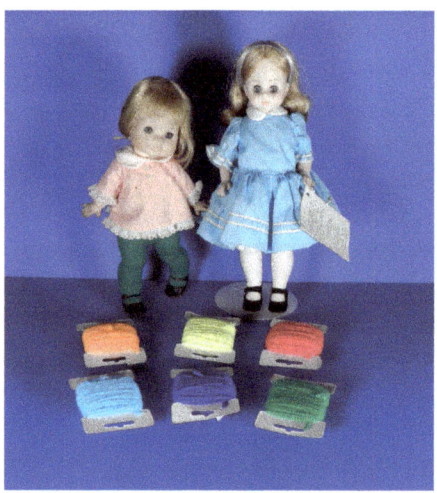

With this setting, you should see a standard rendering of the image, with no emphasis on any particular aspect.

Softer

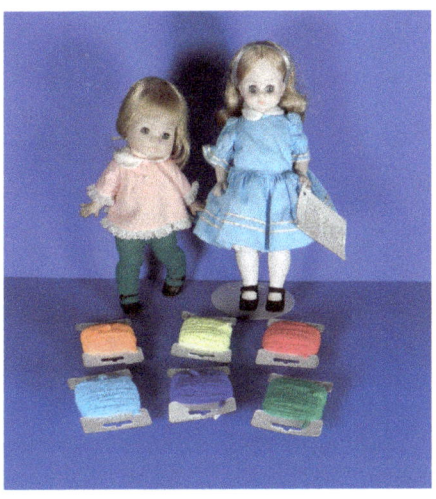

This setting provides reduced sharpening, yielding softer edges. It may be useful for a portrait in which you want to de-emphasize wrinkles or other sharp features on your subject's face.

Vivid

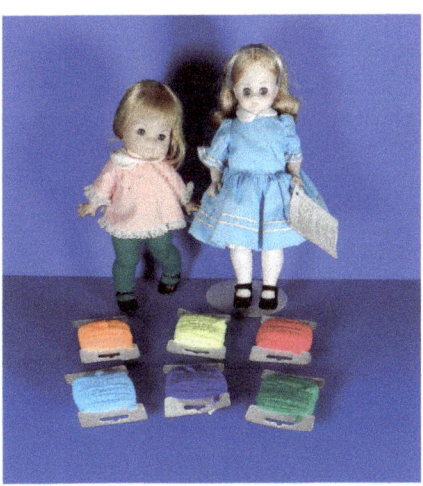

Use this setting to increase the saturation, or intensity, of the colors in the image; it also provides some increase in sharpening and contrast, with the result that the image may "jump" off the page at the viewer with increased impact.

97

More vivid

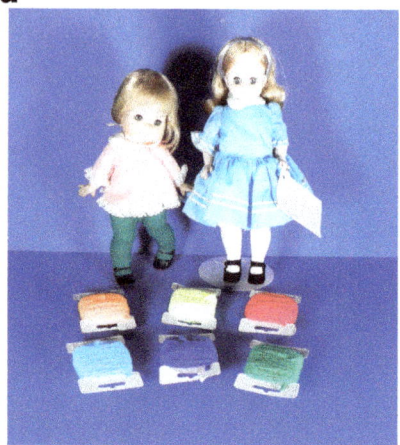

This setting goes beyond the Vivid setting to provide maximum amounts of saturation, sharpening and contrast. In my opinion, the More Vivid option tends to add too much contrast, resulting in a somewhat overexposed or washed-out look, unless you are shooting a dark scene that needs some added emphasis. I generally prefer the Vivid setting when I want to add some extra "punch" to an image.

Portrait

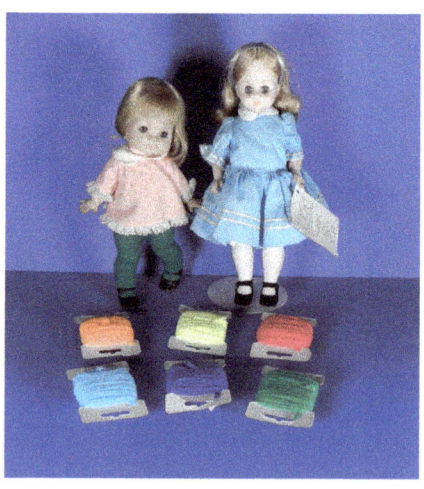

This setting takes a somewhat different approach to portraits than the Softer setting, discussed above. With the Portrait setting, the camera's processing reduces sharpening and contrast so as to render the subject's skin with a soft, textured appearance.

Custom

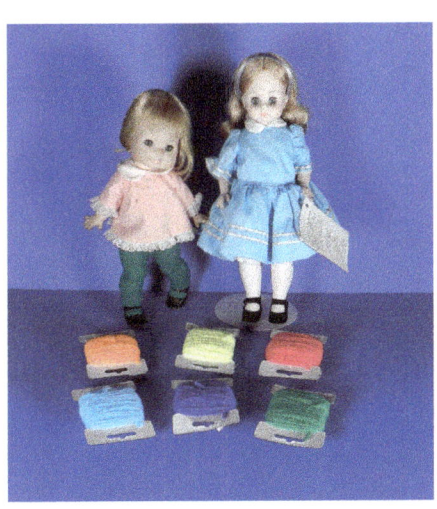

The Custom settings lets you tweak the three available parameters—contrast, sharpness, and saturation—to your individual taste. To do this, select Custom from Optimize image menu, then press the OK button or the right direction button to bring up the menu with these three parameters. Press the right button to get to the list of possible values, which range from -2 to +2 for contrast and sharpening and from -1 to +1 for saturation. For the image above, all 3 options were set to +1.

Black-and-White

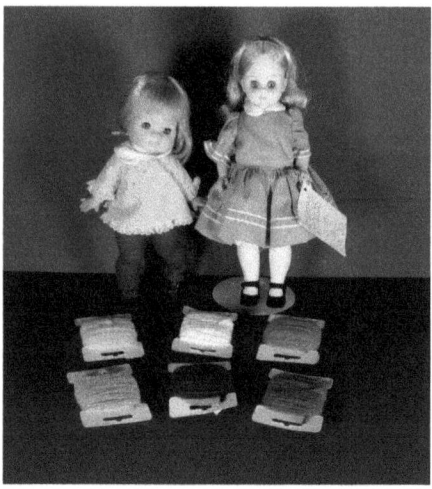

This setting gives you a quick way to set the camera to take black-and-white images. Of course, as with many aspects of digital photography, you can always convert color images to monochrome using software such as Photoshop or Photoshop Elements, but it is convenient to be able to view your images in black-and-white on the camera's display before pressing the shutter button, and you may not want to devote your time and effort to converting images on the computer.

With this setting, you have two sub-options to choose from: Standard and Custom. With Standard, as shown above, the camera sets itself for a normal monochrome rendering of the image. With Custom, you are able to adjust three parameters to your own taste: contrast, sharpening, and monochrome filter. Contrast and sharpening work just the same as with the Custom option, discussed above. The third option, monochrome filter, is a simulation of the use of a glass filter over the lens. The choices are off, yellow, orange, red, green, and sepia. The yellow, orange, and red settings produce increasing degrees of contrast. You may have seen examples of black-and-white photography of a sky taken with filters of these colors; the results can be a dramatically enhanced sky, with clouds

that stand out in sharp contrast to the sky. The green selection produces softer tones in skin colors, which can be useful
for portraits. It's important to note that none of these color
choices actually adds any color to the image. The sepia option,
however, does actually add a sepia tone to the image, producing the old-fashioned look of vintage photographs, as shown
below.

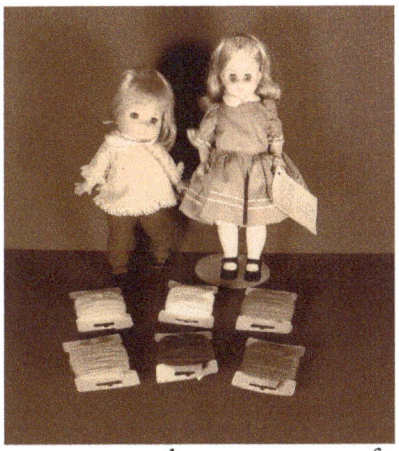

Finally, when you are on the menu screen for selecting between Standard and Custom for the Black-and-White setting,
you will see a band at the bottom of the screen, labeled B&W
+ Color, with a check box at the far left. If you press the down
direction button or turn the command dial to highlight that
band, you can press the OK button to place a check mark in
the box.

If you do that, the camera will take both a color and a black-

and-white image, using the settings you entered for the Black-and-White setting, when you press the shutter button. In that way, you can have the benefit of instant black-and-white results, but without losing the information in the color image, in case you would like to have that version of the image as an extra option.

White Balance

This topic needs a bit of background discussion for those users who are new to digital photography. One issue that arises in all photography is that film, or a digital camera's sensor, reacts differently to colors than the human eye does. When you or I see a scene in daylight or indoors under various types of artificial lighting, we generally do not notice a difference in the hues of the things we see depending on the light source. However, the camera does not have this auto-correcting ability. The camera "sees" colors differently depending on the "color temperature" of the light that illuminates the object or scene in question. The color temperature of light is a numerical value that is expressed in a unit known as kelvins (K). A light source with a lower kelvin rating produces a "warmer" or more reddish light. A light source with a higher kelvin rating produces a "cooler" or more bluish light. For example, candlelight is rated at about 1,800 K; indoor tungsten light (ordinary light bulb) is rated at about 3,000 K; outdoor sunlight and electronic flash are rated at about 5,500 K; and outdoor shade is rated at about 7,000 K.

What does this mean in practice? If you are using a film camera, you may need a colored filter in front of the lens to "correct" for the color temperature of the light source. Any given color film is rated to expose colors correctly at a particular color temperature (or, to put it another way, with a particular light source). So if you are using color film rated for daylight use, you can use it outdoors without a filter. But if you happen to be using that film indoors, you will need a color filter to correct the color temperature; otherwise, the resulting picture will look excessively reddish because of the imbalance between the film and the color temperature of the light source.

With a modern digital camera, you do not need to worry about filters, because the camera can adjust its electronic circuitry to correct the "white balance," which is the term used in the context of digital photography for balancing color temperature.

The Coolpix P500, like most current digital cameras, has a setting for White Balance, which lets you choose the proper color correction to account for any given light source. Here is how to make this setting through the Shooting menu.

Once you have highlighted the White Balance setting, which is the fourth item down on the first menu screen, press the OK button or the right direction button to bring up the list of the following choices for the White Balance setting, each of them represented by an icon or a word or abbreviation: Auto (AUTO); Preset Manual (PRE); Daylight (sun); Incandescent (round light bulb); Fluorescent (rectangular light bulb); Cloudy (cloud); and Flash (lightning bolt).

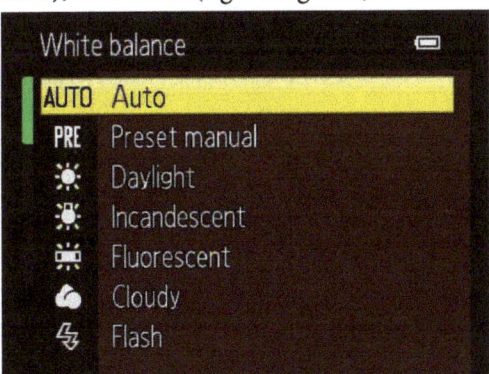

The above labels should be largely self-explanatory, although you need to know a few details about how these settings work. You highlight the choice you want, and press the OK button to confirm. If you select Auto, you are done; there are no further adjustments available. With each of the other selections, though, you can fine-tune the setting, as described below.

103

If you highlight Daylight, Incandescent, Cloudy, or Flash, you can then press the right direction button to bring up a screen with a scale at the left going from -3 at the bottom to +3 at the top.

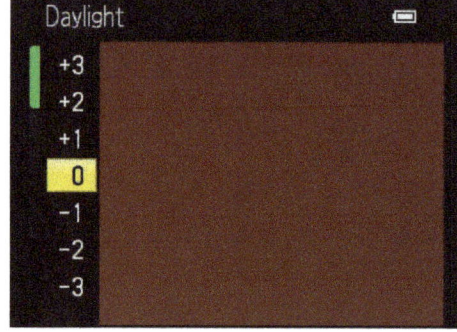

You can use the up and down direction buttons or the command dial to move the yellow selection block up and down this scale to select a value. If the value is positive, the white balance is biased toward a bluish tint, and if it is negative, it is biased toward a reddish tint. If you highlight the Fluorescent option, pressing the right direction button brings up the further choices of FL1, FL2, or FL3. These three sub-varieties of Fluorescent range from white to neutral to daylight. There are no other adjustments available with the Fluorescent setting.

Finally, if you select Preset Manual, you can set the white balance manually. Use this option when you are faced with mixed lighting from multiple sources, or from a reddish or otherwise unusual light source. To make this setting, highlight Preset Manual, then press the right direction button. The next screen will present the options to Cancel or Measure. Highlight Measure, and then aim the square in the middle of the screen at a white or gray surface that is illuminated by the light source you will be using. Then press the OK button, and the camera will measure the white balance and store the setting. To use this setting now or in the future, turn back to the Preset Manual option at any time, even after the camera has been turned off and back on.

Note: You can take advantage of the Preset Manual as a nice way to add a color tint to a scene for creative effect if you want. For example, you can set the white balance manually using a red or orange surface for the measurement, which will result in a pronounced blue tint for any pictures taken under the same light source that you used when setting that white balance value. Just be careful to turn the white balance setting back to Auto or another more normal setting when you don't want that special effect for your images.

Before I leave this topic, I'm going to include a group of images showing how the various white balance settings affect the colors of your shots. All of these were taken under the same incandescent lighting; the only thing that changed from shot to shot was the white balance setting, as indicated.

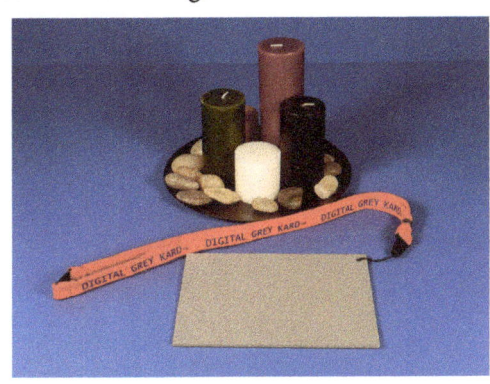

Auto

Preset Manual
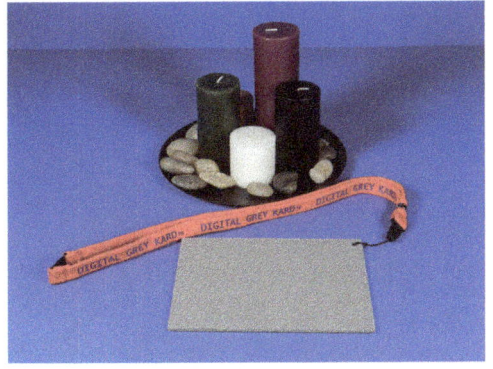

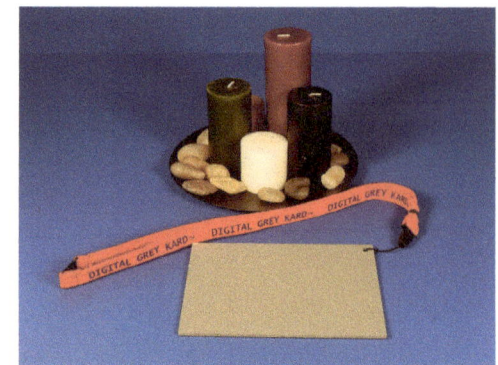

Daylight

Incandescent

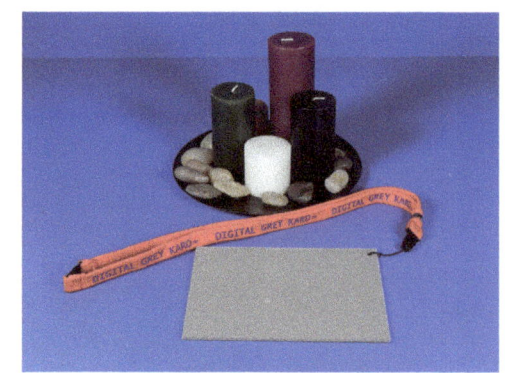

Fluorescent

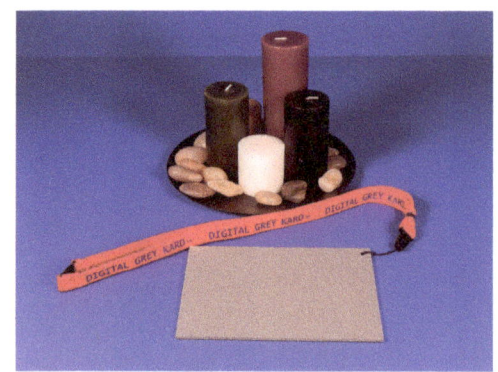

Cloudy

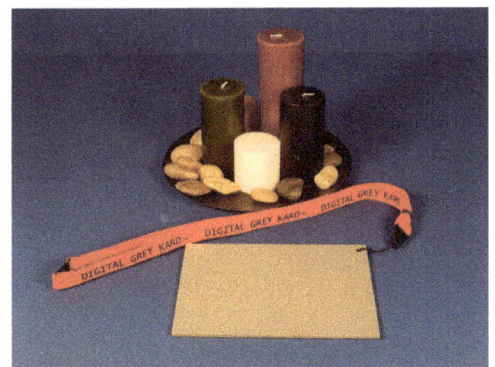

Flash

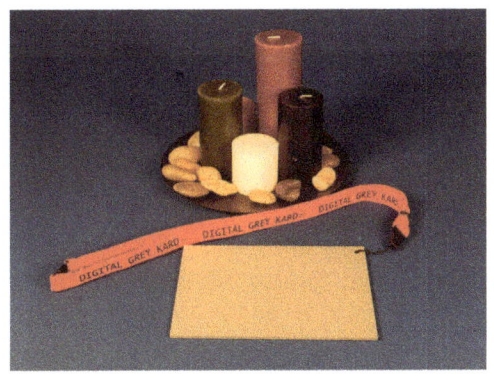

The gray card that you see in each shot is an actual photographic "gray card," a tool used to set a neutral white balance. When the white balance is set properly, the card should appear gray, as it does in the shots with the Preset Manual and Incandescent settings. As you can see, the Auto setting did not do a great job of measuring the white balance, possibly because I had a mixture of light bulbs turned on. This means that you should not rely too heavily on the Auto White Balance setting, particularly with artificial light. The chances are it will do better in outdoors settings, but indoors you should use the Preset Manual setting if the colors of your subjects need to be very accurate. Or, use the Incandescent or Fluorescent setting, but take some test shots to be sure the colors are accurate.

ISO Sensitivity

Before I discuss how to use this setting, I should explain the importance of ISO. These initials stand for International Standards Organization. When I first started in film photography a few decades ago, this standard was known as ASA, for American Standards Association. The ISO acronym reflects the more international nature of the modern photographic industry.

The original use of the ISO/ASA standard was to designate the "speed," or light sensitivity, of film. So, for example, a "slow" film might be rated ISO 64, or even ISO 25, meaning it takes a considerable amount of exposure to light to create a usable image on the film. Slow films yield higher-quality, less-grainy images than faster films. There are "fast" films available, some black-and-white and some color, with ISO ratings of 400 or even higher, that are designed to yield usable images in lower light. Such films can often be used indoors without flash, for example.

With digital technology, the industry has retained the ISO concept, but it applies not just to film, but to the light sensitivity of the camera's sensor, because there is no film involved in a digital camera. The ISO ratings for digital cameras are supposed to be essentially equivalent to the ISO ratings for films. So if your Coolpix P500 is set to its minimum level, ISO 160, there will have to be a fair amount of light to expose the image properly, but if the camera is set to the maximum of ISO 3200, a reasonably good (but "noisier" or "fuzzier") image can be made in very low light.

The upshot of all of this is that, generally speaking, you want to shoot your images with the camera set to the lowest ISO possible that will allow the image to be exposed properly. (One exception to this rule is if you want, for creative purposes, the grainy look that comes from shooting at a high ISO value.) For example, if you are shooting indoors in low light, you may need to set the ISO to a high value (say, ISO 800) so you can expose the image with a reasonably fast shutter speed. Otherwise, if the camera uses a slow shutter speed, the resulting image would likely be blurry and possibly unusable.

To summarize: Shoot with low ISO settings (usually 160 with the P500) when possible; shoot with high ISO settings (say 400 or higher, up to 1600 or even 3200) when necessary to allow a fast shutter speed to stop action and avoid blurriness, or when desired to achieve a creative effect with graininess.

With that background, here is how to set ISO on this camera. Press the Menu button and move to the ISO Sensitivity line, then press the right direction button to get to the screen that lets you select either ISO Sensitivity or Minimum Shutter Speed. For now, select ISO Sensitivity and press the right button again to get to the ISO Sensitivity options.

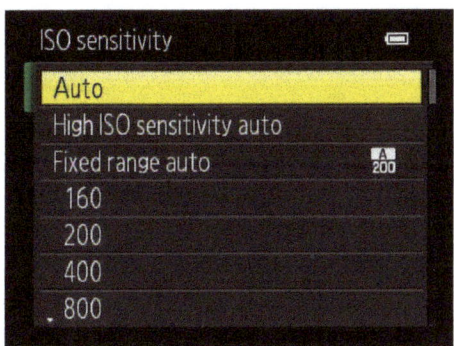

With the first option, Auto, the camera will set the ISO level at 160 in relatively bright light, and it will raise the level as high as 800 as the light grows dimmer. With the next option down the list, High ISO Sensitivity Auto, the level will be set between 160 and 1600. The next option, Fixed Range Auto, has two choices, reached by pressing the right direction button. You can choose from two ranges: 160-200 or 160-400, if you want to constrain the camera's ISO choices to a fairly narrow range of possibilities. You can use this setting if you want the camera to use a certain amount of flexibility, but you want to make sure the ISO value does not go high enough to cause noticeable "noise" in your images. Finally, you can choose any one of the individual ISO values, if you want to specify exactly what ISO setting the camera uses. The choices are 160, 200, 400, 800, 1600, and 3200.

Going back to the first branch on this set of menu screens, you can use the Minimum Shutter Speed setting to specify the slowest shutter speed that the camera will use when the camera is set to the Program or Aperture Priority mode and any of the Auto ISO settings are in effect, before the camera starts to increase the ISO sensitivity.

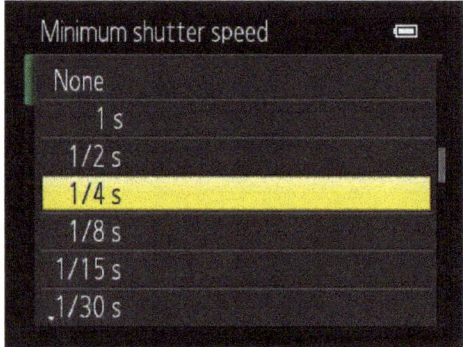

To understand how this setting works, it's helpful to consider an example. Suppose the camera is in Program mode and the ISO Sensitivity setting is Auto. Press the Menu button, use the command dial or the up and down direction buttons to highlight ISO sensitivity on the display, then press the right direction button to get to the next screen. Then highlight Minimum Shutter Speed, press the right direction button, and select 1/30 second from the list of values.

With those settings, the camera will attempt to expose the image properly using a shutter speed no slower than 1/30 second, your Minimum Shutter Speed setting. If the Auto ISO setting increases to its maximum limit and the image is still too dark, then the camera will drop to a slower shutter speed in order to achieve a good exposure. So, in effect, this setting forces

110

the camera to try to keep the shutter speed at 1/30 second or faster, but if that's not possible, the camera will then change to a slower shutter speed. You may want to use this setting to avoid using slow shutter speeds that are likely to result in blurred photos because of camera motion, or to capture images of moving subjects, such as children playing. If you use a setting such as 1/125 second (the fastest setting possible) for Minimum Shutter Speed, along with a setting of High ISO Sensitivity Auto, you are likely to be able to take all of your exposures using the 1/125 second shutter speed, preserving your ability to avoid camera shake and to capture ordinary action.

Finally, one more note on the Auto ISO options. If you select any of the Auto ISO settings in Manual exposure mode, the camera will set the ISO to 160. You can select any other numerical ISO value if you want. In Auto shooting mode and all varieties of the Scene shooting mode, Auto ISO is automatically set, and you cannot adjust it.

Metering

This next option on the Shooting menu lets you choose among the four patterns of exposure metering offered by the Coolpix P500: Matrix, Center-weighted, Spot, and Spot AF Area.

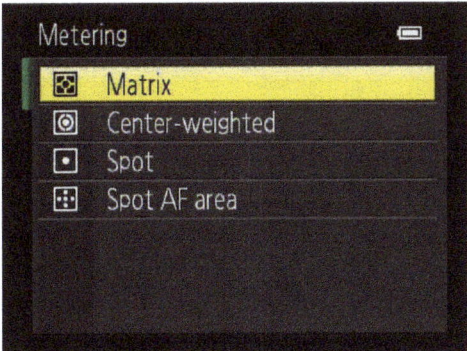

This setting tells the camera's automatic exposure system what part of the scene it should consider when deciding how to set the exposure. If you choose Matrix, the default option, the camera uses the entire scene that is visible on the LCD. If you choose Center-weighted, the camera still considers all of the light from the scene, but it gives additional weight to the center portion of the image, on the theory that your main subject is in or near the center. The camera displays two large arcs to mark the area that is being emphasized. With Spot, as seen in the screen shot below, the camera considers only the light inside the part of the scene covered by the small circle that appears in the center of the screen.

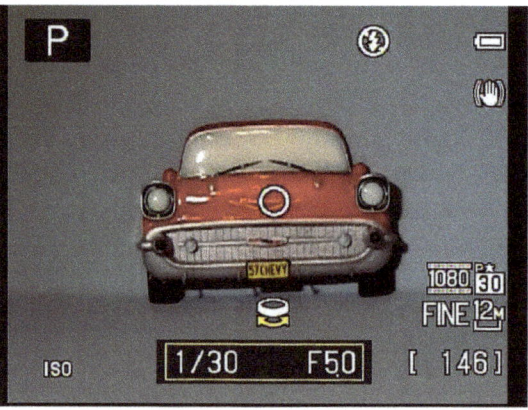

When you set the metering method to Spot, you can see the effects of the exposure system quite dramatically by setting the camera to the Program exposure mode and aiming that small circle at various points, some bright and some dark, and seeing how dramatically the brightness of the scene in the LCD changes. If you try a similar experiment by moving the camera around to aim at differently lit areas in Matrix mode, you will still see changes, but much more subtle and gradual ones.

Finally, if you choose Spot AF Area for the metering mode, the camera measures the light from the same area where the autofocus has been set. This option is not available when the AF Area Mode menu selection has been set to Center or Subject Tracking. If you choose Manual for the AF Area Mode, then, when you move the focus area around the screen, you are also moving the circle for the Spot metering function. So, you can expose for a small area at the side of the scene, for example, if you need to.

Exposure Bracketing

Exposure bracketing is a function that lets you take three pictures with one press of the shutter button, with three different exposure settings, thereby giving you an added chance of getting one good, usable image. In addition, using exposure bracketing is an excellent way to take three pictures that can be combined later in software to produce an HDR (High Dynamic Range) composite, which shows clear details and highlights throughout the image by taking the best-exposed parts of each shot.

To use exposure bracketing, the camera must be set to the Program, Aperture Priority, or Shutter Priority mode. Navigate down in the Shooting menu to the last line on the first screen. Then press the OK button or the right direction button to get access to the next screen, which will present you with four choices: ±0.3, ±0.7, ±1.0, and Off.

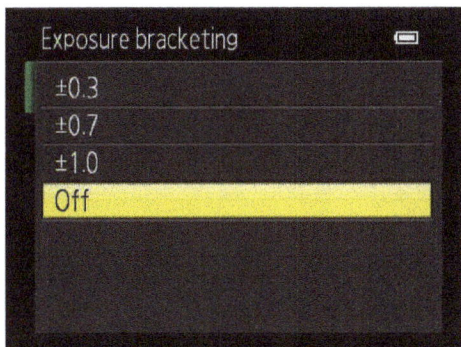

Use the command dial or the direction buttons to highlight the choice you want, then confirm the choice by pressing the OK button. The camera's shooting display will then display a notation such as BKT±0.7, unless you left bracketing turned off. This notation means, for example, that the camera will take three exposures separated by the indicated amount of exposure value (EV, a standard measure of brightness). Adding a single unit of EV, +1.0, has the same effect as opening the aperture by one full f-stop.

When you are ready to shoot, press the shutter button and hold the camera steady (or use a tripod) while it takes the three exposures. The first picture taken is always at the metered level, or 0 change in exposure value (EV); the second is at the lower EV (darker), and the third is at the higher EV (brighter). If you have added exposure compensation, the bracketed exposures are taken at three levels relative to the adjusted exposure.

Note that the flash cannot be used when bracketing is in effect. If you press the Flash button (up direction button) when bracketing is turned on, nothing will happen. If the flash was previously set to forced on, the camera will turn it back off when bracketing is selected.

Be sure to cancel exposure bracketing when you are done using this feature; otherwise, it will stay in effect even after you turn the camera off and back on again.

AF Area Mode

This first option on the second screen of the Shooting menu gives you several options for controlling how the autofocus frame is set up, when the camera is in autofocus mode. Once this menu option is highlighted, press the OK button or the right direction button to get to the next menu screen, and then use the command dial or the up and down direction buttons to select from the four possible options, as follows:

Face Priority

With this option, the camera looks for human faces. If it detects what it believes are faces, it puts a double-bordered frame on the closest face, and single-bordered frames on other faces. When you press the shutter button halfway, the camera then will focus on the main faces and set the exposure and white balance. This is a good option to choose when you're at a picnic or other group function and you need to take a quick snapshot with as many faces in focus as possible. In other situations, you may want to take more time and select the focus point and other options yourself.

Auto

With this option, which is the camera's default choice, the P500 chooses one or more of its nine possible focus blocks as the main focus point(s). When you press the shutter button down halfway to lock in the focus, the camera will select the point or points closest to the camera and display green rectangles on the screen to show which point(s) it chose for focusing.

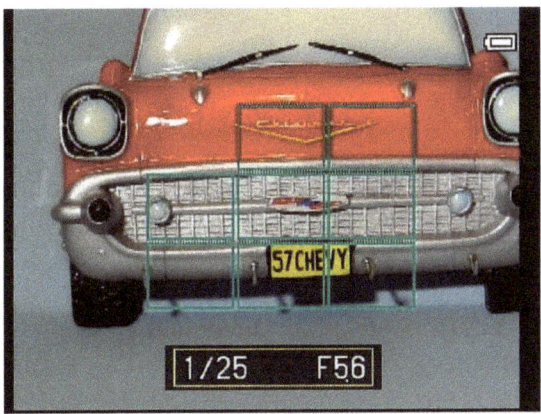

Manual

If you select Manual for the AF Area Mode, the camera displays a focus frame in the center of the screen, with arrows pointing in each direction outside the frame. You can now use the four direction buttons on the multi selector to move the focus frame to any of 99 possible locations around the screen. (There are only 81 locations available if the Image Size setting is 2992 x 2992.)

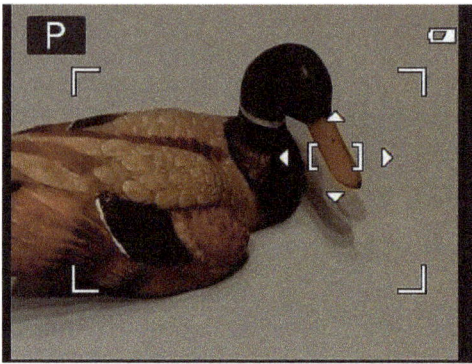

Once you have located the focus frame where you want it, press the shutter button to lock focus and then take the picture. The focus frame will stay in this location as long as the camera is powered on; the location will reset to the center of the frame after the camera is powered off. If you need to use one of the direction buttons for another purpose while using Manual AF Area Mode, press the OK button to return the direction buttons to their other functions (flash mode, focus mode, self-timer, or exposure compensation); then press OK again to return to controlling the location of the focus frame.

Center

With this option, the camera places an autofocus frame in the center of the screen. You can then place this frame over the area of the scene that you want to be in sharpest focus. You can't move this frame around the screen. However, if the point you want to focus on doesn't happen to be in the center of the image, you can lock focus on it by pressing the shutter button halfway while aiming at it, and then keeping the button held halfway down while you move the camera back to compose the shot as you want; the focus will be locked on the target you chose.

116

Subject Tracking

This final option is designed for situations in which you need to track a moving subject, such as a sports competitor or a playing child. Once you have selected this mode, you will see a small, white square-shaped bracket in the center of the screen, with the words OK Start above it.

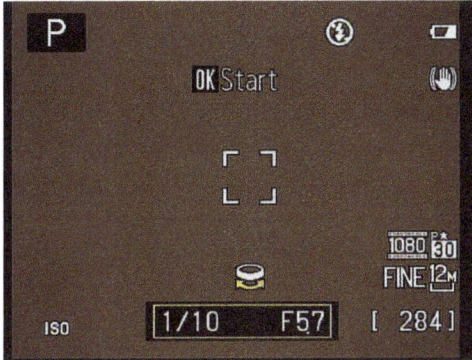

Aim this square bracket at the subject you want to track, and press the OK button. The frame will change to a double set of yellow brackets, which the camera will try to keep centered over the subject, even as the subject (or the camera) moves.

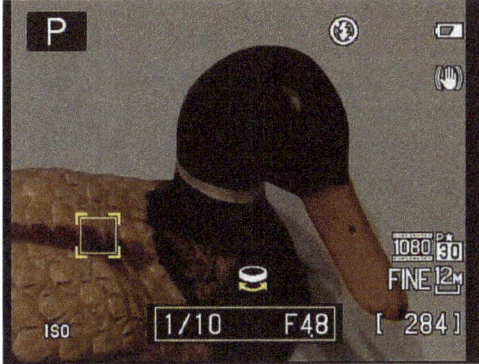

When you press the shutter button down halfway to check exposure, the frame will turn green to confirm exposure, and the tracking will stop. Press the shutter button all the way down when you are ready to take the picture.

117

Autofocus Mode

This feature lets you decide whether the camera will focus just once, when you press the shutter button, or will focus continuously until you press the button. Choose Single AF if you want to conserve the battery and wait until you are ready to take the picture before the camera uses its autofocus mechanism; choose Full-time AF if you want the camera to operate the mechanism continuously. Although the Full-time option will use up your battery more quickly, it has the advantage of keeping the image in focus as you move the camera or your subject moves around; in that way, when you are ready to capture the image, the camera can make the last focusing adjustments quickly when you press the shutter button.

Note that this option does not apply for shooting movies; you need to select an autofocus mode from the Movie menu to cover that situation.

Flash Exposure Compensation

This option works in similar fashion to standard exposure compensation, discussed in Chapter 2. That is, you can dial in an amount of flash exposure compensation up to 2 EV units, in increments of 1/3 EV. When you do that, you are telling the camera, in effect, "Okay, you go ahead and calculate the correct exposure with the flash, but then add in (say) 1 1/3 EV extra, to make the picture brighter." To select this setting, go to its entry on the second menu screen and press the OK button or the right direction button to get to the adjustment screen. At that screen, turn the command dial or use the up and down direction buttons to dial in up to +2.0 EV or -2.0 EV, to make your flash exposures that much brighter or darker. You have to press the OK button to confirm your selection when the value you want to choose is highlighted in the yellow bar in the middle of the screen. When you have activated a positive or negative amount of flash exposure compensation, that value will appear on the camera's display in the upper right-hand corner. That value will remain in effect even after the camera has been powered off and back on, so be sure to cancel it when you no longer need the compensation.

Long Exposure Noise Reduction

This next setting on the Shooting menu is available for use whenever you believe your images may be affected by visual noise, which can be introduced by long exposures. By default, this option is set to Auto, which causes the camera to turn on its electronic noise reduction processing for exposures longer than one second. If you want to have noise reduction applied in every case, you can switch the setting to On, which will cause noise reduction to be applied to all of your shots, though it will not have much, if any, practical effect on the shorter ones. You cannot turn noise reduction completely off. I recommend leaving this setting at Auto unless you find a specific reason to turn noise reduction on for all shots. With the Auto setting, the camera will apply this processing in the cases in which it may really be needed.

Active D-Lighting

This is a very useful option that can help you avoid problems with excessive contrast in your images. Such problems arise because digital cameras cannot easily process a very wide range of dark and light areas in the same image—that is, their "dynamic range" is limited. So, if you are taking a picture in an area that is partly lit by bright sunlight and partly in deep shade, the resulting image is likely to have some dark areas in which the details are lost in the shadows, or some areas in which the highlights, or bright areas, are excessively bright, or "blown out," so, again, the details of the image are lost. One approach to this problem is to use High Dynamic Range, or HDR, techniques, in which multiple photographs of the same scene with different exposures are combined into one com-

119

posite image that is properly exposed throughout the entire scene. I discussed that technique earlier, in Chapter 3.

The Active D-Lighting setting gives you another way to approach the problem of unbalanced lighting, with special processing in the camera that tries to boost the details in the dark areas and reduce the over-exposure in the bright areas at the same time, resulting in a single image with better exposure than would be possible otherwise. If you turn this option on, the camera performs digital processing as it records the image, resulting in some degree of restoration of details in the shadows and in the highlights, to even out the lighting. The menu provides three levels of this processing: High, Normal, and Low, as well as Off, the default setting. In the first image below, Active D-Lighting was turned off; in the second image, it was turned on to the High setting.

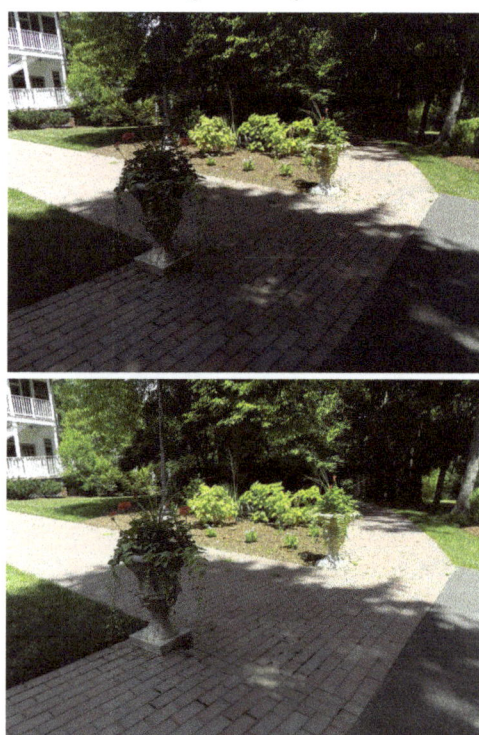

As you can see, with Active D-Lighting turned on, the camera brought out more detail in the shadowed areas without over-exposing the brighter parts of the image.

Note that the Coolpix P500 has a related feature called simply D-Lighting, which is used in Playback mode for images that have already been taken. I'll discuss that feature in Chapter 6.

Save User Settings

I discussed this feature in Chapter 3, in connection with the User Setting sshooting mode, marked by the letter U on the mode dial. To save your current shooting settings for instant recall with the U slot on the dial, navigate to this option on the Shooting menu and press the right direction button or the OK button to save the settings. Be sure you have the settings exactly as you want them before you press the button, because the camera does not ask you to confirm your choice; it just announces "Done" once you press the button.

Reset User Settings

This final option on the Shooting menu lets you reset the settings that are saved to the User Setting mode (U slot on the mode dial) to the default settings without having to go through the menus to adjust each one. For example, choosing this option sets the shooting mode to Program, the flash mode to Auto, exposure compensation to 0.0, the zoom lens to its wide-angle position, and all items on the Shooting menu to their default settings. Note that this option affects only the settings saved for the User Setting mode; if you want to reset all settings for the camera for all modes, you have to use the Reset All menu option, which is found on the Setup menu, as discussed in Chapter 7.

Chapter 5: Other Controls

The Coolpix P500, like many compact cameras, does not have a large number of physical controls. It relies to a great extent on its system of menus to give you the ability to change settings. But, because the P500 is near the upper end of the scale of high-quality compact cameras, it has more actual controls than most cameras of this size, since more advanced photographers generally prefer to be able to make settings with a button or a dial whenever possible, for speed of access. In this chapter, I'll discuss each of these controls and how they can be used to best advantage. I'll start with the controls on the top of the camera.

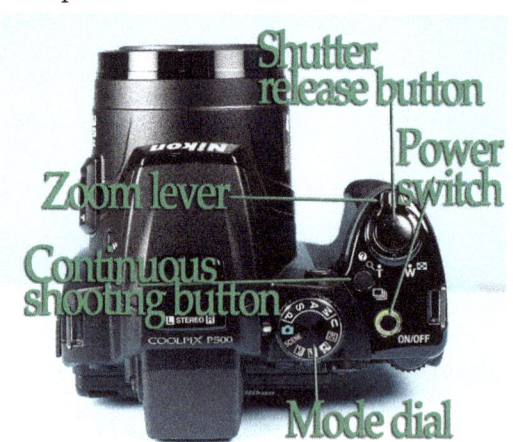

Power Switch

The power switch, located at the right side of the camera's top, may be one of your most often-used controls. Its only function is to turn the camera on and off. When the camera is turned on, the green light around this button turns on. When the camera enters standby mode to save power, the green light starts to blink, and does so for about three minutes. During that time, you can press the power button, the Playback button, the shutter-release button, or the Movie button, or you can turn the mode dial, to cancel standby mode and restore the camera to full power.

Shutter Release Button

The shutter release button is the single most important control on the camera. When you press it halfway down in most shooting modes, the camera evaluates exposure and focus (unless you're using manual focus). Once you are satisfied with the settings, you press the button all the way down to record the image. When the camera is set for continuous shooting, you hold this button down while the camera fires repeatedly. You can also press this button while recording a movie, and the camera will record a single still image (though at a reduced resolution; see Chapter 8 for details).

Mode Dial

The mode dial, located at the right side of the camera's top, is central to the operation of the camera. Its main function is to change the camera from one shooting mode to another. In addition, when the camera has gone into standby mode, and the power light starts blinking, you can cancel standby mode and return the camera to full power-on mode by turning the mode dial (or by pushing the power button or the Playback button).

Zoom Lever

The zoom lever is a small ring with a handle, surrounding the shutter button. Its main function is to change the focal length of the lens between its wide-angle setting of 22.5 mm and its telephoto setting of 810 mm. If you have the camera set for digital zoom, the lever will boost the focal length to a maximum of 3,240 mm. (Though that impressive-sounding zoom amount is illusory, because the image will be distorted by the electronic enlargement of the image.) If you move the lever sharply to either side, the zoom range will adjust quickly; if you move it more gradually, the range will change more slowly.

Note that, when you first turn the camera on, the lens always starts out zoomed back to the full wide-angle position.

In Playback mode, moving the zoom lever to the left produces index screens with increasing numbers of images, and moving the lever to the right enlarges your current image. These operations are discussed in Chapter 6.

When the mode dial is on the SCENE setting and a scene type is highlighted on the menu, you can press the zoom lever to the left, towards the question mark, to produce a screen giving some tips about the scene type. Press the lever to the left again to make the tips vanish.

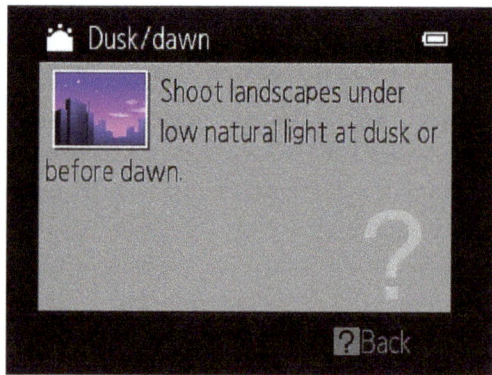

Continuous-shooting Button

This small button, on top of the camera between the shutter button and the power switch, is hard to see, but provides you with great features. In a compatible shooting mode, a press of this button brings up a menu with an impressive array of options. Before describing them, I will provide a brief introduction to the concept of continuous shooting.

With film cameras, continuous shooting involves the use of a special motor to advance the film rapidly, and often the use of an extra-large cassette to hold a large quantity of film. This sort of equipment is bulky and expensive, and, of course, shooting and developing large numbers of exposures is itself quite expensive. With digital cameras like the Coolpix P500, expense is no longer a factor. Continuous shooting is literally available at your fingertips whenever you want to take advantage of it.

The usefulness of rapid bursts of exposures is clearer in some contexts than in others. For example, when you're shooting sports, it's worthwhile to fire off a swift sequence of shots in order to catch the perfect instant when a baseball player tags a runner heading for home plate, or to catch a soccer ball as it bounces off a player's head towards the goal. But continuous shooting also can be helpful in more ordinary shooting, such as pictures of children at play. You have a better chance of capturing a fleeting smile or cute gesture if you keep the exposures rolling. And, even when your subject is not moving, it can be advantageous to take multiple shots. For example, when you're taking a portrait, there may be subtle changes in the subject's expression, or in the way sunlight falls on a cheek. Taking a series of shots gives you some insurance against coming away from the photo session with no winning shots.

Now let's look at the bounty of continuous-shooting options that the P500 provides. To get access to these options, the camera has to be in the Program, Aperture Priority, Shutter Priority, or Manual exposure mode. Press the continuous-shooting

125

button, and a menu will pop up on the screen showing the first group of available settings. If you don't choose an option within about 5 seconds, the menu will disappear.

All of the settings (except the first one, for single shots) offer various ways to take multiple shots while you hold down the shutter button. In each case, the exposure, focus, and white balance settings are fixed when the first image is taken, and they will not vary for later shots, even if the conditions would require different settings. You cannot use the flash for any of the multiple-shot settings except for the last one, the Interval Timer option. You cannot use the self-timer either. Be careful of this limitation; when you select a continuous-shooting mode and then activate the self-timer, the continuous shooting will be canceled, and you may not realize this until you find that your press of the shutter release button resulted in only one image.

By the way, as I discuss in Chapter 6, playing back continuous shots in this camera can be somewhat confusing. In Playback mode, you will see a stack-of-frames icon at the top of the image, indicating that this is one of a continuous set, or, using Nikon's terminology, the "key" image of a "sequence." There also will be a message at the bottom of the screen indicating that you have to press the OK button to display the full set of images. Then, when you press the OK button, you can move through the set of continuous shots using the normal navigation tools—the left and right buttons and the command dial. To return to the main playback screen, press the up direction button. You can then keep navigating through the various individual shots and sequences on the memory card.

Here is the rundown of your wide variety of choices for continuous shooting with the Coolpix P500, starting with the first of the two screens of options.

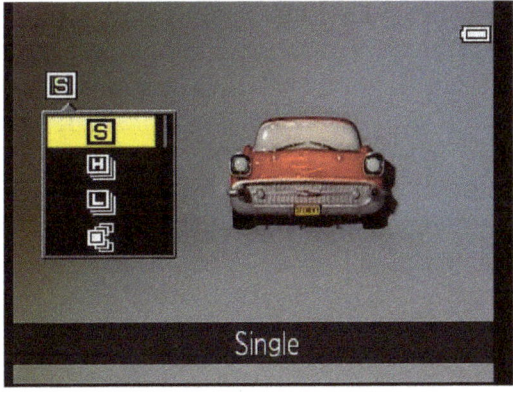

The first option at the top of the continuous-shooting menu is an icon with an S, for single shots. This is the default option. In effect, choosing this first option turns off continuous shooting.

The second option on the menu is the first option for multiple shots. It is marked by an icon that looks like a stack of rectangular frames with the letter H inside, representing high-speed continuous shooting. When you select this option, the camera will shoot up to 5 shots at a speed of up to 8 frames per second, depending on factors such as image size, image quality, amount of lighting present, and the like. You can use any settings for the image quality and size, including the maximum Fine at 4000 x 3000 pixels.

The next icon, marked by an L for low-speed shooting, provides a capability similar to that for high-speed shooting, except that there is a tradeoff of increased capacity versus slower speed. That is, you can take up to 24 images, but at a speed of no more than about 1.8 frames per second.

The next icon down the list looks like a stack of frames branching out into two directions. Selecting this icon activates a novel and fairly amazing feature of the Coolpix P500, which is called Pre-shooting Cache. When you choose this option, the camera actually captures several images before you press the shutter button to take pictures.

127

Actually, this option has its limitations, though it is still a welcome innovation. When you press the shutter button halfway down to evaluate exposure and focus, the camera will take up to 5 images before you press the button the rest of the way down, and up to 20 more as you hold the button down to take the images. The maximum rate is a speedy 15 frames per second, but the catch is that the image size is fixed at a rather small 2 megapixels, or 1600 x 1200 pixels.

The idea here is to give you a tool to use when you are monitoring a scene and waiting for just the right moment to catch a particular action or expression that may come up very quickly, and possibly fade away quickly as well. When it looks as if the action is about to happen, you can press the shutter button halfway down to get ready, and, if the action comes up faster than expected, you won't miss it because of slow reactions. You can then press the shutter button all the way down to capture the rest of the sequence. If you don't mind a sharp reduction in the resolution of your images, this is an interesting option to have available.

Be sure to note one possible pitfall here: If you press the shutter button down halfway but never press it all the way to take any pictures, the contents of the pre-shooting cache will be discarded and no pictures at all will be recorded. You have to press the shutter button down all the way at some point in order to "lock in" the pre-shooting images. Note also that, when you have finished shooting, you may see an hour-glass icon on the screen, indicating that the camera needs time to process the contents of the cache as well as the contents of the other images you have taken.

One more press of the down direction button takes you to the second half of the continuous-shooting menu.

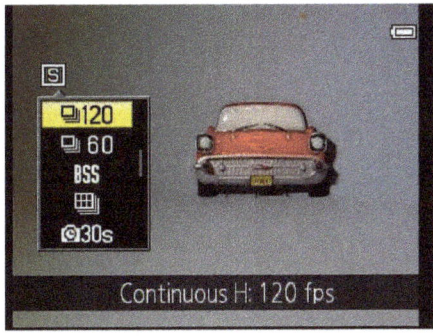

The first choice on this part of the menu is a stack of icons accompanied by the number 120, representing the extremely rapid shooting rate of 120 frames per second. With this setting, the camera emphasizes both speed and volume, giving you up to 50 images at this super pace, but at a drastic reduction in quality, down to one megapixel or 1280 x 960 pixels, which is about the resolution of a modern computer screen. Images shot using this option may look fine on your computer, but they will be quite grainy and will not be suitable for any degree of enlargement. Still, if you need to analyze a golf swing or otherwise shoot a sequence of many pictures over a period of about one-half second, this is the choice for you. Here again, you will almost certainly see the hour-glass icon after shooting, as the camera processes the large quantity of image information that it sucked in like a vacuum cleaner.

The next option is similar to the previous one, except that the numbers are different: This option is marked by an icon with the number 60, for 60 frames per second, and the camera takes up to 25 shots at a somewhat better quality of 2 megapixels, or 1600 x 1200 pixels. Use this option if you need a super-speedy sequence of numerous shots, but need a bit better quality.

The next option down on the continuous-shooting menu is called the Best Shot Selector, marked by the BSS icon. This option is a very useful one, though it is quite different from those discussed above. With the BSS feature, the camera does

129

not emphasize speed. Rather, it takes up to 10 shots at a rather leisurely pace, one after another. When it's done, it "examines" them internally to determine which one is the sharpest, with the most details. The camera then discards all but that "best" shot, and displays it as if it were the only shot taken.

The BSS feature is intended for use with non-moving objects, such as taking a portrait inside a dimly-lit room without flash. (In fact, you cannot use flash when you're using BSS, just as you cannot with most other continuous-shooting options.) The idea is to give you several chances to capture an image that is not marred by blur from camera motion. You can set the image quality and size to their highest levels if you like, and you can control all other settings. (Though, as with all of the continuous-shooting options, the focus, exposure, and white balance will be fixed with the first shot.)

One more notch down on the menu is the somewhat unusual feature called Multi-shot 16, marked by an icon that looks like a frame subdivided into smaller squares. When you press the shutter button with this setting activated, the camera takes a series of 16 images at a speed of about 30 frames per second, and places them all into a single image, arranged in 4 rows of 4 pictures each. So, you end up with something that looks like a proof sheet, or a large set of passport photos.

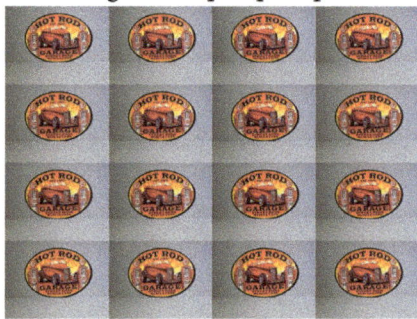

Of course, there may be some variations among the images if the subject moved at all during the half-second it took to capture all the images. This feature seems like a novelty, but you may find a good practical application for it, such as studying the motion of a subject over a short period of time, and this feature might be useful for analyzing some sports actions. The image quality is fixed at Normal, and the image size is limited to 2560 x 1920 pixels, or about 5 megapixels.

Finally, the last entry on the continuous-shooting menu is Interval Timer shooting, which gives the Coolpix P500 a limited capability for time-lapse shooting. When you select this option, the camera displays a small menu with 4 options for the interval between shots: 30 seconds, 1 minute, 5 minutes, or 10 minutes. When you press the shutter button all the way down, the camera takes the first image, then blanks out the display. The green light around the power button will blink slowly to show that interval shooting is active. Shortly before the interval has elapsed, the display will come back to normal brightness, and at the specified time the camera will take the next shot, and so on. If you want to interrupt the sequence of shots before it is complete, you can press the shutter button and the sequence will end.

You cannot take a great many shots with this technique; the maximum numbers for each of the intervals are as follows: for 30 seconds, 600 images; for one minute, 300 images; for five minutes, 60 images; for 10 minutes, 30 images. (That is, the intervals can last for a total of 300 minutes, or five hours.) These images are stored on your memory card in specially designated folders with the letters INTVL in their names. For example, an image might be labeled as 101INTVL-008.

Despite its limited capacity for numbers of images, the Interval Timer option can give you some excellent opportunities for creative photography. For example, you can aim the camera at a site where construction work is taking place, and record all work that is done in five hours. You can then play back these images as a time-lapse movie, using appropriate software such as Adobe Premiere Elements or iMovie. If you used an interval of one minute, resulting in 300 images, you could play back those 300 images at 30 frames per second (the standard video rate in the United States), which would take just 10 seconds to play. So, 5 hours of action would be collapsed into a 10-second sequence. You probably have seen time-lapse sequences of this sort on television, when the program shows weather patterns unfolding at rapid speeds, or shows a speeded-up view of a crowd gathering for an event, etc.

When you use interval shooting, you need to set the camera on a sturdy, steady tripod; the slightest motion of the camera will be magnified and quite obvious when the sequence is played back. Also, you need to be able to keep the camera powered on for 5 hours continuously. The camera does turn off its display between shots, so you might be able to squeeze through, especially if you're shooting for less than the full 5 hours. However, to be safe, you should use the AC adapter designated for this camera, model number EH-62A, which is discussed in Appendix A. Finally, it's generally a good idea to use Manual exposure mode and to set the white balance and ISO to definite settings rather than to Auto settings, so that there is no distracting flickering among the images when the camera adjusts these settings automatically.

Next, I'll discuss the controls and ports on the left side of the camera.

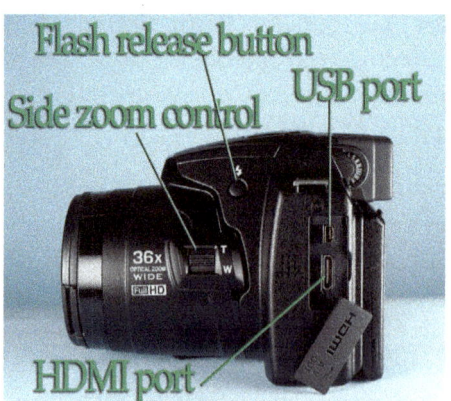

Flash Release Button

This small round button on the left side of the flash housing has just one simple purpose—to release the built-in flash unit so it will pop up and be available for use. If you expect you will be using the flash, you need to press this button to make the unit available; if you don't press the button, the flash will not pop up, and cannot fire. If you select a shooting mode that requires use of the flash, such as Night Portrait, the camera will display a message prompting you to raise the flash. When you are done with the flash unit, press it gently back down until it clicks into place.

Note that the requirement that you press this button to pop up the flash has one clear advantage: When you are in a museum or other location where photography is permitted but the use of flash is prohibited, you can just leave the flash unit stowed away and you can be sure it will never pop up by itself and send out a flash that proves to be embarrassing or gets you ejected from the area. (With some compact cameras, the flash is always available to fire, and you have to remember to set the flash mode properly to avoid having it go off unexpectedly.)

Side Zoom Control

One of the novel and welcome features of the Coolpix P500 is the existence of a second zoom switch, which is located on the left side of the lens barrel as you hold the camera in shooting position. One reason for having this alternative control available is to let you use your right hand to hold the camera firmly, rather than having to reach up to the standard zoom lever on top of the camera. With the super-powerful zoom range of the P500, you need to hold the camera as steady as possible when zooming in to the longer ranges.

Another helpful aspect of the Side Zoom Control is that its function is assignable. That is, you can use this switch to con-

133

trol one of two other functions besides ordinary zooming, depending on your particular preferences. To do this, you use the Setup menu, as discussed in Chapter 7. The first possibility other than standard zooming is to assign the Side Zoom Control to adjust manual focus. If you do so, you still can use the up and down direction buttons to control manual focus, but you then have the option of using the side switch as an alternative. You may like the feel of this control for fine-tuning the focus rather than pressing the up and down buttons.

The other option available for assigning to this switch is a function that Nikon calls "snap-back zoom." Here is how this function works. When you have zoomed the lens in to a powerful telephoto setting, you can "snap" the focal length back to a wider view in a preset amount by a quick press of the side switch down towards the wide-angle (W) position. Another quick press will snap the lens back another definite step towards wide-angle. Then, at any time, as long as you have not used any other controls on the camera in the meantime, you can give a quick press upward on the Side Zoom Control, which will snap the lens all the way back to the original telephoto position.

So, in essence, with the snap-back setting, when you have the camera zoomed in for a magnified, telephoto view, you can experiment with different telephoto settings. You can "snap" the lens back out to a wider view once or twice (or more, depending on how far in the lens was zoomed), and then, once you've checked out those views, which can help you get a sense of your ultimate subject by seeing a wider view, you can snap the camera back to its original telephoto setting without having to use trial and error; that setting has been preserved precisely for you in the camera's "snap-back" memory.

I did not see much need for the snap-back function at first. However, when I was trying to photograph a bird at a long distance using the superzoom lens, I found this feature very useful. When the lens was zoomed all the way in, I found it hard to locate the bird. I eventually realized that I could quickly snap the lens back to a wider view until I found the bird in my field of view. Once I had the bird centered again, I could press the Side Zoom Control back up to snap the zoom back to the full-power telephoto view. So, to help you stay oriented when using the very long focal lengths available with the P500, the snap-back control can be quite useful.

USB and HDMI Ports

These small openings under a little door on the left side of the camera have several functions. The smaller one at the top, the USB port, is where you plug in the charging cable when you charge the battery inside the camera. It also is where you connect the camera to a computer to import photos using the supplied USB cable, and where you connect the camera to a non-HDTV set to view photos or videos using the supplied audio-video cable (the one with red, white, and yellow plugs at one end).

The larger port is where you plug in an HDMI cable (which you need to purchase as a separate option) to view photos or videos on an HDTV set. The end going into this port is a mini-HDMI connector; the end going to the HDTV should be a standard HDMI connector. These cables are available through Amazon.com, at Radio Shack, on eBay, and elsewhere.

Lamp

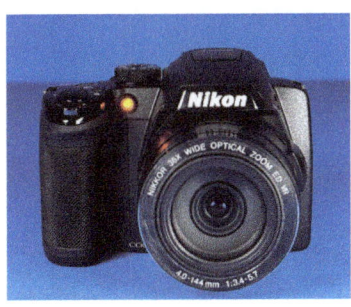

The small lamp on the front of the camera has multiple functions. Its reddish light blinks to signal the operation of the

135

self-timer and smile detection in Smart Portrait mode, and it also turns on in dark environments to assist with autofocusing. You can control the use of the lamp for autofocusing through the Setup menu. You might want to disable it when taking photographs during a religious ceremony or in another environment where this rather bright light could be uncomfortably distracting.

The next group of controls to be discussed are those located on the right side of the camera's back, to the right side of the LCD screen.

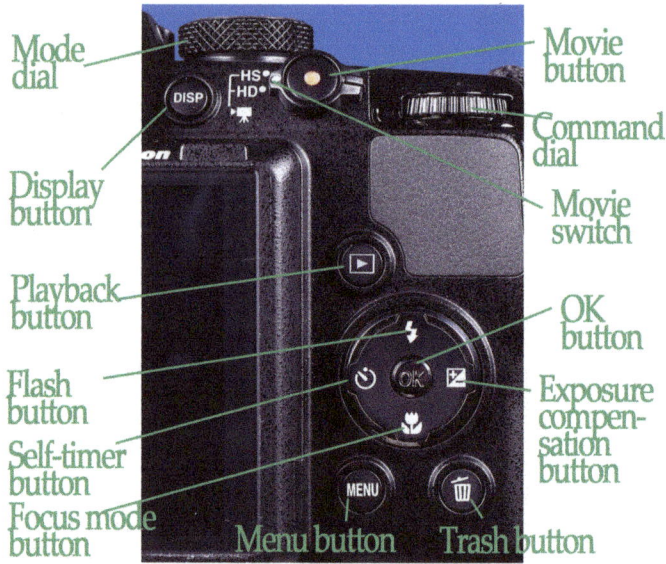

Playback Button

This button, marked with a small triangle, is used to put the camera into Playback mode, which allows you to view your images on the LCD (or in the viewfinder) and lets you get access to the Playback menu. It also can be used in slightly different ways, depending on the context. That is, you can use this button instead of the power button to turn the camera on, placing it immediately into Playback mode. You might want to do this if you know you're only going to view your recorded images, and won't be using Shooting mode. In this way, you won't have to remove the lens cap, because the lens will not extend outward. Of course, if you change your mind and later press the shutter button halfway to go into Shooting mode, you will receive an error message if the lens cap is still on, because the lens will try to extend and will bump into the cap.

If you turn the camera on using the Playback button, pressing it again will not turn the camera off; it will just switch the camera into Shooting mode. When the camera is in Playback mode, you can always press the shutter button down halfway to change into Shooting mode.

When the camera goes into power saving mode and the light around the power button starts to blink, you can press the Playback button to stop the camera from powering off.

Display Button

The button marked DISP, directly to the right of the viewfinder, is used to switch among the various displays of information on the camera's LCD screen or viewfinder, in both Shooting and Playback modes. In Shooting mode, there are three displays available that are called up by successive presses of the Display button: shooting information, which shows the scene before the camera overlaid with icons for shooting mode, flash mode, shutter speed, aperture, image size and quality, number of images remaining, and a few other items; shooting information with a frame overlaid that shows the area of the image that would be used for shooting a movie; and the image alone, with no information except for a lone icon showing battery status.

In Playback mode, there are also three screens available through presses of the button. The first option is photo information, which shows the recorded image overlaid with icons and figures showing the date and time the picture was taken, its identification number, image quality and size, and what im-

137

age number is being shown, out of how many total images. The battery status icon also is shown. The second view is a detailed display of shooting information, which includes a small version of the image along with a histogram that represents the various brightness values in the image along with details about shutter speed, aperture, exposure compensation, ISO value, and image number. The third and final view is of the image only, with just the battery status icon added.

Movie Button and Switch

The red Movie button, at the top of the camera's back just below the mode dial, has one obvious purpose: to start and stop recording of your videos. Press it in once and release it to start recording; do the same action to stop recording. The small switch surrounding the Movie button also has just one purpose: to set the camera for recording either HD (high-definition) video or HS (high-speed and low-speed) video. I will discuss your movie recording options in Chapter 8.

Command Dial

This dial, one of the more versatile controls on the camera, is used to adjust aperture, shutter speed, or exposure compensation when you are using the Aperture Priority, Shutter Priority or Manual exposure modes.

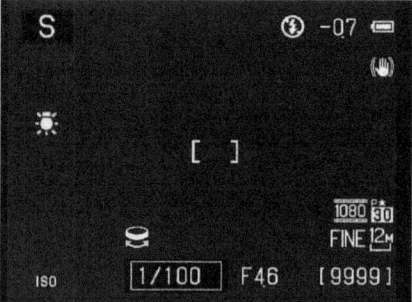

One helpful feature of the Coolpix P500 is that it puts an icon on the screen representing the command dial when there is a value that can be adjusted at that point by the dial. For exam-

138

ple, in the image on the previous page, the icon, which looks like a white disk with a yellow arrow underneath it, is positioned next to the value for shutter speed. This means that you can turn the dial to adjust that setting.

The command dial also has other functions. When you are on a menu screen, you can navigate up and down through the lists of options by turning the dial. In Playback mode, you can use the command dial to navigate through images, adjust the zoom level, and advance or rewind in movies.

Menu Button

The Menu button, to the lower left of the multi selector, is quite straightforward in its basic function. Press it to enter the menu system, and press it once more to exit back to whatever mode the camera was in previously (Shooting mode or Playback mode). There are several different menus available, depending on what mode the camera is in. The three main menu systems are for Shooting, Playback, and Setup, but there also are more specific menus for various shooting modes, including Scene, Night Landscape, Night Portrait, and others, as well as a separate menu for Movie mode. I discuss the menu systems in Chapters 4, 7, and 8.

Trash Button

To the right of the Menu button is a round button marked with a trash can icon. This is the Delete button, which can also be called the Trash button. Its operation is quite simple; this control has no other function other than to delete items. When the camera is in Playback mode, press the Trash button and the camera will display a short menu of choices: Current Image, Erase Selected Images, or All Images. Use the command dial or the up and down direction buttons to highlight your choice. If you select Current Image and press the OK button to, the camera will display one more message, asking you to confirm. You can cancel out of this (or any) deletion message by pressing the Menu button. When you are using the Trash button to delete images in this way, note that, if the image displayed is the key image for a sequence of continuous shots (see discussion of continuous shooting in Chapter 5), choosing Current Image will delete all images in the sequence. (If the images in the sequence are displayed individually, only one image at a time will be deleted.)

If you choose Erase Selected Images and press OK, the camera will display an index screen showing thumbnail versions of all recorded images. Navigate through those and use the up or down direction button to mark or unmark those you want to delete. A check mark will appear on any image marked for deletion. You can enlarge any of the thumbnails to get a better view of it by turning the zoom lever towards the telephoto position; turn it back the other way to reduce the image back to the thumbnail size. When all selected images have been marked, press the OK button, and the camera will ask you for one final confirmation before deleting the selected images.

If you choose to erase All Images, the camera will delete all images that are not protected using the Protect function, as discussed in Chapter 6.

The Trash button also is used to delete voice memos from images with voice memos attached, as discussed in Chapter 6. Finally, this button can delete movies, as discussed in Chapter 8.

Also, when the camera is in Shooting mode, if you press this button, the camera will ask if you want to delete one image. The camera will then display the last image that was recorded, and present a Yes/No choice. If you select Yes, that image will be deleted and the camera will return to Shooting mode.

Multi Selector and its Buttons

The most prominent set of controls on the back of the camera is contained within the perimeter of the multi selector, the cir-

140

cular area with raised edges that function as the four direction buttons. Each of these four buttons also has another purpose designated by an icon on the button. In the center of the multi selector is the OK button. I will discuss each of these controls in turn.

OK Button

This button, which is one of the most-used controls on the camera, serves as a selection, confirmation, or "set" button when you choose certain options. For example, whenever you use the camera's menu system and highlight a desired menu option, you press the OK button to confirm and set your selection. Similarly, when you press the focus mode button (bottom direction button) and then highlight a focus mode on the pop-up menu (autofocus, macro focus, infinity, or manual focus), you press the OK button to confirm that choice. You also use this button to get access to sub-menus. For example, when you highlight Image Quality on the Shooting menu, you then press the OK button to bring up the sub-menu with the list of choices: Fine, Normal, and Basic. Then, you can press the OK button again to make the actual selection.

In Playback mode, when the first frame of a movie is displayed on the screen, the OK button is used to start the movie playing. The button also is used to select any one of the playback controls that appear at the top of the screen during movie playback. (You use the direction buttons to highlight one of these controls, such as play, stop, or rewind, and then press OK to choose that function.)

Direction Buttons

Each of the four directions—top, bottom, left, and right—on the multi selector is also a "button" that you can press to get access to a setting or operation. This may not be immediately obvious, and sometimes it can be tricky to press in exactly the right spot, but these four direction buttons are very impor-

141

tant to your control of the camera. You use them to navigate through menus and through screens for settings, whether moving left and right or up and down.

You also use them in Playback mode to move through your images and, when you have enlarged an image using the zoom lever, to scroll around within the magnified image.

In addition to these navigational duties, the direction buttons are used for several miscellaneous functions in connection with various settings. For example, when you are shooting in Manual exposure mode, you use the right direction button to switch the function of the command dial between controlling shutter speed and controlling aperture. In addition, when you are navigating in the menu system, you can use the left direction button to move back one screen in the system. When you are on the main screen of a given menu system (Shooting, Playback, Scene, etc.), pressing the left direction button moves the yellow selection block to the left column of the screen, which contains the icons that identify the currently available menus. For example, when you are on the main screen of the Shooting menu, pressing the left direction button takes the selection block to the column that contains an S for Shooting menu, a movie camera icon for the Movie menu, and a wrench for the Setup menu. You can navigate up and down through these icons to select the icon for the menu you want to use. You can then press the OK button to select that menu.

The up direction button also has an unexpected extra function. When you are viewing a "sequence" of continuous shots, as described later in this chapter and in Chapter 6, pressing the up button returns the camera to normal Playback mode, in which you view only the "key" image from the continuous set (assuming the Sequence Display Options setting on the Playback menu is set to show key images rather than individual images from sequences).

Finally, each of the direction buttons has its own separate

identity, as indicated by the icon that appears on each of the buttons, as discussed below.

Up Button

Flash Settings. When the camera is in Shooting mode, pressing the top button brings up a small menu showing the options for setting the behavior of the flash unit. (If the flash unit is not popped up, the camera will display a brief message telling you to raise the flash.) Depending on the shooting mode, these options may include Auto, Auto with Red-eye Reduction, Off, Fill Flash, Slow Sync, and Rear-curtain Sync, or possibly just two of those. In some cases, such as when you have selected one of the dedicated Scene modes on the mode dial (Night Landscape, Night Portrait, Backlighting, or Smart Portrait), the top button will not bring up any flash menu at all; the camera makes all flash decisions for you in those modes.

Right Button

Exposure Compensation/Toggle Shutter Speed and Aperture Settings. When not acting as the right direction button, this control has two functions. In Shooting mode, it serves as the exposure compensation button. As I discussed in Chapter 2, you press this button to bring up an EV scale on the screen, and then use the up and down buttons on the multi selector to adjust the value.

Also in Shooting mode, when the mode dial is set to M for Manual exposure, the right button serves as the switch to toggle between having the command dial control shutter speed or aperture, as discussed in Chapter 3.

Down Button

Focus Mode. In Shooting mode, press this button to bring up the small menu of options for the camera's focus mode: autofocus, macro focus, infinity, and manual focus. After you press the down direction button, use the up and down buttons or the command dial to navigate to the icon for your desired mode, then press the OK button to confirm. You have to move quickly, because the menu disappears after a few seconds.

Left Button

Self-timer. This final button is labeled with an icon showing the dial of a timer. Press this button in Shooting mode and the camera displays a small menu of the three available choices for setting the self-timer: 10 seconds, 2 seconds, and Off. If you set a delay of either 10 seconds or 2 seconds, the camera will delay the specified amount of time before taking the picture, after you press the shutter button. Choose 10 seconds if you need a substantial delay so you can get into a group picture after pressing the shutter button; choose 2 seconds if you just need to avoid touching the camera during the exposure, to minimize the camera shake that can accompany a shutter press. You might need to use the 2-second delay when you're taking extreme close-ups, because any camera motion could be magnified by the closeness to the subject. Or, the 2-second delay could help when you're shooting in a dim light and a slow shutter speed is needed, because any camera motion during the long exposure could blur the image.

Unfortunately, with the Coolpix P500 you cannot use continuous shooting in conjunction with the self-timer, so you are limited to having the camera take just one shot after the self-timer delay period runs out. If you need another shot, you will have to press the shutter button again. However, the self-timer does function with movie recording, so you can turn on a delay with the self-timer, and then press the red Movie button to start a movie recording after the specified delay.

Finally, there are a few other controls that are located in their own particular areas, described below.

Monitor Button

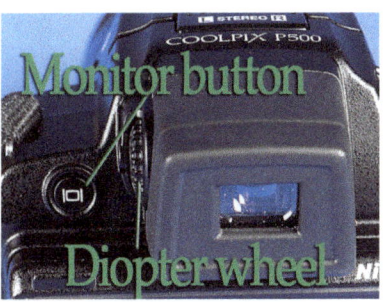

The button at the top of the camera's back, to the left of the viewfinder, has just one function—to switch your view between the 3-inch LCD screen and the electronic viewfinder. Press the button to toggle back and forth between these two views. The default view is the LCD display, with its generously sized, high-resolution screen. But when you're taking photos in bright sunlight it can be very hard to view the image on this screen. Also, some photographers prefer to hold the camera up against their forehead and look through the viewfinder, at least in some situations. So, it's good to have two options.

Note that the Coolpix P500 does not provide any automatic switching between the viewfinder and the LCD screen when your head approaches the viewfinder, as some cameras do; the only way to switch views is by pressing this button.

Diopter Adjustment Wheel

The small wheel on the left side of the viewfinder is used to dial in optical correction to the viewfinder, so you can see a sharply focused image in the viewfinder window. Just press the Monitor button to activate the viewfinder display, and then turn this little wheel in either direction until the image is at its clearest for your eyesight. In some cases, if you wear glasses, you may be able to dial in enough of an adjustment that you can take your glasses off and still see the image clearly through the viewfinder. (I am a glasses wearer, and this works for me,

145

though I usually just keep my glasses on.)

Swiveling LCD Screen

The last item to be discussed in this chapter is not really a "control," but it does allow some physical adjustment, so I will discuss it here. This is the swiveling, or articulated, LCD display on the back of the camera. This screen, even without its swiveling ability, is a notable feature of the camera. It has a diagonal span of 3 inches (7.5 cm), and provides a resolution of about 921,000 pixels, giving a very clear and sharp view of your images before and after you capture them.

With its ability to move up and down vertically, the monitor gives you a considerable amount of added flexibility for your shooting. If you pull it back and fold the screen underneath the camera so it aims downward, you can hold the camera high above your head and view the scene as if you were an arm's-length taller, or were standing on a small ladder. If you attach the camera to a monopod or other support and hold it up in the air, you can extend the camera's vertical height even further and still view the LCD screen quite well.

On the other hand, if you need to take images from a very low vantage point, near ground level, you can fold the screen so it tilts upward towards your eye, and hold the camera down as far as you need to get a mole's eye view of the world.

Also, as I discuss further in Chapter 9, the swiveling display can be quite useful for street photography, because it lets you fold the screen upward so you can look down at the camera while taking long-zoom photos of people on the streets without drawing undue attention to yourself.

Chapter 6: Playback

If you're like me, you take the images you've created and import them into your computer, where you manipulate them with software, then post them on the web, print them out, e-mail them, or do whatever else the occasion calls for. In other words, I don't spend a lot of time viewing my pictures in the camera. But that doesn't mean it's not a good thing to know about. Depending on your needs, there may be plenty of times when you take a picture and then need to examine it closely in the camera. Also, the camera can serve as a viewing device like an iPod or other gadget that is designed, at least in part, for storing and viewing photos. So it's worth taking a good look at the various playback functions of the Coolpix P500.

Normal Playback

Let's start with a brief rundown of the basic playback techniques. First, you should be aware that, when you take a new photo, your image stays on the screen for a couple of seconds for review. If your major concern with viewing images in the camera is to check them right after they are taken, this feature is somewhat helpful, but the review time is very brief, and there is no way to adjust its duration. You can turn this feature off using the Monitor Settings item on the Playback menu.

If you want to control how your images are viewed, you need

to work with the settings that are available in normal Playback mode. Besides normal Playback, there are 3 other Playback modes, which are activated through the Playback Mode menu, as discussed later in this chapter: Favorite Pictures; Auto Sort; and List by Date.

For plain vanilla review of images in normal Playback mode, the process is simple. Press the Playback button, marked by a right-facing triangle, to the right of the LCD screen on the camera's back. Once you press that button, the camera is in Playback mode, and you will see the most recent image saved to the memory card that is in the camera (or, if no card is inserted, to the internal memory). To move back through older images, press either the left direction button or the up direction button or turn the command dial (the dial at the top right of the camera's back) to the left. To move through the increasingly more recent images, use the right direction button or the up direction button, or turn the command dial to the right.

Index View and Enlarging Images

In normal Playback mode, you can press the zoom lever on top of the camera to view an index screen of your images or to enlarge a single image. When you are viewing an individual image, press the zoom lever once to the left, and you will see a screen showing four images, one of which is outlined by a yellow frame.

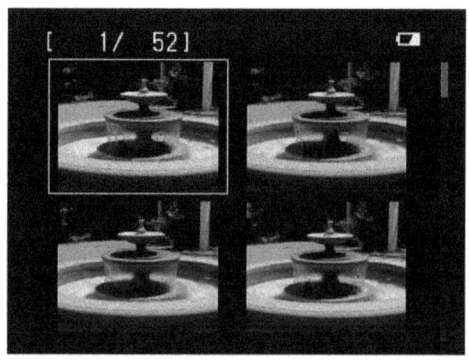

You can then press the OK button to bring up the outlined image as the single image on the screen, or you can move through your images with the 4-image index screen by pressing the four direction buttons or by turning the command dial.

If you press the zoom lever to the left once more, the camera will display an index screen of 9 images; another press brings 16 images; and a last press brings a 72-image index screen (assuming in each case that you have that many images; if not, there will be blank spaces on the screen). You can maneuver through any of these screens to select a single image for viewing. If you want to reduce the number of images per screen, just press the zoom lever to the right repeatedly to reverse the progression of index screens.

Once you are again viewing a single image, another press of the zoom lever to the right enlarges that image.

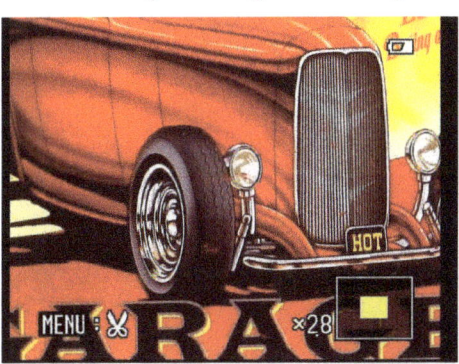

You will see a display in the lower right corner showing an inset yellow block that represents the portion of the image that is now filling the screen in enlarged view. If you press the zoom lever to the right repeatedly, the image will be enlarged up to a maximum of about 10 times normal. While the image is magnified, you can scroll around within it using the four direction buttons; you will see the inset yellow block move around within the white rectangle that represents the whole image. To reduce the image size again, just press the zoom lever to the left as many times as necessary. You can also increase or decrease

149

the zoom level by turning the command dial right or left.

While the image is displayed in an enlarged view, you will see the word MENU in the lower left corner of the screen next to a scissors icon. When you see that display, you can press the Menu button to save the visible, enlarged portion of the image as a separate file. This is actually a rather neat capability, which gives you a rough-and-ready way to edit your images in the camera. So, if you want to crop a group photo to save just the face of a single person, you can enlarge the image and scroll it around until just that face is visible, and then press the Menu button to save a separate file with that face as the only subject. This process is no match for editing with a computer, but it could come in very handy in a pinch, when no computer is available and you need a particular part of an image for a special purpose, such as a business presentation.

Calendar View

Once you have moved the zoom lever to the left repeatedly so the screen displays 72 thumbnail images, one more press of the lever to the left will put the camera into calendar view, in which the screen shows a calendar for the current month, with yellow lines under each date on which images were taken.

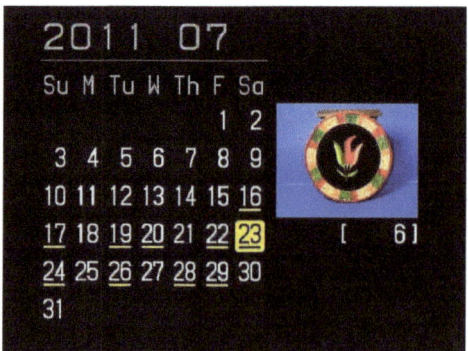

You can scroll through the dates using the 4 direction buttons or the command dial. When you reach the date you want, press OK to begin displaying the images from that date. (Pressing the zoom lever to the left will not take you to calendar view, however, if you are viewing your images using the List by Date option, discussed later in this chapter. That limitation makes sense; there's no need to use the calendar when you're already viewing the images from one selected date.)

Different Playback Screens

When you are viewing an image in normal display mode, pressing the Display button repeatedly cycles through the three different screens that are available: the full image with no added information except battery status; the full image with basic information, including date and time it was taken, file name, image number, image size and quality; and a reduced-size image accompanied by detailed recording information, including aperture, shutter speed, ISO, recording mode, exposure compensation, and other data, plus a histogram.

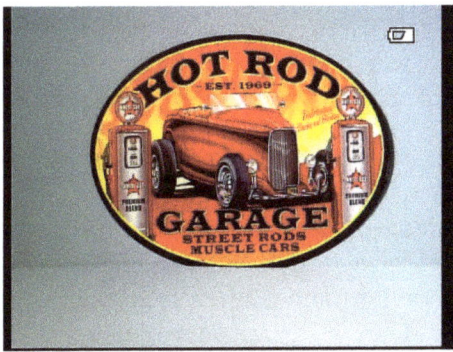

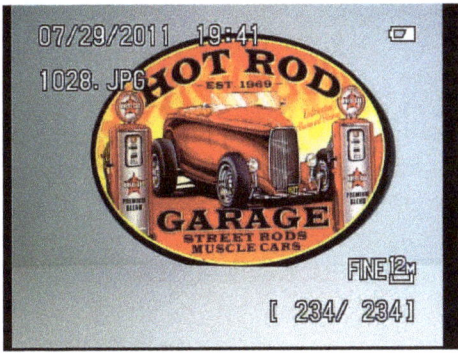

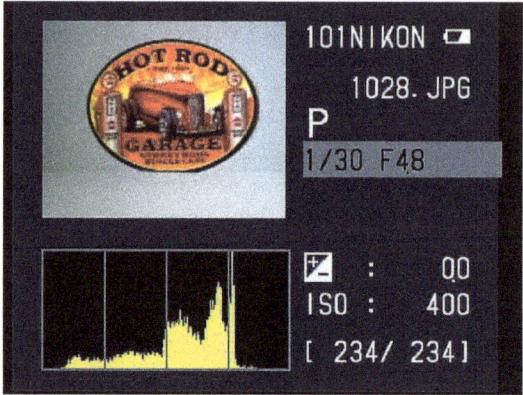

The third display screen includes a histogram for the image. The histogram is a graph, or chart, representing the distribution of dark and bright areas in the image that is being displayed on the screen. The darkest blacks are represented by vertical bars on the left, and the brightest whites by vertical bars on the right, with continuous gradations in between. Also, if any of the highlights in the image are excessively bright, those areas will flash to warn you of the overexposure.

If you have a histogram in which the pattern looks like a tall ski slope coming from the left of the screen down to ground level in the middle of the screen, that means there is an excessive amount of black and dark areas (high points on the left side of the histogram), and very few bright and white areas (no high points on the right). A ski slope moving from the middle of the screen up to the top of the right side of the screen would mean just the opposite—too many bright and white areas.

A histogram that is "just right" would be one that starts low on the left, gradually rises to a medium peak in the middle of the screen, then moves gradually back down to ground level at the right. That pattern indicates a good balance of whites, blacks, and medium tones. The three illustrations on the next page show histograms for shots of the same scene that are underexposed, overexposed, and properly exposed.

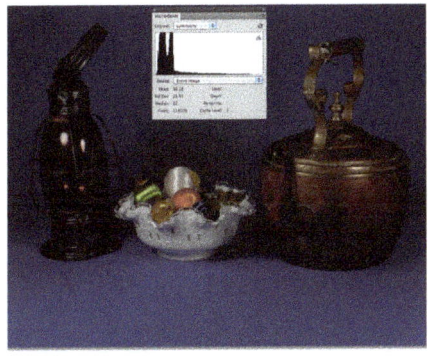

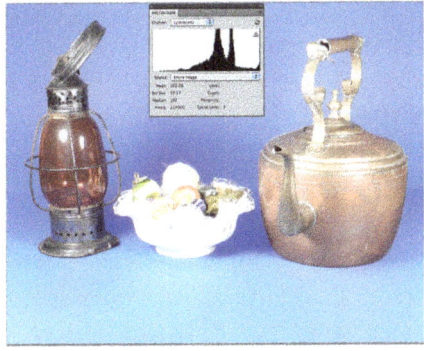

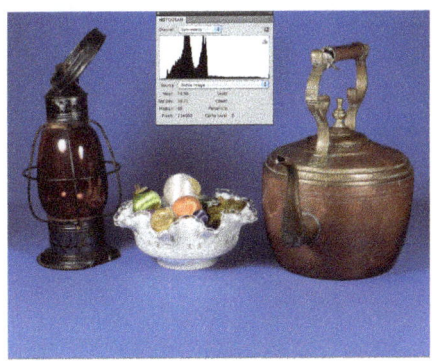

The histogram is an approximation, and should not be relied on too heavily. It may be useful to give you some feedback as to how evenly exposed your image is likely to be.

Viewing Shots Taken in a Sequence

When you take photos with the Coolpix P500 in certain shooting modes or with certain functions, the images become part of what Nikon calls a "sequence." When you enter Playback mode to view those images, you ordinarily will see only the "key" image of the sequence, usually the first one of the group that was taken. To see the rest of the images in the sequence, you have to take other steps. I'll discuss this process in some detail, because it can be a bit confusing at first.

Let's start with an example, which will make it easier to illustrate the way the P500 handles sequences of still photos. Suppose you have placed the camera in Program mode by turning the mode dial to P, and then selected continuous high-speed shooting by pressing the continuous-shooting button and selecting Continuous H from the menu. We'll say you have selected Fine for the image quality and the maximum image size, 4000 x 3000 pixels, from the Shooting menu. Now, when you aim the camera at your subject and hold down the shutter button for a second or two, you will hear the sounds of the camera operating. The LCD display (or viewfinder) will display one of the captured images for a few seconds and then revert back to the view of the live image.

When the camera has settled back to the live view, you can press the Playback button to start viewing your images. If everything worked as expected, there should be five images to view, because that is the maximum number of shots the camera can take using the Continuous H setting. However, when you press the Playback button, you will see only one image from this sequence. If you press any of the direction buttons or turn the command dial, you will move to an entirely different image, assuming one exists; you will not see the other 4 images from this sequence.

Where did those other images go? Well, look at the display on the screen, which has a few unusual aspects. For one thing, if

154

you press the Display button, nothing happens, because you are viewing the "key" image of a sequence. For another thing, you will see the notation OK at the bottom of the screen with a triangle, indicating the Play function, to its right. Finally, you will see a continuous-shooting icon at the top of the frame— an icon looking like a stack of frames, which means that this frame is the key frame of a continuous sequence. What these notations mean in practice is that, in order to view the images in this sequence, you need to press the OK button.

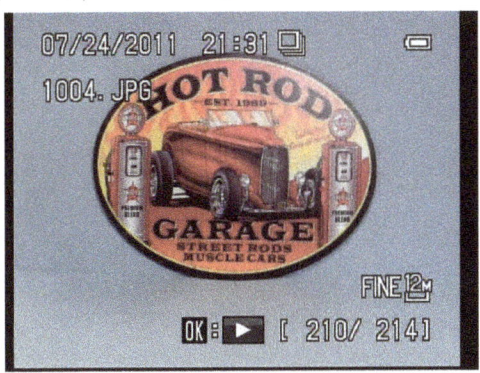

So, go ahead and press the OK button. You will see the same image as before, but now pressing the Display button will cycle through the 3 possible views of the image, because you are viewing this photo as an individual image, rather than as the key image.

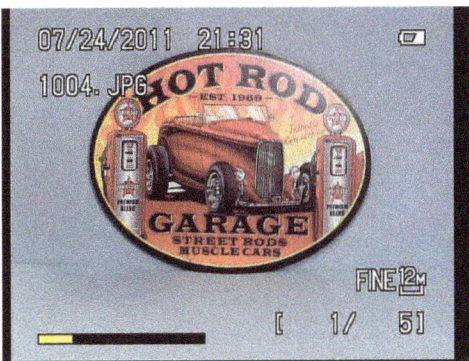

You will no longer see the OK notation; instead, you will see a short yellow bar at the lower left, and the numbers 1/5 at the lower right. The yellow bar will progress across the bottom of the screen as you navigate through the 5 images in this sequence using the left and right (but not up and down) direction buttons or the command dial, and the numbers will increase up to 5/5 as you move to the most recent images in the sequence. You can then magnify each individual image by moving the zoom lever towards the T position, but you (naturally enough) cannot call up an index screen by pressing the zoom lever in the other direction, because only the images in the single sequence are available for viewing at this point.

Once you have "entered" the sequence by pressing OK, you will be "stuck" inside it—you can keep navigating through the images, but you will continue to navigate through the same 5 images, over and over, until you exit from the sequence, back to viewing the key image. There is no prompt on the screen that advises you how to do this; you have to remember the secret: Press the up direction button. That is, when you want to stop viewing these individual images and return to the key image, so you can navigate through the rest of the images on your memory card, you have to press the up button—the one marked with a lightning bolt, which also controls flash functions.

The "sequence" mode of playback applies to the following continuous-shooting types: Continuous H, Continuous L, Pre-shooting cache, Continuous H: 120 fps, and Continuous H: 60 fps. It also applies to shots taken with exposure bracketing and to continuous shots taken in the Sports or Pet variety of Scene mode.

If you would rather not have the camera display your continuous-mode shots in sequences, but would prefer to have them displayed as individual shots, you can switch to that option using the Sequence Display Options item on the Playback menu, as discussed later in this chapter. If you take many sequences using a feature such as Continuous H: 120 fps, which takes 50 shots at a time, you may appreciate the ability to display just the key frame from the sequence when you browse through your images in Playback mode.

The Playback Mode Menu

As I noted earlier, the Coolpix P500 has a Playback menu, in addition to the Shooting and Setup menus, and the subsidiary shooting menus, including Scene, Night Landscape, Night Portrait, and others. Later in this chapter, I will discuss the options on the Playback menu, which control various functions such as image rotation, voice memos, slide shows, protecting images, and others.

When the camera is in Playback mode, there is another play-back-related menu option available, called the Playback Mode menu.

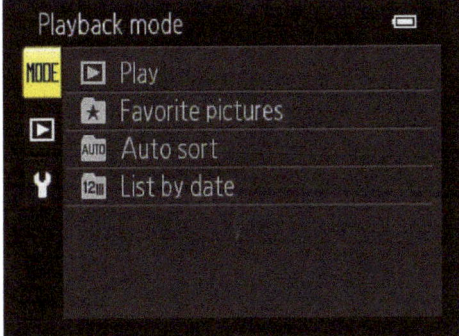

This menu contains options that control which images are displayed, or in what order they are displayed, rather than functions that protect images or otherwise affect them. The Playback Mode menu, designated by the word MODE at the left of the menu screen, contains 4 entries: Play, Favorite Pictures, Auto Sort, and List by Date, all of which are described below.

Play Mode

This first option on the Playback Mode menu, called simply Play, is the default choice. When you select Play mode, you are returning the camera to its normal method of playback, as described earlier. In this mode, all images are displayed, and you get access to them by scrolling with the direction buttons or the command dial.

Favorite Pictures Mode

Using the Favorite Pictures feature, you can categorize your stored images into various numbered Albums of favorites, which you can then recall for viewing whenever you wish. This process does not alter, copy, or move your images; rather, it is just a way of sorting them so you can call them up in organized groups.

To use the Favorites feature, first set the camera to any of the Playback modes except Favorite Pictures mode. That is, press the Playback button to switch from Shooting mode to Playback mode, then press the Menu button and make sure the camera is in Play, Auto Sort, or List by Date mode. (If you need to change modes, use the left direction button to navigate to the far left menu column, select the MODE item at the top of the left column, and then use the right button to move the yellow selection block back to the right and highlight the Play option at the top of the menu list, or the Auto Sort or List by Date option, if you prefer.)

Once the camera is in one of these Playback modes, press the Menu button again to call up the Playback menu (not the Playback Mode menu). If necessary, navigate to the left column to select the right-facing triangle that indicates the Playback menu, then navigate back to the right, to the several screens of the Playback menu. Use the command dial or the up and down direction buttons to scroll to the very bottom of the Playback menu. (It may be faster to scroll up in the menu so you can wrap around past the top, to the bottom item.) That bottom item is called Favorite Pictures. When it is highlighted by the yellow selection block, press the OK button or the right button to select it.

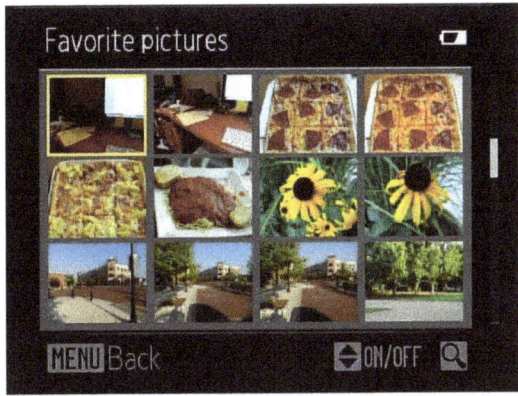

Now you will see the notation Favorite Pictures at the top of the screen and the camera will display a group of your images (if there are enough to display). Move through these images using the command dial or the left and right direction buttons. When an image you want to save as a Favorite is highlighted by the yellow selection frame, press the up or down direction button, and a yellow check mark will appear on the image. Press the opposite button (down or up) to remove the check mark. Move through your images until you have placed check marks on all those you want to save to an Album.

Next, press the OK button, and you will see a screen with a group of numbered blocks, some of which may show a thumbnail image and some of which may be blank. These blocks represent the Albums available for storing your images. Use the command dial or all four direction buttons to navigate to the numbered Album you wish to use to store the images you have just marked as Favorites, and press OK. The camera will display a message telling you to wait while it stores the images. It will then return to the Playback menu.

Now, whenever you want to view the images in a particular numbered Album, return to the Playback Mode menu and select Favorite pictures, and you can select the numbered Album of images to view. When that Album's numbered block is highlighted, you can press OK to start viewing the images in the

Album in full-screen mode. You can also remove images from an Album and change the designation of each Album block from a number to an icon that represents the type of images in that Album; see the P500 user's manual at pages 125-127 for detailed instructions.

Auto Sort Mode

Another useful way to categorize your images is Auto Sort mode. Whenever you take pictures, the Coolpix P500 automatically assigns your images to various categories. When images are taken in the various Scene modes, they are automatically placed into the following categories: Smile, Portraits, Food, Landscape, Dusk to Dawn, Close-ups, Pet Portrait, Movie, Retouched Copies, and Other Scenes. To view images from any of these categories, press the Playback button to put the camera into Playback mode, then press the Menu button, navigate to the Mode tab in the left column, select Auto Sort, and press the OK button.

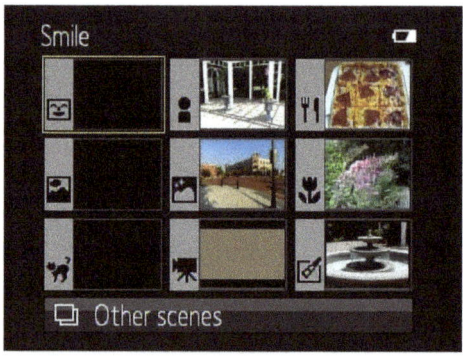

You will see a screen with 9 blocks for these categories, and a tenth item at the bottom of the screen for Other Scenes. Navigate to your selection and press OK, and the camera will display only the images (or movies) from that category. For further information about Auto Sort mode, see the P500 user's manual at pages 129-131.

List by Date Mode

The last of the four entries on the Playback Mode menu, List by Date, lets you select a single date on which photographs were taken and view just those images. Select this option from the Playback Mode menu and press the OK button. The camera will display a screen showing a list of dates on which photos were taken, with a thumbnail image at the left showing the first image captured on that date, and a number at the right showing how many images are available for that date.

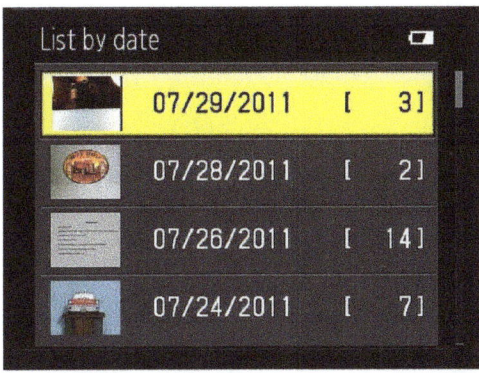

Once you have highlighted a given date, you can press the OK button and browse through those images, or you can press the Menu button, which will give you the options to view them in a slide show, protect them, or take other actions. The camera will list only up to 29 dates; if there are more than 29 dates available, all images taken before those dates will be lumped together as Others. For more information about the List by Date mode, see the P500 user's manual at pages 132-133.

The Playback Menu

We have just looked at the options for basic review of your images in Normal Playback mode, and we have looked at the three other modes that are available for playing back your images: Favorite Pictures, Auto Sort, and List by Date. Now it's time to discuss the numerous options that are available through the Playback menu. Again, it's important to distinguish between the Playback Mode menu and the Playback menu. The Playback Mode menu gives you options for controlling which images (or movies) are displayed—that is, those in a particular category, those from a particular date, or those that you have assigned to Albums as Favorites. The Playback menu, on the other hand, gives you options for controlling how those images or movies are displayed, or what operations are performed on them.

As you recall, to get access to this menu, the camera must be in Playback mode, entered by pressing the Playback button (right-facing triangle). Then press the Menu button and, if necessary, move the yellow block on the screen to the left column and navigate to the triangle icon to select the Playback menu.

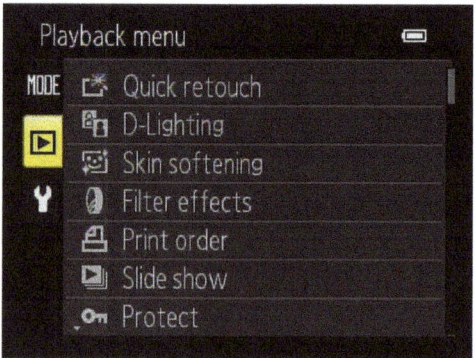

Then move the yellow block back to the right to highlight the various entries in the menu. I'll go through the options on the Playback menu one by one.

Quick Retouch

The Quick Retouch option gives you a way to add "punch" to your recorded images with in-camera processing. You can apply this enhancement to any individual image. If the image you want to enhance is displayed as part of a sequence, you have to use the technique described earlier (pressing the OK button) to display the individual images from the sequence. When the image you have selected is displayed, press the Menu button and choose Quick Retouch. You can then use the up and down direction buttons or the command dial to choose the desired amount of alteration—Low, Normal, or High.

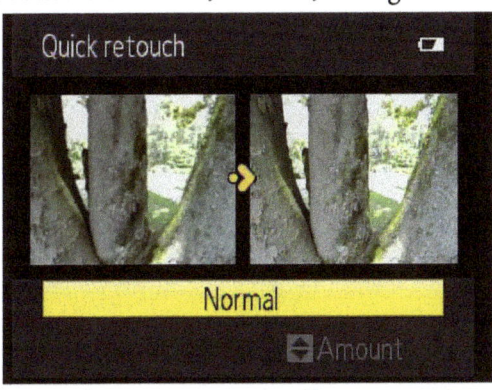

As you change the amount, you will see a preview of the finished product in a thumbnail on the right of the screen, and the original on the left, for comparison. When you have selected the amount of change, press the OK button to confirm, and a new image will be saved with the retouched appearance and a new file number. It will have the Quick Retouch icon on the left side, underneath the file name.

You cannot make any choices other than the level of the retouching. When it applies this processing, the camera increases the image's contrast (amount of difference between light and dark areas) and saturation (intensity of the colors).

This is one of those features that I don't find too much use for myself, because I prefer to do my processing with computer software. But there could be situations in which you take images at a party and want to display them on a TV set during the party. You could use this function to brighten up some muddy images and make them livelier for the audience.

D-Lighting

The D-Lighting option works in exactly the same way as the Quick Retouch feature. Select an image that is being displayed individually (not as the key frame of a sequence), press the Menu button, and then choose Low, Normal, or High for the degree of enhancement. In this case, the camera will attempt to add details in both the shadow and highlight areas, as it does when you use the Active D-Lighting option in Shooting mode. (That option was discussed in Chapter 4.)

Skin Softening

This next entry on the Playback menu presents you with another opportunity to modify your already-recorded images. In this case, you can add a softening effect to the areas in an image that the camera considers to be human faces. As with the previous two menu options, you select the image, press the Menu button, and then select how strong the effect should be. One difference with this feature from the other ones is that the camera will decide whether or not there are any faces in the image you have selected. If it does not detect any, it will display an error message that the image cannot be modified, and return you to the menu without carrying out any processing.

Filter Effects

The Filter Effects menu selection has five sub-options, giving you a considerable variety of additional tricks the camera can perform to create copies of your images with altered aspects.

First on the list is the Soft effect, which blurs the focus of the image to a varying degree, leaving the center of the image sharp and spreading the soft-focus area outward in a pattern you can select: either Narrow, Normal, or Wide, in order of increasing range of the blur effect. You can use this option to create a nice vignetting effect for a portrait, introducing an attractive blurred area with a sort of halo effect.

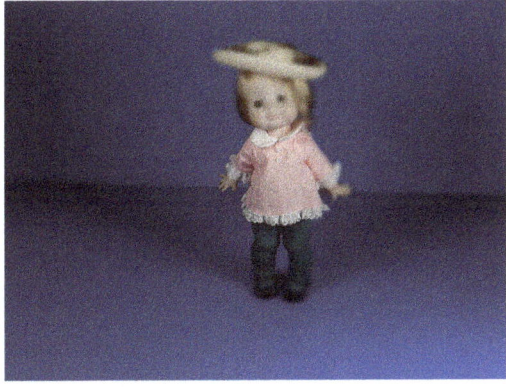

The next option under Filter Effects is called Selective Color. When you display an image on the screen, the camera places a vertical spectrum of colors to the left of the image, with a pointer that you can move up and down the scale using the command dial or the up and down buttons. As you move the pointer next to a color on the scale, the image changes to preserve only the portions that are approximately that color. If no parts of the image are that color, the image turns completely black-and-white. If you use this effect carefully, you can take an image with one area of bright color, remove all other colors using this effect, and end up with a photo that dramatically highlights the single colored object or area that remains, surrounded by a monochrome environment.

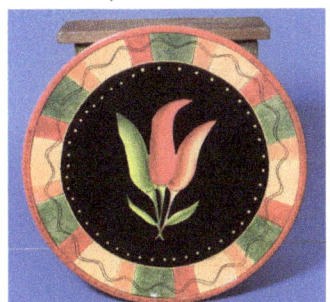
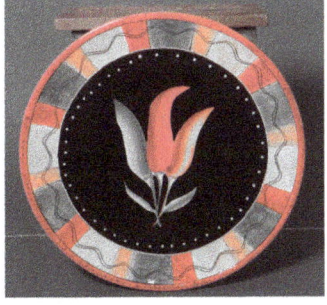

The third choice on this menu is Cross Screen. With this option, there are no adjustments to make; you either save a copy of the image using this processing feature, or you cancel out of the selection. If you choose to go ahead, the camera makes a copy of your selected image that has rays of light radiating outward from bright objects such as lights. If there are no bright objects of that nature in the image, this option will not produce any changes at all.

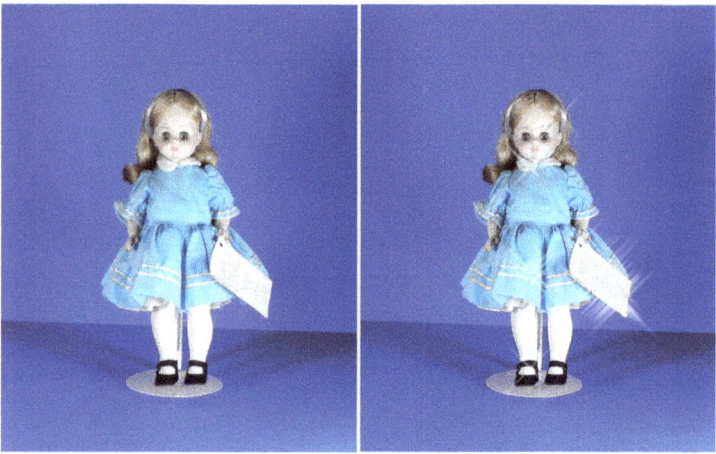

Next down on the list of Filter Effects is the Fisheye effect. You have probably seen photographs taken with a fisheye lens, a super wide-angle lens that greatly distorts the image, making it look spherical as if seen through a fishbowl. With this option, the camera applies processing that simulates this effect. The result will not look attractive unless you choose your subject wisely. It can be appealing or entertaining to distort a person's face or a building, perhaps; it generally works best with a single, clearly identifiable subject. If you use the Fisheye effect on a busy or cluttered scene, it may be difficult to make out the subject at all, because of the distortion.

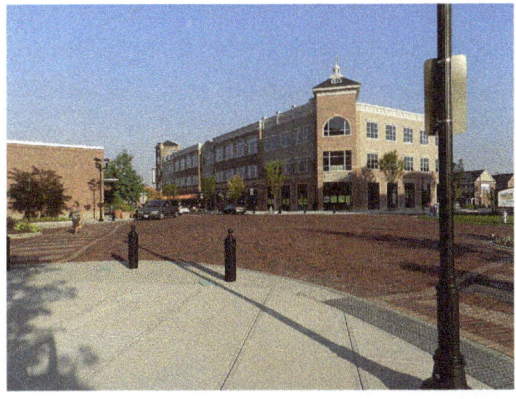

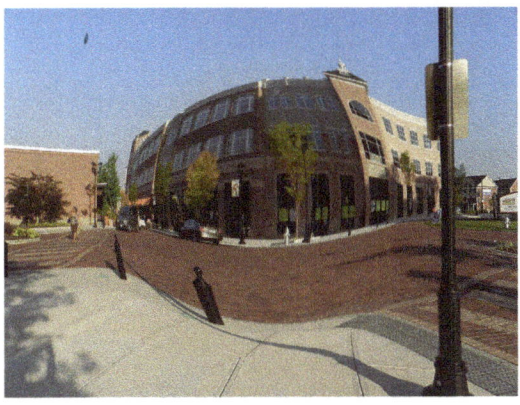

The final effect available is called Miniature effect. When you apply this option to an image, the camera adds blurring at the sides, to simulate the appearance of a photograph of a tabletop model or miniature. Such images often appear blurred at the edges, either because of the narrow depth of field of these close-up photos, or because of the use of a tilt-and-shift lens, which causes blurring at the edges. This is a rather odd and specialized effect, but I have seen it show up on television commercials and elsewhere, so it evidently is becoming increasingly popular. Here, again, you need to choose an appropriate subject. I have found that you are best off selecting something like a street scene or a house, which might actually be reproduced in a tabletop model. For example, if you are able to get a high vantage point above a road intersection, you may be able to get a very effective photo of the traffic at the intersection, and then apply this processing to make it look as if you had photographed a high-quality mock-up of an intersection with model cars.

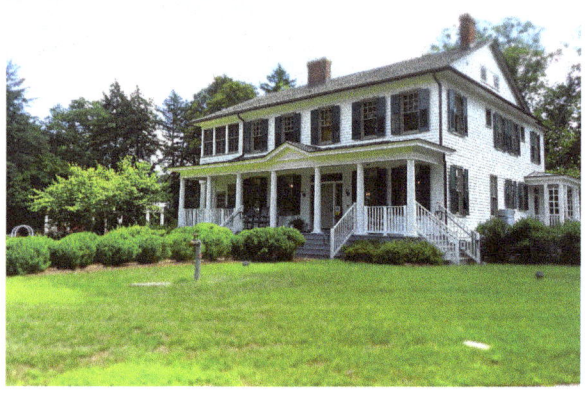

Print Order

If you want to select multiple photographs before sending them to the printer, use the DPOF (Digital Print Order Format) function, which is built into the camera. The DPOF system lets you mark various images on your memory card to be added to a print list, which can then be sent to your own printer. Or, you can take the memory card to a commercial printer to print out the selected images.

To add images to the DPOF print list, select the Print Order option from the Playback menu, then choose the Select Images option from the next screen, and the camera will display thumbnail versions of your images in groups of 12 per screen. Use the command dial or the left and right direction buttons to move through the images. When an image you want to have printed is highlighted with a yellow frame, press the up direction button to mark it for printing; press it repeatedly to in-

168

crease the number of copies up to nine. Press the down button to decrease the number of copies or to unmark the image. You can then keep browsing through your images and adding (or subtracting) them from the print list.

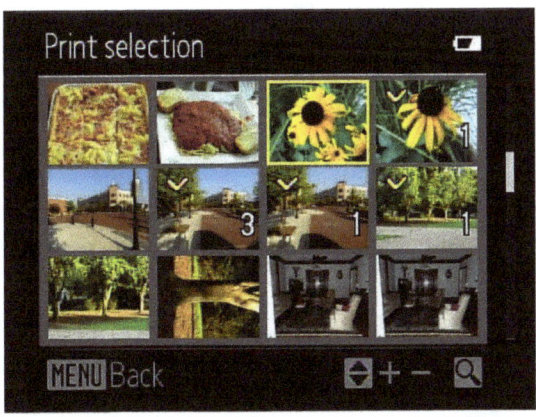

When you have finished selecting images to be printed, press the OK button to confirm your choices and exit from the selection screen. On the next screen, you can navigate to boxes for Date and Info to specify whether the printed images will include the date and shooting information. Then highlight the Done message on that screen and press the OK button. You can take the memory card to a service that prints photos using the DPOF system, or you can connect the camera to a Pict-Bridge compatible printer to print the selected images.

Slide Show

Like most modern digital cameras, the Coolpix P500 has a capability for displaying the images on your memory card (or in the camera's internal memory) in a slide show that plays back on the camera's display or on a connected TV or HDTV. The P500 does not offer elaborate options such as music or a variety of transitions; your pictures are played back with straight cuts between them, and in silence. The only choices you can make from the Slide Show menu option are the length of time between images and whether the show should repeat in a loop.

169

(The loop is not endless; the show will repeat for a maximum of 30 minutes.)

To start a slide show, you need to take one action before you select the Slide Show option from the Playback menu. Your first step should be to select the images to be included in the show, which you do using the Playback Mode menu, discussed earlier in this chapter. Go to that menu and select one of the four available choices: Play, Favorite Pictures, Auto Sort, or List by Date. If you choose Play, the show will display all images. With the other options, you can select a subset of your images, according to how you have categorized your photos. For example, with the Favorite Pictures option, you may have several Albums of photos, and you can select any one of those Albums as the subject matter for the slide show.

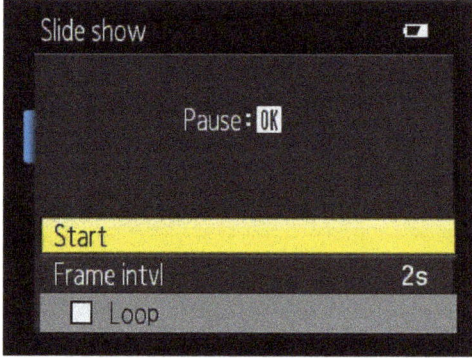

Once you have made your selection from the Playback Mode menu, go to the Playback menu and choose Slide Show. You can then navigate to the option for Frame Intvl and select 2, 3, 5, or 10 seconds for the time between images; then press the left direction button to go back to the previous screen, and press the OK button while the Loop option is highlighted, if you want the show to repeat. After selecting these options, highlight the Start option and press OK to start the show. To pause the show while it is running, press OK again.

Protect

With the Protect feature, you can "lock" selected images so they cannot be erased with the normal erase functions using the Trash button. However, if you format the memory card using the Format command, all data will be erased, including protected images.

To protect images using this menu option, the procedure is similar to that for selecting images for Favorite Pictures or for Print Order. You navigate through your images and use the up and down direction buttons to mark or unmark any image that you want to protect.

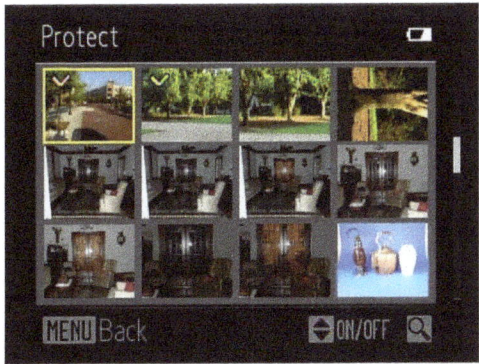

Then press the OK button to apply the protection. An image that is protected will have a key icon in the upper left corner to the right of the file name.

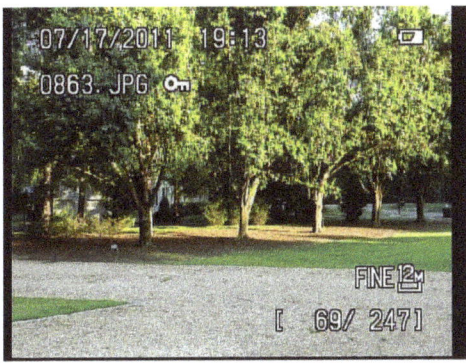

That icon will be visible when the image is viewed with the basic information screen; the icon will not appear in the image-only view or in the detailed view with the histogram.

Rotate Image

Using this option, you can rotate your still photos 90 degrees clockwise or counter-clockwise. You cannot rotate the key image of a sequence when it is displayed in sequence mode; you have to display the pictures from the sequence individually in order to rotate them.

After you select the Rotate Image option from the Playback menu, the camera displays the Select Image screen. Navigate with the command dial or the left and right direction buttons until you have highlighted with a yellow frame the image you want to rotate, then press the OK button to select it.

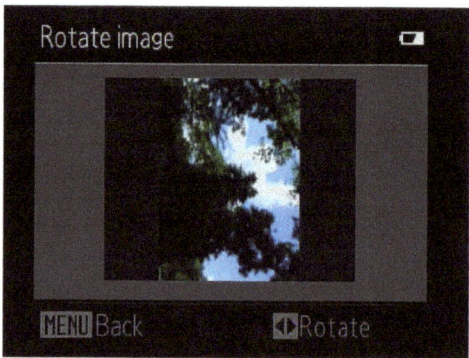

On the resulting screen, you will be prompted to use the left or right button to rotate the image counter-clockwise or clockwise. (You can also do the rotation using the command dial.) Press OK when it is rotated to the orientation you wish, then press the Menu button to display it on the full screen.

Hide Image

This somewhat unusual feature lets you set your images so they cannot be played back in the camera. When you select this menu item, the camera lets you mark (or unmark) the images on the familiar selection screens, applying check marks with the up or down direction button. Once marked, these images will not show up. You can go back into the Hide Image menu option to un-hide any image. Even though they are hidden from view, these images will be erased if you format the memory card they are stored on.

I'm not sure what the main purpose is for this feature; it seems to allow you to select a group of "un-favorite" images. I guess it could come in handy if you wanted to assemble a quick slide show of all your images, but just wanted to exclude a few that did not fit the theme or purpose of the show.

Small Picture

This option provides you with another way to do a rudimentary form of in-camera editing. This feature could be quite useful. It allows you to take any of your saved images and create a new version in a small file size that is suitable for sending by e-mail or posting on the internet. This function could come in handy if you need to take a quick photo and then e-mail it to a friend or colleague. If you don't have software available on your computer to edit the image down to a smaller size, you can let the camera take over this task. Of course, you could take the image in the small size to begin with, but you might want to have a higher-resolution version available for later editing or printing, and be able to create a small version for e-mailing after you have already recorded the original version.

To use this feature, you first have to navigate to the image you want to alter. Once it is displayed, in either full-frame or thumbnail view, press the Menu button, then select the Small Picture option. On the next screen, you can choose from 3 options: 640 x 480 pixels, 320 x 240 pixels, or 160 x 120 pixels. Each of these sizes represents a low-resolution image, well under 1 megapixel in size. If you confirm the operation, the camera will make a copy of the selected image at your chosen size, and copy it to the end of the images on the memory card (or in internal memory). The image will be displayed in the camera with a large, black border area around the image itself, to signify that this is a "Small Picture" copy. This border does not become part of the actual image; it displays only in the camera.

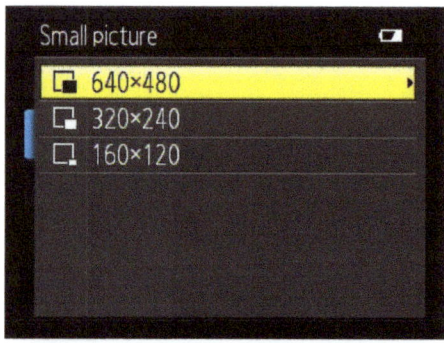

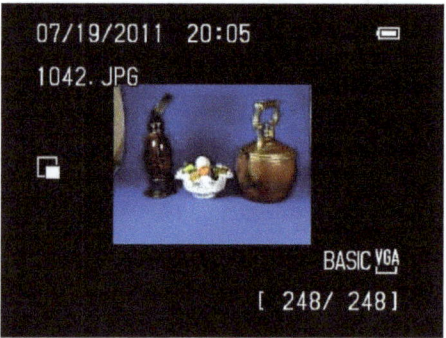

Voice Memo

This option gives you the ability to record a memo of up to 20 seconds with any picture that is stored on your memory card; the image must have been taken with the Coolpix P500, not with another camera. When the image is displayed on the screen, press the Menu button, select the Voice Memo option, and press the OK button or the right direction button to get to the voice memo recording screen. You will see a microphone icon in the upper left corner and another one in the bottom center of the screen, with the word OK next to it. When you're

174

ready to record, press and hold the OK button and talk into the microphone, which is on top of the viewfinder housing. The recording will stop when you release the button, or after 20 seconds, whichever comes first. Make sure you actually hold the button down; if you just press and release it, nothing will be recorded.

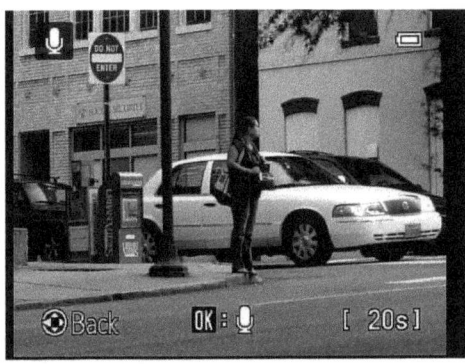

To play back a voice memo, display an image that has a voice file attached; the image will have a musical note icon in the upper left, below the file name. When it is displayed, press the Menu button and select the Voice Memo option. Press OK or the right button, and then press OK on the next screen to play the audio file.

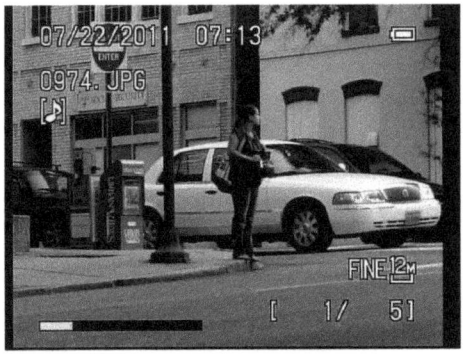

To delete a voice memo, display an image that shows the musical note icon and press the Trash button, then select Current image on the next screen. The camera will display the message,

175

Erase 1 image? at the top of the screen, with three choices at the bottom: Yes, No, and a musical note icon. To erase just the voice memo, select the musical note icon and press OK. The voice memo will be erased, but the image will remain.

Copy

The Copy option lets you copy your images from the camera's internal memory to the currently installed memory card, or from the memory card to the internal memory. When you choose this menu option, the camera first displays a screen with these two choices, represented by icons for the internal memory (a camera icon with the word IN on it) and for the memory card, with an arrow indicating in which direction the copying will take place.

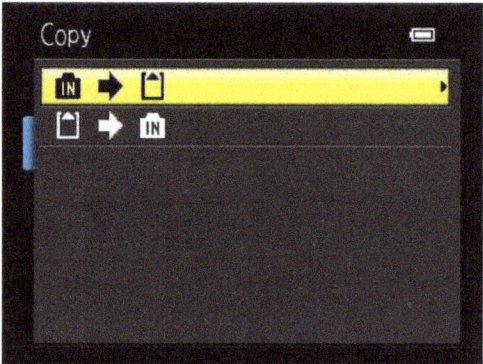

Highlight one of those options and press OK or the right button to move to the next screen. The camera will then give you the choice of copying all your images or just selected ones. If you choose the latter, the camera will take you to the familiar image selection screen. There, you can mark (or unmark) each image to be copied using the up or down direction button. Then press OK, and the camera will ask you once more to confirm the operation. Of course, if you choose to copy all images or a large volume of images from a memory card to the internal memory, they will not all fit, and the operation will terminate with an error message.

176

If you regularly copy your images to a computer, you probably won't have much need for this option, but, like many of the options on the Playback menu, it can serve as a backup procedure when a computer is not available. Also, if you have taken a few images with the internal memory, it can be quite convenient to copy them to a memory card so you can save them, and then format the internal memory for future use.

Copying from an SD card to the internal memory is not likely to be a function you need often, but it could be useful if you're at an event with another photographer who got some great shots with another camera (even if it's not a P500) that you need copies of. You could copy several shots from his or her SD card to your internal memory to take home with you.

Black Border

This is yet another way the Coolpix P500 gives you the ability to perform some types of editing of your images inside the camera. In this case, the menu option lets you create a new copy of an image with a black border around it. To use this feature, you first have to select the image you want to copy and display it, either in full-screen or thumbnail mode. Then select this menu option, and, when prompted, choose from a thin, medium, or broad border. The camera will ask you to confirm your decision, and then it will create a new image with the chosen width of border.

The border will overlap and cut off some parts of the original image. Also, when you view the new image on the camera's screen, it will appear as if you had created a white border, not a black one, because the camera displays the bordered image on a light background, so you can see the black border against that background.

For me, this is not an important option, though it could be useful if you like to have bordered images to display in a slide-show.

Sequence Display Options

This menu option lets you control how the camera displays images that were taken in one of the continuous-shooting modes such as Continuous H, Continuous L, Pre-shooting Cache, and others, which normally are displayed as "sequences." This option is a very straightforward one: You have just two choices—Individual Pictures or Key Picture Only. If you choose Key Picture Only, then, as you navigate through your images, when you come to a sequence, only the key image will display; it will have a multi-frame icon, indicating that it is the key frame of a sequence. You cannot change the display of that image with the Display button or use any of the Playback menu options to manipulate the image; you first have to press the OK button to "enter" the sequence and display the individual images. If you choose the Individual Pictures option, all sequences will automatically be opened up, so the images from the sequence all display as you scroll through your saved images; you will not see any key images or have to "enter" into the sequences.

Choose Key Picture

This option is provided for a very specific purpose—to change the key picture that displays when you select a sequence. Ordinarily, the first image in a sequence is used as the key picture. If you have a sequence in which you would prefer to display

178

one of the other images when the shots are being displayed in sequence mode, you can use this feature. First, you have to make sure the previous menu option, Sequence Display Options, is set to Key Picture Only. Then, you have to display the sequence whose key picture you want to change. Select this menu option, and press the OK button or the right button to activate it. The camera will display all of the images from the sequence; navigate through those images using the command dial or the left and right direction buttons. Press the OK button when the picture you want to choose is highlighted.

Because of the nature of continuous shooting, which captures a stream of images rapidly, in most cases the images will be quite similar. However, there may be occasions when one image stands out above the others in quality and you will want to have it display as the representative of its sequence, so it will show up in slide shows, for example.

Favorite Pictures

This final option on the Playback menu is provided so you can add images to your Albums of Favorite images, for easy recall. I discussed this option earlier in this chapter, in connection with the discussion of the Favorite Pictures option on the Playback Mode menu. Essentially, what you do with this option is select still images (not movies) to be Favorites, and then store up to 200 of them in each Album of Favorites.

Printing Images from the Camera

There is a great deal of variation among photographers with respect to how often they print their photographs on a printer. Some people are content to view their images on the camera's screen; many save them to a computer and share them on sites such as Flickr and Facebook; others send them to friends by e-mail. Still others print enlargements on fine photo paper.

If you want to produce copies of digital photographs on paper, there are various approaches to getting that done. You can import the photographs into a program such as Adobe Photoshop or Photoshop Elements, or use the software supplied by Nikon with the Coolpix P500, or any of many other programs that are available for photo editing. Once you have edited the images to your satisfaction, you can print the finished products from that software.

However, in some cases you may not be willing or able to spend the time to manipulate the pictures in software before printing them out. You may have access to a printer that will connect directly to the camera, and you may need or want to print out copies on photo paper without going through the time-consuming process of transferring the images to a computer first. Or, you may want to try a service that will take your memory card and produce high-quality prints directly from that card. The following discussion will cover the high points of these procedures.

Printing Directly from the Camera

The Coolpix P500 uses the PictBridge printing protocol, which lets it communicate directly with a wide variety of printers. The basic procedure is quite simple: Just plug the black USB cable that came with the camera into the mini-USB port inside the door on the left side of the camera. (This is the upper of the two ports in that location.)

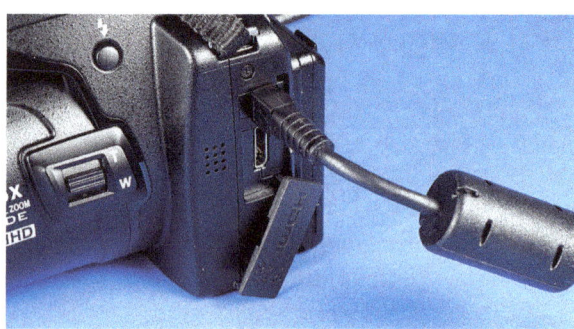

Then plug the other end of the cable into the USB port of a PictBridge-compatible printer. (This USB port is different from the one for the cable that connects the printer to a computer; this one is rectangular; the port for the cable to the computer has more of a square shape.) The printer does not have to be made by any particular company; I plugged the camera directly into my HP Photosmart C6180 printer, and the two devices communicated with no problems.

Once the connection is made and the printer is turned on, the camera should turn on automatically and display a special screen that appears only when it's connected to a PictBridge printer.

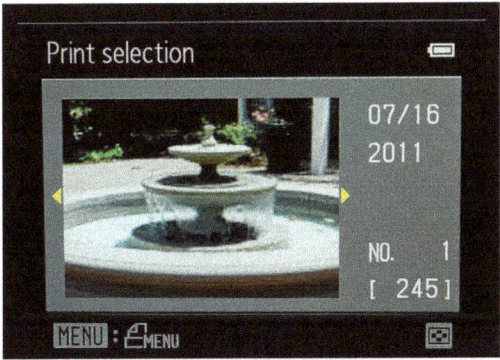

To print an individual image, navigate to the one you want to print and press the OK button; the camera will prompt you for the number of prints and the paper size. To print multiple images, when the print display screen initially displays, press the Menu button to bring up the Print menu, from which you can select images to print, print all images, or use the DPOF selection of images, as discussed earlier in this chapter. For further details about these procedures, see the Nikon P500 user's guide at pages 179-184.

Once you have all of the settings as you want them, press the OK button on the camera to print out the photograph or photographs.

Chapter 7: Setup Menu

Now I have discussed the options available to you in the Shooting menu and Playback menu systems. The next menu system to discuss is the Setup menu. (I'll discuss various menu options for Movie mode in Chapter 8.) The Setup menu gives you various choices for housekeeping matters such as screen brightness and operational sounds, but it also includes some important settings that affect your images, including vibration reduction and red-eye settings. In addition, this menu is where you perform the crucial operation of formatting a memory card.

As a reminder, you enter the menu system by pressing the Menu button. The available menus change depending on whether the camera is set to Shooting mode or Playback mode, and, in Shooting mode, which exposure mode is selected (Program or Scene, for example). However, no matter what other options are available, you can always enter into the Setup menu. After you first press the Menu button, use the left direction button to highlight the wrench icon at the far left of the screen, indicating the Setup menu. Once that icon is highlighted, use the right button to move the yellow selection block back into the list of menu items, and then use the command dial or the up and down direction buttons to navigate through the various options on the menu. I'll discuss those choices in turn.

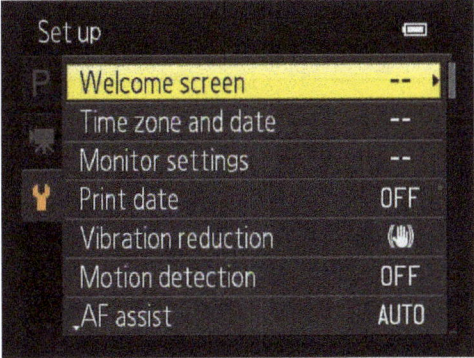

Welcome Screen

When the camera comes from the factory, it does not display any start-up image when you turn on the power. This menu option gives you a way to have it display a standard Nikon start-up logo or one of your own images. Choose this item on the Setup menu, then use the right button or the OK button to move to the next screen, where you can select from None, Coolpix, or Select an Image. If you want the standard Nikon image, select Coolpix, and the next time the camera is powered on it will display the Coolpix logo in a nice-looking graphic on the screen for a few seconds.

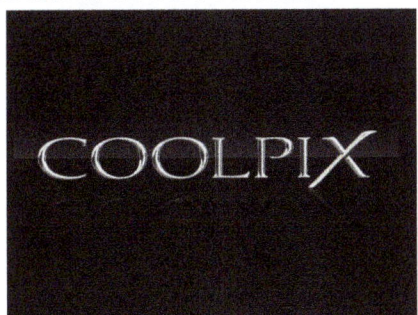

If you want to select one of your own images, the image must be stored in the camera's internal memory or on the memory card that is in the camera. Choose the Select an Image option from the Welcome screen menu, and then navigate through your images. When you find the image you want, press the OK button to select it. That image will then appear every time you start up the camera, unless you change it again using the same process. There are certain limits on the size of image you can select. For full details, see the Nikon P500 user's manual at page 187.

Time Zone and Date

Chances are you set the date, time and time zone when you first set up the camera. If you haven't done so or need to change them, use this menu option and navigate through the various selections using the left and right direction buttons; change the values using the command dial or the up and down buttons.

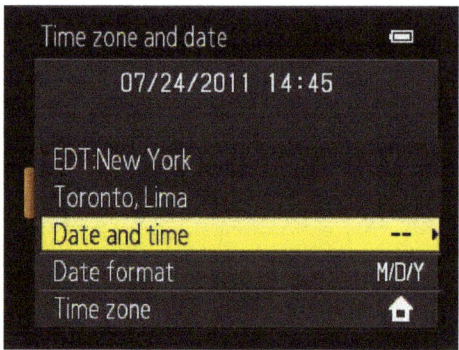

When you get to the time zone option, you have two choices—the home time zone and the travel destination. Set the home zone to the location where you spend most of your time, and set the travel zone for an area you are most likely to travel to. Then, whenever you travel, just select the travel time zone from this menu option, and the camera's time and date will change as required, so your images will have the correct dates and times when you take pictures in your destination time zone.

Monitor Settings

With this menu item, you are able to control several aspects of the way your camera's monitor (LCD screen or viewfinder) displays images.

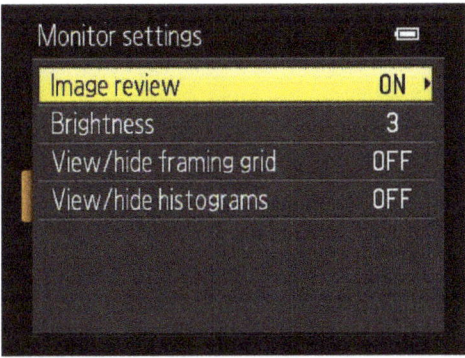

First, you can turn the Image Review feature on or off. If it is turned on, a new image shows up on the screen for about a second when you first take the picture. If it is turned off, the display immediately goes back to the shooting screen when you take a picture. There is no way to control the length of time the image displays; this feature is either on or off. If you want to view a new image for a longer period of time, just press the Playback button and use the normal playback procedures.

The next option, Brightness, lets you select from 5 levels of brightness for the LCD monitor on the back of the camera. Just choose this option and navigate to the setting you prefer. Note that this setting has no effect on the brightness of the display in the viewfinder window or on a TV set; if you have activated the viewfinder using the Monitor button to the left of the viewfinder or have the camera connected to a TV set, the Monitor Settings option will be unavailable for selection.

Next, the View/Hide Framing Grid option lets you turn on or off a grid of vertical and horizontal lines that divide the screen into nine blocks. You may appreciate having this grid available to help you compose your images according to the Rule

185

of Thirds, which calls for placing your most important subject close to the intersections of these lines, to increase visual interest in the photo. The grid also may help you keep a subject properly horizontal or vertical by lining it up against one of the lines on the screen. If you don't find the grid useful, just leave it turned off.

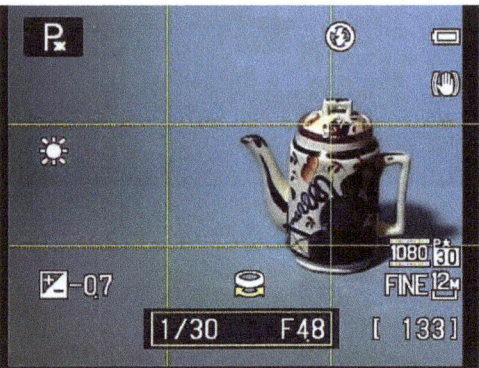

The final option under Monitor Settings, View/Hide Histograms, gives you a way to control whether or not the histogram is displayed when the camera is in Shooting mode. If you turn this option on, the histogram appears in the upper quarter of the screen whenever the camera is set to Shooting mode.

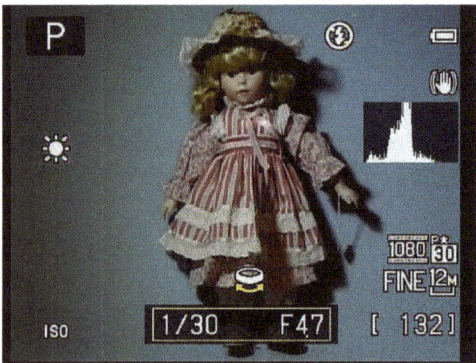

Even when this option is turned on, the histogram does not display under certain conditions, including when you are recording a movie or when the flash mode, self-timer, or certain other screens are displayed.

186

Note that, if this option is turned off, you can still display the histogram in Shooting mode by pressing the exposure compensation button (right direction button) to adjust the exposure. The histogram will turn on in that situation to help you gauge how much exposure compensation to apply.

You should also note that the histogram will always display for still images in Playback mode when you have selected the histogram display screen by pressing the Display button, as discussed in Chapter 6.

Print Date

With this option, you can control whether the camera places the current date, or date and time, on the image when the image is recorded. Note that this option places this information permanently on the image, and the information cannot be deleted (unless you use Photoshop or similar software to edit it out). You might want to use this option if you are taking images as part of a scientific experiment in which you need to record this information as part of your data, but you ordinarily would not want to use it for general picture-taking, because the date (or date and time) information will mar the image. For ordinary images, you can always use editing software to retrieve the date and time information, which is recorded invisibly with the images (assuming the camera is set to the correct date and time). To use this feature, go to the Print Date option on the menu, then select either Date, Date and Time, or turn the option off altogether.

Vibration Reduction

This is one of the more important settings for the camera, particularly because of the extreme telephoto capability of the P500's lens. When you activate Vibration Reduction (VR), the camera uses one of its two systems to stabilize the image. When you are hand-holding the camera, there is bound to be a slight amount of camera motion or shake. At slow shutter speeds, this motion can cause blurring of your images. Any such blurring is magnified at higher telephoto levels, as you can see if you look through the lens at a zoomed-in level. The slightest motion can make the image appear to jiggle uncontrollably.

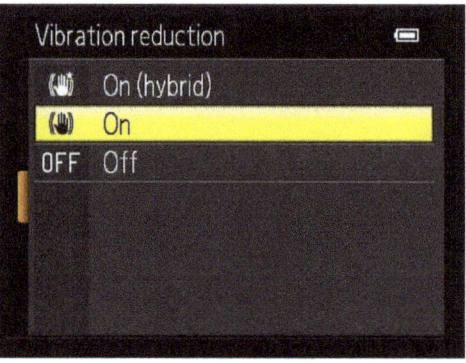

There are three available settings for the VR system: Off, Hybrid, or On. When you have the camera placed on a tripod, you should make sure the VR setting is Off, because the camera's circuitry can get confused and attempt to correct for camera shake when there is none, thereby degrading the image.

For most shooting, you can probably do best with the default setting of On. With this setting, the Coolpix P500 uses just one of its two VR systems—the sensor-shift system. With this system, when the camera detects motion, it causes the digital sensor to shift slightly in a direction to compensate for that motion, so that the optical image that is captured by the sensor is, ideally, free of motion blur. In addition, if you are panning the camera (moving it steadily in a horizontal direction for a panoramic view) or tilting it (moving it vertically in a steady way), the camera will detect that motion, and not attempt to compensate for it; it will only try to negate any movement that is not part of the panning or tilting motion.

If you set the VR system to the Hybrid setting, the camera uses the normal optical (sensor-shift) system and also uses a secondary, electronic system. This system will activate only under certain conditions, including when the flash is off and only single shots are being taken.

I was not able to tell any difference between the On and Hybrid settings, but it may be that the Hybrid setting offers advantages in some situations. You certainly should use at least the On setting whenever you're using the camera without a tripod, particularly when zooming in with the P500's super-telephoto lens.

When you are taking movies with the P500, the normal VR system is not available; you need to choose Electronic VR from the Movie menu in that case, if you want the camera to provide stabilization.

Motion Detection

The Motion Detection option on the Setup menu is a rather interesting feature. It is related to Vibration Reduction, but operates quite differently.

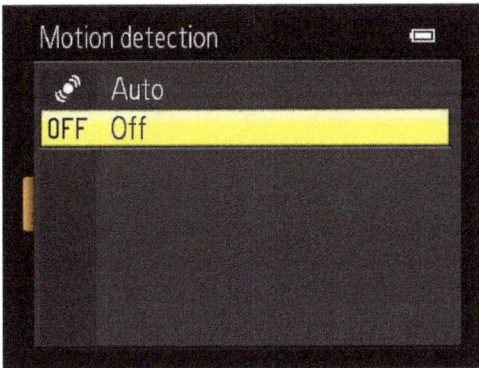

Just as with the VR system, the camera detects motion of the camera that could cause blur and takes action to counteract the possibility of image blur. However, instead of making adjustments to the image processing, the camera makes adjustments to its settings for capturing the image in the first place. That is, when motion is detected, the camera automatically raises the ISO sensitivity level and sets a faster shutter speed in an attempt to use an exposure that is brief enough to avoid blur.

For example, if the camera would normally take a picture at 1/15 second at f/3.4, if the Coolpix P500 detects motion, the camera may increase the ISO level so that the sensor's sensitivity to light is increased and less light is needed to expose the image. In that way, the camera may be able to take the picture at 1/50 second rather than 1/15 second, resulting in an exposure that is short enough to prevent any camera motion from blurring the image.

There is one somewhat unusual aspect to this setting: It is not available in any of the more advanced shooting modes—Program, Aperture priority, Shutter priority, or Manual exposure. It is available only in Auto mode and some (but not all) of the Scene modes.

When this setting is in effect, an icon that looks like a ball with curves emanating from it displays in the upper right corner of the screen. When the motion detection system actually causes the camera to change its settings, the icon turns green to let you know.

In my opinion, this is a useful setting, because it can possibly rescue a shot that would be unusable because of motion blur. Given that it is only available when you are using the more automatic shooting modes, I recommend turning it on. If you want to exercise more control over the camera's settings, you can shoot in Program or one of the other advanced shooting modes and use the Vibration Reduction feature instead of Motion Detection. When you are shooting in Auto or the Scene modes, the Motion Detection setting can be of considerable benefit if you're shooting in dim light where the use of a slow shutter speed may result in motion blur.

AF Assist

This menu option lets you turn on or off the reddish light beam that emanates from the AF Assist/self-timer lamp on the front of the camera. This beam comes on when the camera is trying to focus in a dark area; the light helps the autofocus mechanism find the patterns and shapes it needs to evaluate in order to achieve proper focus. You should usually leave this setting turned on, but you may want to turn it off when you're taking pictures in a place where the beam could be distracting or annoying to others, or where it might alert the subjects of your candid photography. The choices for this setting are Auto or Off. With the Auto setting, the lamp will fire when needed, except with some focus settings and some Scene modes in which it is disabled and cannot activate.

Red-eye Reduction

This next option lets you adjust the camera's approach to solving the scourge of "red-eye" in your images—the red cast to human eyes that results when on-camera flash lights up the blood vessels on the retinas. When you set the flash mode to Auto with Red-eye Reduction, the camera fires the built-in flash unit several times at low intensity before the image is captured with the full flash; these "pre-flashes" are intended to cause the subject's pupils to narrow, thereby reducing the ability of the full flash to enter them, bounce off the retinas, and produce the unwanted red glow in the eyes.

With this menu option, you can control whether or not the pre-flashes fire when this flash mode is active. If you want to turn off the pre-flashes, select Pre-flash Off from this menu item. With that setting, the camera will attempt to digitally remove unwanted red areas from the image after it is captured. If you don't want even that level of red-eye correction, you can just choose a different flash mode, such as Auto or Fill flash.

Digital Zoom

This feature lets you zoom in on a scene electronically, beyond the magnifying power of the camera's optical zoom capability. Because it is an electronic zoom and not an optical one, it does not really increase the information received by the camera; instead, it just enlarges the image digitally, which can result in a blocky, pixellated look. That's not to say that digital zoom is completely useless. It can help you to compose a scene the way you want to, or to measure the exposure on a small part of the scene before you zoom back out to take the picture without the digital zoom effect, for example. And, in some cases, the use of digital zoom does not actually degrade the quality of the image; it just uses a smaller portion of the image sensor's surface, resulting in a lower-resolution image, but without the pixellation of an artificially magnified image.

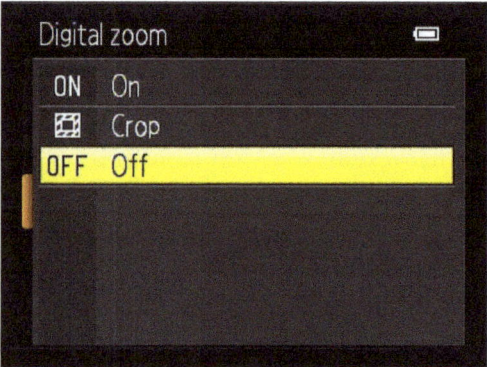

Here is how to use this feature. There are three settings available on the Setup menu for this item: On, Crop, and Off. If you choose Off, the camera will be limited to using its optical zoom, which is really not too much of a limitation, since the P500's lens has the impressive range of 22.5mm to 810mm.

If you choose On, the lens will "zoom" electronically beyond the optical limit of 810mm, up to a maximum of an amazing (though illusory) 3,240mm. With this unrestrained digital zoom setting, beyond a certain level of magnification the camera will use its electronic circuitry to "interpolate" pixels—that is, it will use an educated guess to create new pixels in between those that are actually produced by the image sensor, in order to be able to expand the image to a greater magnification. When the camera is using interpolation, the image naturally deteriorates to some extent because the camera is showing you pixels that are not part of the original image. When this interpolation is taking place, the zoom scale in the upper part of the screen turns yellow to show that the image may be degraded.

Finally, if you choose Crop, the camera takes a different approach to magnifying the image electronically. Instead of interpolating new pixels among the existing ones, the camera crops out the actual pixels that appear on a portion of the image sensor, and enlarges that area to fill the entire area of the sensor. In this way, the resolution of the image is decreased, because the smaller number of pixels from the central area has to cover the entire area of the sensor. Therefore, the Crop option for Digital zoom is available only when the image size is set to certain levels, which allow for cropping. When the Crop feature is in effect, a small camera icon appears on the zoom scale. You can then zoom the lens in so the zoom scale reaches as far as that camera icon. The camera icon will appear further to the right as you set the image size to smaller levels, because there is more capacity for the camera to enlarge the image and still preserve that image size. The scale will stay white in color.

How should you use the Digital Zoom setting? Well, the optical zoom range of this lens is so phenomenal (810mm) that there really should be no need to zoom beyond that. It becomes very difficult to maintain a completely steady image, even with a tripod, at magnifications greater than that. However, if you are trying to capture an elusive bird or other creature with your lens, or have some other special photographic need, I recommend you use the Crop feature if it will help you, bearing in mind that you will have to settle for some of the smaller image sizes. I suggest you stay completely away from the full digital zoom, with its yellow zoom scale. The image deterioration is not pleasant, and there is no need to push the camera to this limit.

Assign Side Zoom Control

I mentioned this option briefly in Chapter 5, in discussing the Side Zoom Control. This switch, on the left side of the lens, ordinarily serves as an alternate zoom control. When you leave it set to that function, you may find that you can hold the camera more steady by using the side control rather than the zoom lever around the shutter button. (Personally, I don't notice much difference; when using the regular zoom lever I can hold the camera quite steady.)

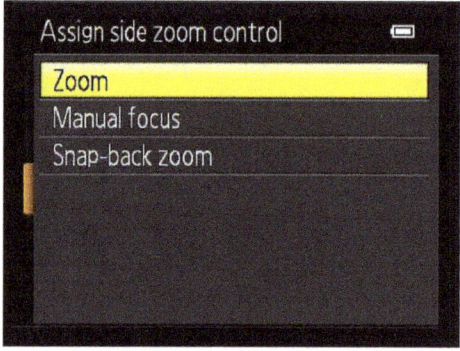

If you want to use the Side Zoom Control for one of its two other possible purposes, use this menu option to choose either manual focus or snap-back zoom. If you choose manual focus, the side control can be used to adjust the focus point, but you can still use the up and down direction buttons to focus. If you choose snap-back zoom, the Side Zoom Control can be pushed toward the W side to "snap" the zoom length back to about half of what it was, in several stages. Then, when you press the switch back in the T direction, the zoom reverts all the way back to its original length. In this way, you can experiment with various focal lengths, or maybe just get a broader perspective on your scene before going back to the original focal length to take the shot. Of the three possibilities for this switch, I tend to prefer snap-back zoom, because it gives the camera a capability it does not otherwise have.

Sound Settings

This next option on the Setup menu gives you a quick way to silence all of the electronic beeps and chirps that sound off when the camera performs certain actions, such as turning on, achieving focus and exposure, or having the shutter pressed to take a picture.

There are not many options here—first, you can turn the "Button sound" either on or off. This option controls whether or not the camera beeps when it starts up, when settings are successfully made, when it achieves focus, and when an error occurs.

The other option for this item is whether to turn on or off the Shutter sound, which ordinarily is heard when you press the shutter button all the way down to take a picture. This sound is automatically disabled in the Pet Portrait mode, during continuous shooting, and during movie recording.

Auto Off

This option lets you control the length of time before the camera enters Standby mode to save power. By default, the camera will stay fully powered on for 1 minute when you are not touching the controls; after that time, it enters Standby mode, in which the green light around the power button blinks continuously about twice per second. After about three minutes in that mode, the camera turns completely off. During Standby mode, you can bring the camera back to full-power mode by pressing the power button, the shutter release button, the Playback button, or the Movie button, or by turning the mode dial.

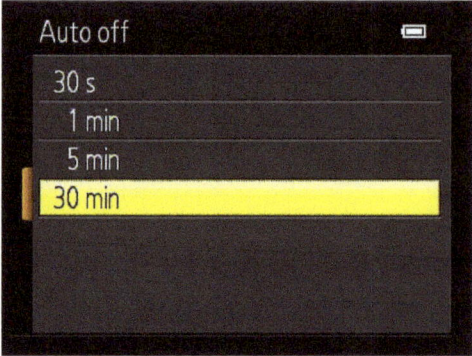

If you would like to set a different interval before the camera enters Standby mode, you can choose 30 seconds, five minutes, or 30 minutes with this menu item. Note, however, that those times apply only when the camera is in Shooting mode, displaying the shooting screen. When menu screens are displayed, the camera will enter Standby mode in three minutes, no matter what setting is chosen for Auto off. Also, during slideshow playback, the camera will stay active for up to 30 minutes, and when the AC adapter is connected, the time before entering Standby mode will always be 30 minutes.

Format

This is one of the more important of all menu options. Choose this process only when you want or need to completely wipe all of the data from a memory storage card. When you select the Format option, the camera will warn you that all images currently on the card will be deleted if you proceed. If you reply by highlighting Format and pressing the OK button to confirm, the camera will proceed to format the card that is in the camera, and the result will be a card that is empty of images and properly formatted to store new images from the camera.

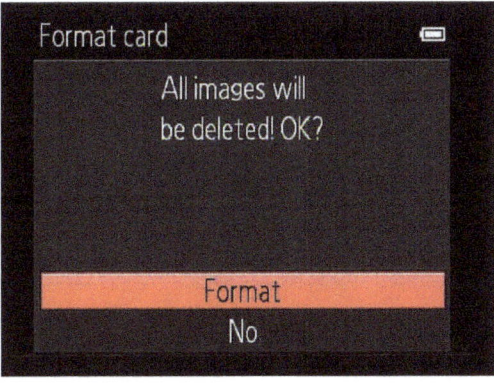

With this procedure, the camera will erase all images, including those that have been protected from accidental erasure with the Protect function on the Playback menu. It's a good idea to periodically save your good images and videos to your computer or other storage device and then re-format your memory card, to make sure it is properly set up to start recording new images and videos. It's also a good idea to use the Format command on any new memory card when you first insert it in the camera. Even though it likely will work without that procedure, it's best to make sure the card is set up with Nikon's own particular method of formatting.

If you want to format the camera's internal memory instead of a memory card, just remove the card from the camera. Then, when you select the Format command, the camera will format the internal memory.

Language

This option gives you your choice among 26 languages for the display of commands and information on the camera's display. Once you have selected this menu item, scroll through the numerous language choices using the command dial or the direction buttons and press the OK button when your chosen language is highlighted.

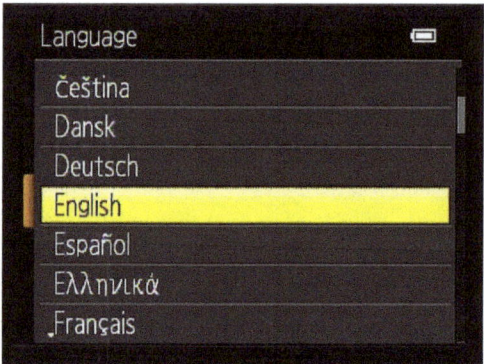

TV Settings

This menu item lets you choose settings for three video-related items. First, the Video Mode setting gives you the option of selecting the appropriate system for the television to which you are connecting the camera by means of the audio-video cable. There are only two options available: NTSC and PAL. NTSC is the system used in the United States, Canada, most of South America, South Korea, Japan, Taiwan, and some other countries; PAL is used in Europe and most other areas. A third standard, SECAM, used in some countries, is not available on the Coolpix P500.

The second sub-option for this menu item is HDMI, which can be set to Auto, 480p, 720p, or 1080i. Ordinarily, the Auto setting will work best; the camera will set itself for the optimum display according to the resolution of the high-definition (HD) TV set it is connected to. If you experience difficulties with that connection, you may be able to improve the image on the HDTV's screen by trying one of the numerical settings on this menu option.

The third and final setting under this menu item, HDMI Device Control, is of use only when you have connected the camera to an HDTV set, and you want to control the camera with the TV's remote control, which is possible in some situations.

If you want to do that, set this option to On, follow the in-structions for the TV and its remote control, and see the list of items that can be controlled at page 172 of the Coolpix P500's user's guide.

Charge by Computer

By default, when you connect your Coolpix P500 to a com-puter using the USB cable, the camera's battery is gradually charged by power coming from the computer over the cable. If you want to disable this capability, choose Off from this menu item, and the camera will not receive power from the comput-er. You may want to turn this charging ability off when you are using a laptop computer on battery power and you don't want to run down the computer's battery unnecessarily. In addition, some users of the P500 have reported getting better battery life by turning this menu option off. So, unless you have some par-ticular need to charge your battery through a USB connection, I recommend going into this menu item and setting Charge by Computer to Off.

Reset File Numbering

This menu option gives you the ability to reset the file num-bering system back to 0001. Ordinarily, the camera assigns in-creasingly higher file numbers to your images, even when they occupy numerous folders on your memory card.

For example, when you start out with a new camera and a freshly formatted memory card, your first images will be stored on that card in a folder named 100NIKON. The first image will be named 100NIKON-0001.jpg. Once the 100NIKON folder has 200 files stored in it, the camera will automatically create a new folder called 101NIKON. If none of your files had been deleted, which would interrupt the numbering scheme, the first file in the new folder will be numbered 101NIKON-0201. jpg. That is, each folder can hold only 200 files before a new folder is created, but the individual files' numbers will keep increasing, even over multiple folders, until the individual file numbers reach 9999. Thus, after roughly 50 folders are filled with files, the individual numbers start over again at 0001.

If you don't like the idea of your folder and file numbers continuously increasing, you can use this menu option at any time to reset the file numbering back to the beginning. That is, if the file numbers have increased to a number such as 0476.jpg, and you don't want to wait until the numbers reach 9999 before they start over, you can invoke this procedure, select Yes when prompted by the menu, and the camera will start numbering your next image back at 0001.jpg. The folder numbers will continue to increase, however; whenever the newest folder contains 200 files, a new folder will be created.

Blink Warning

This feature gives you an automatic alert if the camera detects that a person blinked his or her eyes in a picture that has just been captured. If you turn this option on, then it will operate in certain conditions—that is, when you are using Face Priority for the AF Area Mode, including when you are shooting in the Night Portrait, Scene Auto selector, or Portrait variety of Scene mode.

If this option is turned on, the camera will display the message "Did someone blink?" on a special screen if it detects what appear to be closed eyes in the newly captured image. On this screen, the camera will place a yellow frame around the culprit's face. You can then zoom in on that face using the zoom lever and take whatever other action you wish, including deleting the image or re-shooting the picture.

Reset All

Choose this menu option when you want to reset all of the

camera's settings back to their original (default) values. This action can be useful if you have been experimenting with different settings and you find that something is not working as expected. It will give you a fresh start with known values for all of the major settings on the menus and for shooting. There are a few settings that will not be reset, including items such as date and time, time zone, language, and video system. The complete list of these items is at Page 208 of the Coolpix P500 user's guide.

Firmware Version

The final entry on the Setup menu gives you a way to find out the current version of the firmware that is installed in your camera. The Coolpix P500, like other digital cameras, is programmed at the factory with firmware, which is a semi-permanent set of computer instructions that are electronically implanted in the camera. These instructions control all aspects of the camera's operation, including the menu system, functioning of the controls, and in-camera processing of your images. The reason you might want to check to see what version is installed is that, in many cases, the manufacturer will release an updated version of the firmware that may fix problems or bugs in the system, provide minor enhancements, or, in some cases, even provide major improvements, such as including new shooting modes or menu options.

In fact, the Coolpix P500 has had one significant firmware upgrade since I purchased my camera. The original version was 1.0; the upgraded version, 1.1, addressed some issues with battery life, display of images shot with continuous-shooting settings, compatibility of some memory cards, and others.

To determine what firmware version is currently installed in your camera, highlight this menu option, then press the OK button or the right direction button, and the camera will display the version number.

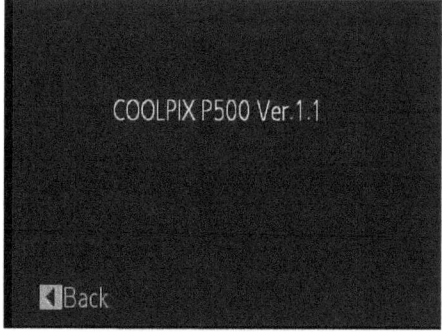

If you still have version 1.0 installed, I recommend that you visit Nikon's support web site; for United States customers, the address is http://support.nikonusa.com; for Europe, the site can be found by starting at http://www.europe-nikon.com. Find the Download Center, and look for the link to current firmware versions. The site will provide detailed instructions for downloading and installing the new firmware. You also should check periodically for any further upgrades beyond version 1.1.

Chapter 8: Motion Pictures

Nowadays it seems that it's a necessity for any DSLR or advanced compact digital camera to include movie-making capabilities. Most recently, it's become standard practice for camera manufacturers to incorporate high-definition (HD) video recording into their premium cameras, and the Coolpix P500 is one example of that trend. And, along with HD video, the P500 offers some extra benefits such as high-speed video recording, which results in slow-motion footage when you view it. I will explain the various options for movie-making in this chapter. Before I get into the specific settings you can make for your movies, I'll begin with a brief overview of the process.

Movie-making Overview

In one sense, the fundamentals of making videos with the Coolpix P500 can be reduced to four words: "Push the red button." Having a dedicated motion picture recording button makes things easy for the user of this camera, because anytime you see a reason to take some video footage, you can just press that easily accessible button while aiming at your subject, and you will get results that are very likely to be usable. So, if you're more of a still photographer and not particularly interested in movie-making, you don't need to read any further. Be aware that the red button exists, and if flying saucers start to land in your neighbor's back yard, the red button will be there for you.

But for those P500 users who would like to delve further into their camera's motion picture capabilities, there is considerably more information to discuss. Even though you can just press the red button at any time to start recording a video sequence, there are several settings that can have a significant impact on your footage. The shooting mode the camera is set to for still images, and the menu settings you make, all have some effect on your movie recordings. So, it is helpful to be aware of the current settings, even if you just want to capture a brief clip of a scene during your vacation.

Quick Guide to Recording a Movie Clip

I will discuss the details of movie-related settings later in this chapter. For now, here are some suggested guidelines for quick settings when you just want to record the action and you don't care about fine-tuning the menu options and other settings. I'll discuss these steps with a bit of extra detail, in case you have turned to this section before reading about the camera's various controls and menus.

1. Locate the red Movie button at the top right of the camera's back and find the small black handle that sticks out to the right of the button. Turn that handle so the white dot on the other side of the red button lines up with the letters HD to the left of the Movie button, for high-definition video. (The letters HS represent high-speed video, discussed later in this chapter.)

2. Turn the mode dial on top of the camera, to the right of the viewfinder, so the green camera icon is at the white indicator mark, putting the camera into the Auto shooting mode.

3. Remove the lens cap and turn on the camera with the power button.

4. Press the Menu button at the bottom left of the control area on the right side of the camera's back. Next, press the left direction button (left edge of the silver-colored round area), then

press the down direction button, which will cause the yellow selection block to move to the movie camera icon in the left column of menu icons, representing the Movie menu.

5. Press the right direction button to move the yellow selection block into the list of menu options. Using the direction buttons or the command dial (the wheel just below the power switch on the camera's back), highlight the top line of the menu, Movie options.

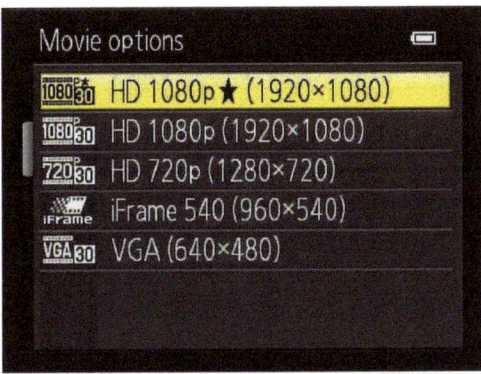

Then press the right direction button to get to the next menu screen, and make sure the top line is highlighted. It should say HD 1080p, with a star, and (1920 x 1080). Press the OK button to select this option.

6. If necessary, press the left direction button to return to the main Movie menu screen. (The yellow rectangle should already be on that screen.) Scroll down through that menu, using the command dial or the direction buttons, until you reach the Electronic VR item, near the bottom of the menu. Use the direction buttons, if necessary, to set that option to On, as opposed to Off, so the image stabilization system will be activated. You can leave the other menu settings as they are for now. Press the Menu button to go back to shooting mode.

7. Aim at your subject and use the zoom lever on top of the camera to frame the scene as you want, zooming in or out as needed. Press the shutter button halfway down until you hear

a beep, to have the camera evaluate the exposure and focus. When the action starts or you're ready to begin, press the red Movie button to start the recording. Then take your finger off the button and hold the camera as steady as possible.

8. Continue to hold the camera steady, and pan (move the camera from side to side in one direction) slowly and smoothly if appropriate to take in the scene before you. When the scene has ended, press the red Movie button again to end the recording.

Other Settings for Movies

The above steps will get you started recording video with the Coolpix P500 using the highest quality recording format and standard settings for white balance, autofocus, and other options. Once you have become familiar with the basic steps for movie-making, though, you may want to experiment with some of the other available settings. There are quite a few items that can be adjusted for recording videos with this camera.

Still Photo Settings Available for Movies

When you are recording movies with the Coolpix P500, several of the settings that you make for still photos, either through use of the controls or through the Shooting menu, carry over to your movies, provided that the camera remains set to a shooting mode in which that setting remains in effect. For example, if, as discussed above, the camera is set to the Auto shooting mode, the Auto mode settings will be in effect, including autofocus and auto white balance. If, on the other hand, the camera is set to the Program mode, the settings for focus and white balance will be whatever you have set through the Shooting menu. In Program mode you can select manual focus, any white balance setting you want, and several other options, although not all items on the Shooting menu will carry over to affect your video recordings. I will discuss below the settings you can make that will work for movies.

Focus Mode

The first setting that carries over to video shooting is the focus mode, set by pressing the down direction button. You can adjust this setting to some extent in Auto mode and you can adjust it more fully in the advanced shooting modes (Program, Aperture Priority, Shutter Priority, and Manual exposure.) You cannot adjust it in any of the Scene modes. Whatever setting you make will remain in effect for video shooting, as long as the camera stays set in the mode in which you made the setting. So, for example, you can set macro focus if you are taking close-up footage. Also, in the P, A, S, or M shooting mode, you can select manual focus. In that case, you have to adjust the focus before you start recording the video; there is no way to adjust the manual focus once the video recording starts.

Exposure Compensation

The next adjustment you can make that stays in effect during video recording is exposure compensation, which is available in all shooting modes except Manual exposure. Whatever adjustment you make before pressing the red Movie button, to either brighten or darken the image, will stay in effect during video recording, and you will see the effects on the screen in the brightness level of the image. You cannot make any changes to this setting during the video recording.

Optimize Image

Turning to menu options, the first item on the Shooting menu that works for movie recording as well as stills is the Optimize Image feature. The availability of this selection for movies is a considerable advantage, because it lets you add a distinctive style to your video footage. You can shoot in black-and-white, for example, or you can use one of the Vivid settings to enhance colors. If you are taking video of people's faces, you may want to opt for the Softer or Portrait setting. Of course, you can only use this setting for movie recording if you set it while

207

the camera is in the P, A, S, or M mode, and if the camera remains in that mode during the video recording.

White Balance

The second menu option that carries over to video shooting is White Balance. Generally, Auto White Balance is adequate, so you can usually use the Auto shooting mode with no problem in this respect. However, if you happen to be shooting your movie indoors, perhaps with non-standard artificial lighting, you may want to turn to the P, A, S, or M mode and use one of the specific preset White Balance settings or even the Preset Manual option. Also, being able to set white balance however you want it gives you the option of purposely setting a "wrong" white balance in order to achieve an unusual color cast. For example, if you set your manual white balance using a blue surface as your standard rather than a gray or white one, your footage will take on an eerie reddish appearance, suitable for some science fiction or horror scenes, perhaps.

Metering

You can set the Metering option however you want it for movies, if you set it while the camera is in one of the advanced shooting modes (P, A, S, or M). Here, as with White Balance, the standard setting (Matrix) is likely to be quite satisfactory for most of your shooting. However, having the option to use Center-weighted or Spot metering may be of use in some specific lighting situations. (You can't use the Spot AF area setting for video recording.)

Self-timer

The self-timer works normally for video recording; just press the self-timer button to activate it and select either a two-second or a 10-second delay. Then, when you press the red Movie button, the delay will take place before the recording starts.

Zoom

The optical and digital zoom work during video recording. Not all digital still cameras with video capability are able to zoom during video shooting, so your P500 is at the head of the pack in this respect. However, to use digital zoom, you have to stop at the limit of optical zoom, release the zoom control, and then start zooming again to cause the digital zoom to start working. I have to say that I don't have much of a problem with this limitation of the P500. My own preference is to zoom in, if necessary, before starting the recording. I try to avoid zooming while shooting a video if at all possible, because I find that motion can be unsettling to the viewer. Also, as Nikon points out in its user's guide, the noise of the zoom mechanism is likely to be audible on your recording. So, unless you're following action that requires you to adjust your zoom range, you're probably better off adjusting it before you start recording. (Though, of course, if you don't mind using editing software, you can later edit out the parts where you adjust the zoom range.)

Shutter Release Button: Taking Stills During Video Recording

When you are shooting movies with the Coolpix P500, you can, in some circumstances, press the shutter button and take a still photo. You cannot do this when taking HS movies, or HD movies in the iFrame format. With the other settings, though, you can just press the shutter button and capture a single still frame. The image quality will be normal, and the image size will be the same as that of the video format you are using. You cannot take another still photo until you see the camera icon re-appear in the upper left corner of the screen.

Settings that Are Not Adjustable for Video Recording

Although, as discussed above, several settings for still photography are available for use during video recording, several others are not. You cannot adjust the ISO, aperture, shutter speed, Autofocus Area Mode, or Active D-Lighting. Several other settings from the Shooting menu do not apply for shooting movies, either because there are specific settings for movies (Image Quality, Image Size, and Autofocus Mode) or because, by their very nature, they apply only to still photography (exposure bracketing, flash exposure compensation, and long exposure noise reduction).

The Movie Menu

Whenever the camera is in Shooting mode, you can get access to the Movie menu, which is represented by the movie camera icon. To reach this menu, press the Menu button, then use the left direction button to move the yellow selection block to the left column on the screen and use the up or down direction button or the command dial to navigate to that icon. Then use the right button to move the yellow block back into the list of menu options on the main part of the screen. I will describe below each of the options on this menu.

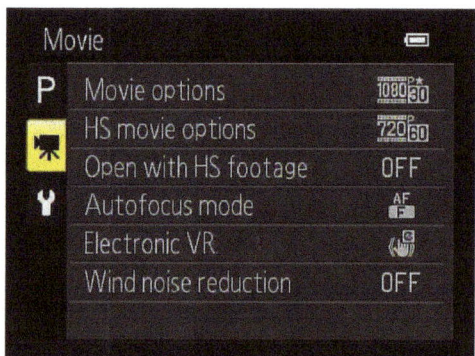

Movie Options

The first choice on the Movie menu lets you choose the size, aspect ratio, and quality of your video footage from 5 possibilities. Before I discuss the specifics of these options, I should point out a limitation of the Coolpix P500 with respect to the length of its video sequences. Like many modern digital cameras that are not primarily video cameras, the P500 is limited to recording only about 29 minutes of video in any single sequence. You can store quite a lot of video on a large SD card (for example, you can fit 140 minutes of the highest-quality HD video on a 16GB card), but you can only record 29 minutes at a time; you have to then stop and re-start your recording. So, choosing a video format that lets you store a great deal of video may not mean as much as it would if you could store a very long single sequence.

With that introduction, here are the details about your various movie format options.

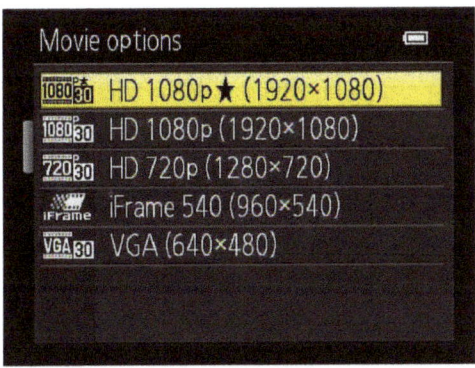

The top two selections look very similar on the menu; they both are designated as HD 1080p, which means they provide high-definition video with 1080 vertical pixels and 1920 horizontal pixels, the same amount on the highest-quality HDTV sets. This standard is sometimes called "Full HD" to distinguish it from the lesser-quality HD that provides only 720 vertical pixels and 1280 horizontal pixels. The letter "p" following the number 1080 stands for "progressive," which provides higher quality than 1080i, where the "i" stands for "interlaced." The only difference between the two 1080p settings is indicated by the presence of a star on the top one. The top setting is of a higher quality because it provides a higher "bit rate" than the second setting. The bit rate represents the volume of data

211

recorded per second: 14 megabits per second for the top option versus 12 megabits per second for the second one.

To reduce all of this technical information to its essence, both of the first two choices display your video in the standard 16:9 "widescreen" aspect ratio common to HDTV sets and both provide excellent results. Choose the top option, which is the default choice, when you want the highest-possible quality for your HD videos. For example, if you plan to show them on a high-quality HDTV set, you have ample storage space on your memory card and computer, and you have a fast SD card to record to, choose the top option. If you need to conserve storage space but still want the highest level of quality, choose the second one.

The third option down on the Movie menu screen, HD 720p, produces footage with 720 vertical and 1280 horizontal pixels, which still provides high-definition video in the 16:9 aspect ratio, but with fewer pixels and somewhat reduced quality. Choose this option if you want HD, but with less-taxing storage and speed requirements for your memory card and computer.

Next, you can chose the iFrame standard, which records your footage with 960 horizontal pixels and 540 vertical. This choice still provides the HD quality and the 16:9 widescreen aspect ratio of the standards discussed above. This format was developed by Apple Computer, Inc.; its purpose is to provide increased ease of editing your footage in Apple's iMovie software. So, if you plan to edit your video on a Macintosh using iMovie, you may want to try using the iFrame format. Otherwise, there probably is no advantage to using it.

Finally, you can select the bottom option on the list, VGA. This is the only non-HD format offered for normal (non-high-speed) video recording with the Coolpix P500. The VGA format is named after the standard resolution of an old-fashioned computer monitor, which has a display of 640 horizontal pixels and 480 vertical ones, resulting in an aspect ratio of 4:3, like that of the camera's LCD display. This format has the advantage of using virtually all of the area of the camera's display, but, of course, it does not provide the quality of high-definition video. Its appearance will be noticeably coarse and rough in comparison to that of HD footage. You may want to choose this option if you don't need high quality, and just need to record some information, such as doing a video inventory of your household goods. Or, you may choose this option if your memory card is running out of space or does not provide the speed that is required for recording HD formats. Also, if you plan to send the footage by e-mail, this format will be easier to deal with than the HD ones.

HS Movie Options

The second choice on the Movie menu lets you choose the speed at which you record HS movies with the Coolpix P500. I have not discussed the HS capabilities of the camera before now, so I will take this opportunity to explain the use of this very interesting feature.

First, the use of the abbreviation HS, for high-speed, is something of a misnomer. Actually, the HS choices include both high-speed and low-speed options. It would be more accurate to use a term such as "non-standard-speed," but that would be rather awkward. HS is a convenient shorthand, but you just have to bear in mind that it is not precisely accurate.

With that introduction, here is a brief explanation of how the HS feature works. The standard rate for recording and playing back video (in the United States) is 30 frames per second. That is, the camera takes 30 individual images each second and then plays them back at that same rate. When your eyes see those images, the pictures follow each other so rapidly that it seems as if the motion in the scene is continuous, rather than 30 separate still photos, which is the actual situation.

If you have seen old silent movies, they sometimes seem un-naturally fast and jerky. That happens because those movies were recorded at a slower speed than movies of today, but sometimes are played back on modern projectors at a faster rate. So, if a movie were recorded at, say, 15 frames per second, and then played back at 30 frames per second, the action in the movie would appear to be twice as fast as normal, resulting in a jumpy, jerky, speeded-up appearance.

Similarly, if you were to set a camera to record at 60 frames per second, and then play back the footage at 30 frames per second, the action would appear to be slowed down to one-half its normal rate.

The Coolpix P500 gives you the ability to either increase or decrease the frame rate at which it records video footage. It's important to note that the video will always play back in the camera at the standard 30 frames per second; the only factor you can change is the speed at which the video is recorded.

To use this feature, you turn the switch around the red Movie button to point to the HS option, instead of the HD one.

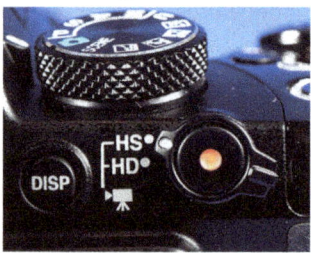

Then, of course, you have to use the Movie menu to choose from the available options on the HS movie options line. Once you have made those choices, just press the red button when you are ready to start recording.

With that introduction, I will discuss each of the options on the HS movie options menu.

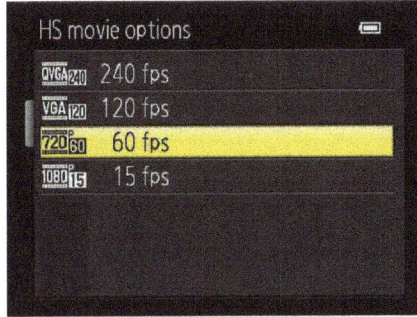

The first choice, 240 fps, sets the camera to record video at 240 frames per second, which, of course, is 8 times faster than the normal 30 fps. When this footage is played back in the camera, any movement will appear to be at one-eighth normal speed. This setting provides an excellent capability for true slow-motion video, which you can use to analyze a golf swing, slow down the beating of a hummingbird's wings, or for any of a myriad of sports and nature applications. Or, you might just like slow-motion for its dreamlike, underwater-style motion.

The one major caveat with this setting is that, not surprisingly, the use of this setting requires a sharp tradeoff of speed against quality. When you set the camera to record 240 frames per second, it automatically reduces the quality to QVGA, standing for one-quarter VGA, which is a very low quality, with 320 horizontal pixels and 240 vertical ones, only one-quarter the pixels of even the VGA standard. The aspect ratio is 4:3. There also is another limitation: The camera can only record for 10 seconds at this rate, which results in a playback time of 80 seconds. However, for many applications, that amount of time should be sufficient.

The next setting, 120 fps, gives you half as much slow-motion capability as the first one, at greater quality. In this case, your footage will play back at one-quarter normal speed, and at full VGA quality. You are limited to recording at this speed for 15 seconds, resulting in one minute of playback time.

Moving down the menu list, the next choice is 60 fps, which is the first option that lets you record slow-motion HD footage. You can record HD quality at 1280 by 720 pixels (in the 16:9 aspect ratio) for 30 seconds, giving you one minute of half-speed playback time.

Finally, we come to the final option on the list, which turns the whole exercise in a different direction. This option, 15 fps, is the only one in which the camera records at a slower than normal speed. In this case, when played back at the normal 30 frames per second, the footage will appear to be speeded up to twice the normal speed. And, as a bonus, because the camera is actually doing less work in terms of speed, it can provide higher-quality video: full HD, at 1920 by 1080 pixels, recording for 2 minutes, with a playback time of one minute.

Open with HS Footage

The third option on the Movie menu lets you control the way the camera records video when the switch around the red Movie button is turned to the HS setting. As discussed above in connection with the various HS recording options, the camera is quite limited in the length of time it can record in any of the HS formats, ranging from 10 seconds at the 240 fps setting to 2 minutes at the 15 fps setting. With the Open with HS Footage option, you can decide whether the camera immediately starts using the HS setting you specified in the Movie menu, or whether it waits until you press the OK button to start using that setting.

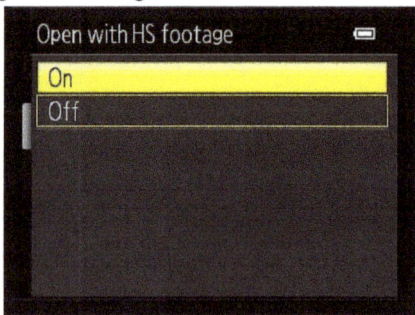

This option is needed because of the limited time available at the HS setting. So, for example, if you are taking footage of a bird in a birdbath, and you want to wait until it starts flying to use the 240 fps setting, you can set the Open with HS Footage option to Off. Then, when you turn the movie switch to the HS indicator and then press the red Movie button, the camera will start out recording footage at the normal speed of 30 frames per second, at the QVGA quality that it will use for this setting. The screen will display the message OK: HS 240, meaning that, when you press the OK button, the camera will switch to recording at 240 frames per second. Of course, it will only do so for its maximum of 10 seconds. After the 10 seconds at 240 fps, the camera will go back to recording at 30 fps for a short time, but then, once it has "recovered," it will again display the message to press OK to go into 240 fps mode. So, you can take multiple sequences at 240 fps, but you have to let the camera revert to 30 fps to catch its breath in between those sequences.

A similar situation exists for each of the other HS modes. For example, if you choose 60 fps, the camera will start recording in 720p format at 30 fps. When you press OK, the camera will record at 60 fps in that quality.

If you set the Open with HS Footage option to On, then the camera will immediately start recording in the selected HS format when you press the red Movie button. Thereafter, the camera will switch between formats when it reaches the time limit for each format, as discussed above.

Autofocus Mode

This next choice on the Movie menu controls how the camera focuses when you are recording videos. Your focus options for movie-making are a bit tricky, so I'll go through them again here. First, it's important to remember that the shooting mode you select has an impact on video recording in this area. That is if you choose the Auto shooting mode, the camera will use autofocus for video shooting. However, if you choose the Program, Aperture Priority, Shutter Priority, or Manual exposure mode, you have the option of choosing manual focus, and that choice will carry over to video shooting.

So, if you want to use the Autofocus Mode option on the Movie menu, you have to make sure that you have the camera set for autofocus, not manual focus. If the camera is set for manual focus, you will find that you cannot get access to the Autofocus Mode option on the Movie menu. You will not see any indication such as MF on the screen when you are shooting videos, though, so you need to be careful not to leave the camera set for manual focus when recording video (unless, of course, you want to use manual focus for your video shooting).

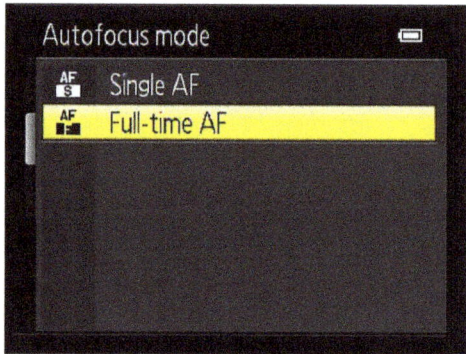

Assuming the camera is set for autofocus shooting, you can use this menu option on the Movie menu to choose either Single AF or Full-time AF. If you choose Single AF, the camera will use autofocus just once, when you first press the red Movie button to start recording video. Then, even if the distance to the subject changes, the camera will not re-focus at all. If you choose Full-time AF, the camera will continue to focus as the distance changes, keeping the image in focus to the best of its ability. The possible problems with this mode are that the camera is likely to pick up the sound of the autofocus mechanism and that the battery will run down more rapidly than with Single AF.

Electronic VR

This option lets you turn on an electronic form of vibration reduction for video recording. With video shooting, the standard setting of optical (sensor-shift) vibration reduction is not available. You can, however, turn on electronic VR using this option. It is available only when the Movie switch is turned to the HD setting; it is not available when recording HS movies.

Wind Noise Reduction

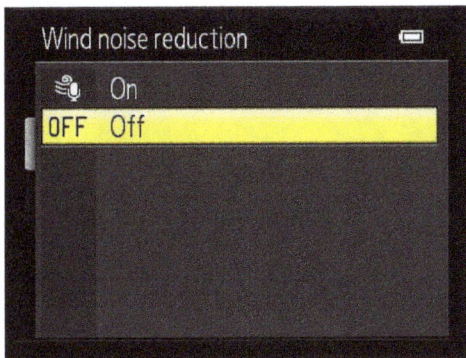

This last Movie menu option lets you minimize the effects of wind noise on the sound tracks of your videos. Turning on this option may reduce the interference from the sounds of wind, but it also may cut back on other, more desirable sounds at similar frequencies, so you probably should experiment with both settings to see which one works best for your purposes.

Movie Playback and Editing

In Chapter 2, I discussed the fundamentals of movie playback. Now it's time to go into more detail about that topic and to discuss how to edit your video footage in the camera.

Playback

When the camera is in full-screen Playback mode, you can

recognize a movie by the movie format icon on the right side of the display. When the camera is displaying thumbnail images in screens of four or 16, you can recognize a movie by the sets of small gray blocks that look like movie film sprockets on the sides of the images. (When the camera shows screens of 72 thumbnails, there is no way to distinguish movies from stills; you need to move the zoom lever to the right to get to a screen with larger thumbnails to tell which ones represent movies.)

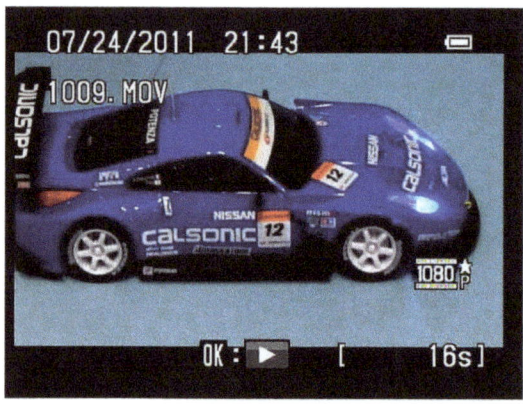

With a movie's frame on the display, press OK to start it playing. You will see a line of VCR-like icons at the top left. Use the left and right direction buttons to move to any of those icons, then press OK to choose that function. The controls are, from left, rewind, play, stop, and fast-forward. You can also turn the command dial to the left or right to rewind or fast-forward the movie.

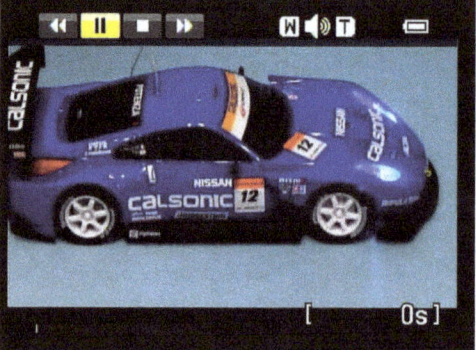

Once the movie starts playing, the icons will disappear. You can then press the OK button again to pause the playback and bring the icons back on the display. At that point, while the movie is paused, there will be a somewhat different group of icons.

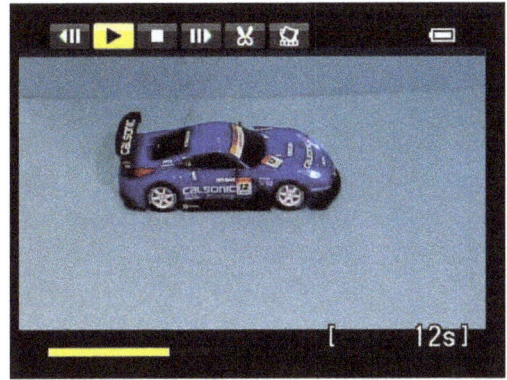

From the left, they will be single-frame back, play, stop, single-frame forward, edit, and extract and save a single frame. If you hold down the OK button while highlighting the single-frame forward or back icon, the frames will advance continuously, one at a time, at a slow rate. You can also use the command dial to advance and rewind the frames at that rate.

Editing

Of course, you cannot do anything like full-blown video editing in the camera; if you want to get really involved in editing, you need to import your video footage into a computer program that has serious editing capabilities, like Adobe's Premiere or Premiere Elements, or Apple's Final Cut or Final Cut Express. If you don't want to purchase a dedicated editing program, if you're a PC user you may already have Windows Movie Maker; Mac users generally have iMovie available. Finally, if you purchased your Coolpix new, you have Nikon's software suite, which includes Nikon Movie Editor software.

However, if you're out on a camping trip away from your computer or you need to put together a quick video show to play on a hotel's TV screen, you have the ability to perform some rudimentary trimming of your P500 video files in the camera. (You cannot perform any in-camera editing with videos recorded in the iFrame format.) Here is what you can do.

First, you can save a portion of an original video to a new file by trimming away footage at the beginning and/or end of a clip. To do this, start by playing the video to the approximate location where you want the new, shorter clip to start. Then pause the clip by pressing the OK button, and quickly (while the icons stay on the screen), use the right direction button to highlight the scissors icon and press OK to select that icon.

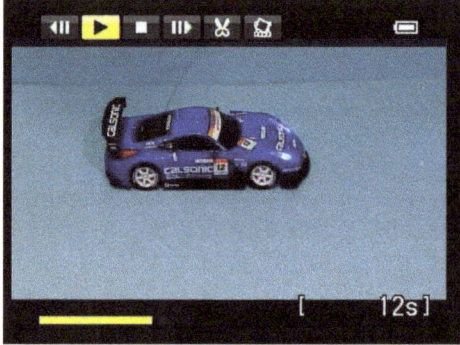

You will now see a vertical menu of icons, representing, from top to bottom: Choose Start Point; Choose End Point; Preview; Save; and Back. You will also see a yellow bar at the bottom of the screen, with a white pointer at the left end and a gray pointer at the right end.

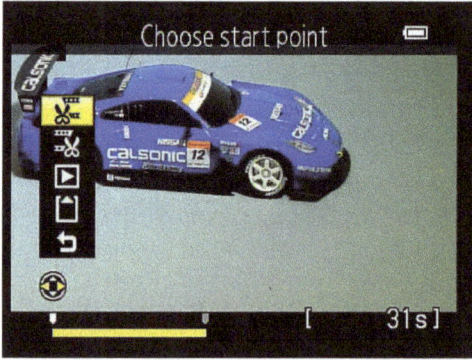

222

The top icon, Choose Start Point, will be highlighted. You can now use the left and right direction buttons to adjust the position of the white pointer, indicating the starting point for the new clip. If you prefer, you can use the command dial to move the pointer. If you have to move the start point more than a few seconds, it may take you quite a while to do so, because each press of the direction buttons moves the pointer only a small fraction of a second in the clip.

When you have finished moving the left (start) point, press the down direction button to highlight the second icon down in the menu, for Choose End Point. Repeat the previous procedure, but move the right (end) point in towards the center of the yellow bar.

When both the start and end points are set as you want them, highlight the third icon, which looks like a Play button; here, this control lets you preview the adjusted clip. If the preview looks okay, press the OK button to stop it if necessary, and move down to the next icon, a rectangle with a small triangle at its top. When that icon is highlighted, press the OK button, and the camera will ask if you want to save the clip in its new length. If so, highlight the Yes bar and press the OK button. The camera may take quite a while to save the new, shorter version of the clip; the original will remain untouched.

Finally, you can save a single frame from any video clip taken with the P500, except for clips made in the iFrame format. To do this, start playing the movie to the approximate point where you want to extract a frame, then press the OK button to pause the movie. You will then (briefly) see the icons for playing, advancing or reversing by single frames, as well as editing and saving a single frame. (If the icons disappear before you can use them, press the OK button to bring them back on the screen.)

Use the advance and reverse controls to move to the exact frame that you want to save. Then, if necessary, press the OK button to bring the icons back onto the screen, highlight the one at the far right that looks like a frame next to some movie footage, and press the OK button. When the camera displays a message asking if you want to copy that frame as a still image, highlight the Yes bar and press the OK button to confirm. The camera will then display your new still image with a .jpg file name. The still picture is saved in the Normal quality, with the same image size as that of the format of the movie it was extracted from.

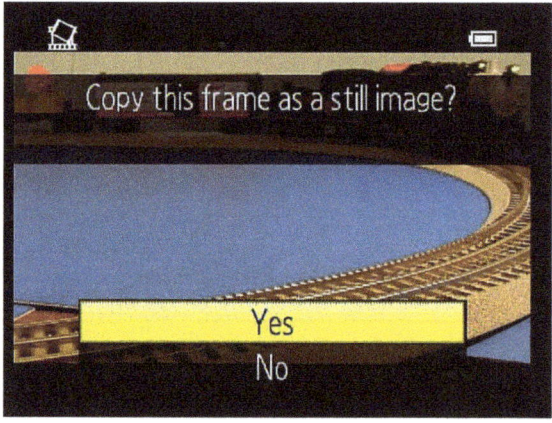

Chapter 9: Other Topics

Using the Superzoom Lens

The first special topic to discuss for the Coolpix P500 is, naturally enough, its lens, which is remarkable for its range at both ends—wide-angle and telephoto.

To put it in non-technical terms, the focal length of a lens is a measure of how wide is its view of a scene and of how powerfully it enlarges the view. The standard for stating focal lengths for cameras such as the P500 is called "35mm equivalent," meaning the focal length is stated as if the camera were a 35mm SLR or rangefinder camera from the days of film. With those cameras, a "normal" lens—one that is used for everyday shooting of family scenes, portraits, and the like—is often considered to be a 50mm lens. Using that system, a "wide-angle" lens would be in the range of 35mm or lower, and a telephoto lens would be one with a focal length of 100mm or greater. The P500, of course, has a "variable focal length" lens, more commonly known as a "zoom" lens. The 35mm equivalent focal lengths of this lens range from an extremely wide 22.5mm to an astounding 810mm at the telephoto end, for an overall range of 36 times optical zoom. (None of this discussion will involve digital zoom, which is not a "real" zoom capability, as discussed in Chapter 4.)

Of course, as with many things in life, there are tradeoffs for having this tremendous zoom range. It is not possible to provide the same quality in a zoom lens of this type as in lenses used by professional photographers at professional sporting events, for example. A good Nikon zoom lens for a DSLR can easily cost more than $1,000, and a top-quality Nikon telephoto (non-zoom) lens can cost more than $10,000. However, for everyday photography, the P500 provides you with the ability to capture scenes with an array of focal lengths that is practically unmatched in the world of consumer cameras.

At the wide-angle end, the P500's lens gives you several millimeters more than most cameras in its class. A wide-angle range starting at 28mm is often considered quite adequate, and only a few compact digital cameras have been available in recent years with a range starting as low as 24mm. The 22.5mm focal length of the P500 is very useful when you need to photograph a large group of people without standing back a great distance. Also, if you need to photograph the interiors of rooms, this focal length is a great bonus, because you will likely be able to capture an excellent overall view of the entire room by standing in one corner.

But it is the telephoto range of the P500's lens that is the most dramatic feature of the camera, so I will concentrate on discussing its use.

First, and maybe most obvious, the extreme telephoto range of the P500's zoom lens is so powerful that it can capture details that you cannot even begin to see with the naked eye. For example, the top image on the next page was taken with the P500's lens zoomed all the way out to its 22.5mm wide-angle setting. You cannot see this, but slightly to the right of the large tree in the foreground, out in the water, and to the left of the next tree to the right, there is a channel marker topped by a red triangle.

226

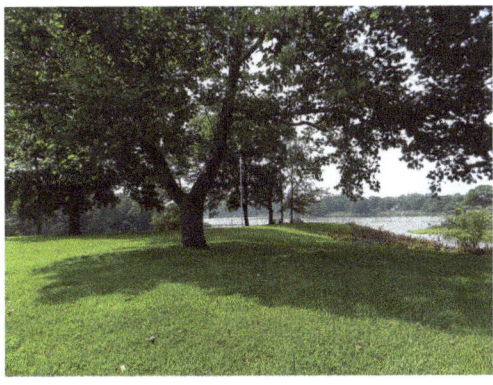

Now look at the image below, taken from exactly the same place, with the P500's lens zoomed all the way in to its 810mm telephoto setting. There is the channel marker—invisible at wide-angle range, and clear enough to read its number at the long end of the zoom.

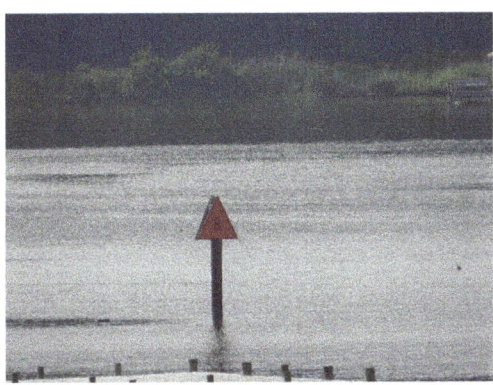

When you use the powerful zoom lens at its highest power, you will encounter some issues. For one thing, as you may be able to tell from the shot of the channel marker, images shot at this power suffer somewhat from the compression of the atmosphere; in other words, you're shooting through a lot of air, which can add a hazy aura to the image.

The photo on the next page, also taken at the full optical zoom range of 810mm, illustrates the haze effect as well as another

227

phenomenon—flattening of the objects you are photographing. In this case, I was using the P500 for street photography at some distance. The result of using such a powerful zoom in this case is that everything appears flattened up into a single plane, even though the objects actually are separated by some distance. So, if you take photographs that show people or objects at various distances from the camera, don't be surprised if they are flattened out with this two-dimensional effect.

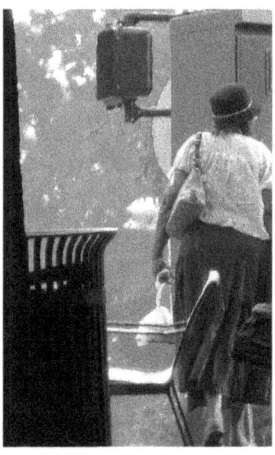

However, you very well may find creative uses for this flattening effect, which can give a distinctive look to your photos.

Another positive side of the super-long zoom range is its ability to isolate a single subject. If you use the zoom to focus on a particular person in a crowd or on a particular animal in a pack, you can fill the frame with that single subject, thereby emphasizing its importance.

Perhaps the greatest overall benefit of the superzoom lens on the Coolpix P500 is that it gives you the equivalent of a whole range of focal lengths without the need to carry around a bag crammed full of lenses. In practical terms, with the P500 you have at your fingertips every focal length that a photographer could reasonably want or need for everyday photography, ranging from the super wide-angle 22.5mm with a strong macro capability to the super 810mm telephoto.

228

Here is one more use for the superzoom lens—astrophotography. Of course, the Coolpix P500 is not a camera that a dedicated sky photographer would likely choose; a more likely choice would be a DSLR with a telescope adapter, or a specialized astrophotography camera. However, because of its very long zoom range, the P500 actually can achieve some pleasing results for subjects that are easy to track, such as the moon. The shot below was taken at the full 810mm zoom range of the P500, at f/6.3 with a shutter speed of 1/100 second and an ISO setting of 160. As you may expect, I used a tripod.

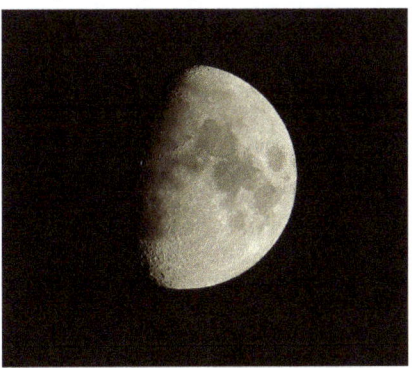

If you were to work for National Geographic or a professional photography firm, you would not use a P500 to capture your images. But, if you have a chance to go on a safari or a cruise around the world and you want to be able to bring back a complete photographic record of your trip using one lightweight, easy-to-use camera, the P500 fills the bill very nicely.

Now, let's discuss how to avoid some of the problems that come along with a superzoom capability.

First, and probably foremost, is the problem of camera movement. When the lens is zoomed in to its full 810mm focal length or anywhere close to that range, any slight motion of the camera is multiplied because of the magnification of the image. You will notice how jittery the image looks on the display, and you will find it hard to keep the picture steady.

There are several steps you can take to reduce the effects of camera movement. First, if possible, use a tripod. It can be inconvenient to do, but using a solid tripod is one of the best ways to ensure high-quality images. If you can't manage a full-blown tripod, use a monopod, a lightweight travel tripod, or any support available, such as a fence post, or just sit on a bench and hold the camera steady on your lap, folding the LCD display up toward your face to view your image.

Suppose, though, that you are walking through a field in search of wildlife shots and there is no physical support available. There are several things you can do to minimize the effects of camera shake. First, you should make sure that the Vibration Reduction feature is turned on through the Setup menu. This system counteracts camera movement quite effectively, up to a point. Also, you may find you can hold the camera steadier if you activate the electronic viewfinder (using the Monitor button to the left of the viewfinder), so you can hold the camera against your forehead and look into the viewfinder, rather than using the LCD display at some distance from your face.

Next, use the fastest shutter speed you can. If the shutter is open for only a very brief instant, there will not be time for camera motion to register on the image. According to one rule of thumb, when hand-holding a zoom lens you should use a shutter speed no slower than the fraction of a second with the focal length of the lens as the denominator. So, if the lens of the P500 is zoomed all the way in to 810mm, you would use a shutter speed of 1/800 second or faster. In the case of the P500, the choices faster than 1/800 are 1/1000, 1/1250, and 1/1500.

Of course, if you want to control the shutter speed, you should use Shutter Priority as your shooting mode, as discussed in Chapter 3. You also could use Manual mode, if you are willing to accept the added task of setting the aperture correctly. Or, if you would like to use Program mode, you can let the camera set the shutter speed and aperture initially, and then use the Flexible Program feature, which lets you turn the command dial to select new combinations of shutter speed and aperture that are equivalent to what the camera selected.

However, you are quite likely to run into a problem if you use the camera's standard settings and try to set a fast shutter speed. One of the unfortunate characteristics of the superzoom lens on the P500 is that, as was discussed in Chapter 3, its maximum aperture when zoomed in is quite narrow. When the lens is zoomed all the way out to wide-angle, the maximum (widest open) aperture is f/3.4, which is not very wide to start with, though it is wide enough for most purposes. But, when the lens is zoomed in, it rapidly loses the ability to use a wide aperture.

When the lens is zoomed all the way in, the maximum aperture is f/5.7. In order to use a shutter speed of 1/800 second or faster at that rather narrow aperture, there will have to be a good deal of light, unless you change some of the other settings. If the lighting is not sufficiently bright to expose your images well at a fast shutter speed, you still have some options available.

In this case, your best option probably is to increase the ISO sensitivity of the camera, which will mean that the camera's image sensor will require less light to expose the picture, at the risk of increased visual noise in the image. Using the ISO setting in the Shooting menu, you may want to try using the setting for High ISO Sensitivity Auto, or you might prefer using a specific level, such as ISO 800 or 1600.

If you prefer not to boost the ISO, one strategy you can employ is to zoom back out somewhat until the camera can use a wider aperture, such as, say, f/5.1 or f/4.6. Later on, when editing your photos with software, you can crop them to achieve the same field of view you originally saw with the zoomed-in lens, though with some loss of quality because of the cropping.

Another possible strategy for getting good, clear images with the superzoom lens is to take advantage of the P500's excellent array of continuous-shooting options. With some of these settings, the camera will take multiple shots in rapid succession, increasing the likelihood that one or more shots will be usable. In addition, with two of these settings, Continuous H: 120 fps and Continuous H: 60 fps, the camera will use a shutter speed that can range up to a super-fast 1/4000 second, a speed that is not available with any other settings.

One more excellent feature of the Coolpix P500, also found on the list of continuous-shooting options, is the Best Shot Selector (BSS), the 7th choice down on the menu of those options. When you select BSS, the camera takes a series of 10 consecutive shots and preserves only the single shot that includes the most sharp detail. The downside to this feature is that you can't second-guess the camera; you will never see the nine shots it discarded. However, using BSS is a great way to increase your chances at getting a good, clear shot. Also, it is available in the more advanced shooting modes, so you can, for example, use Shutter Priority mode and select a fast shutter speed while using BSS to cast a wide net for a super-sharp shot.

If you are not comfortable making so many settings through the menu system and otherwise, all is not lost. You can set the camera to the Auto shooting mode by turning the mode dial to the icon of the green camera, and then make just one setting: Go into the Setup menu and set the Motion Detection item to Auto. Then, if the camera senses motion, it will automatically raise the ISO level and use a faster shutter speed in order to counteract the effects of camera motion.

One more note: Don't forget that the Coolpix P500 offers the very useful U slot on the mode dial, for User Setting. If you use the lens zoomed in frequently, you may want to save your preferred settings for those occasions, so you can quickly call them up just by turning the mode dial to the U setting. For example, you may want to set up the camera in Shutter Priority mode, with a shutter speed of 1/800 second, with an ISO setting of 1600 and with BSS enabled.

Finally, I recommend that you take advantage of the Side Zoom Control on the P500—the switch on the left side of the camera, below the flash release button. As discussed in Chapter 5, this switch can be of use in two ways in connection with your use of the zoom lens. First, with its default function as an alternative to the zoom lever around the shutter button, this switch can let you hold the camera more firmly in both hands. If you zoom with the left-side switch, you can use your right hand to keep a tight grip on the right side of the camera without having to reach up to the zoom lever.

Second, if you use the Setup menu to assign the snap-back zoom function to this control, you gain a different benefit. In that case, you can use this switch to quickly pull back from a zoomed-in view, so you can get your bearings and see exactly where your subject is in relation to its surroundings, before quickly zooming back in to take the picture. It can be very difficult to locate your subject when the lens is zoomed all the way in to its 810mm maximum; use the snap-back zoom to get the wider view quickly when you need it for orientation.

Macro (Close-up) Shooting

Macro photography is the art or science of taking photographs when the subject is shown at actual size (1:1 ratio between size of subject and size of image) or slightly magnified (greater than 1:1 ratio). So if you photograph a flower using macro techniques, the image of the flower will be about the same size as the actual flower. You can get wonderful detail in your images using macro photography, and you may discover things about the subject that you had not noticed before taking the photograph.

233

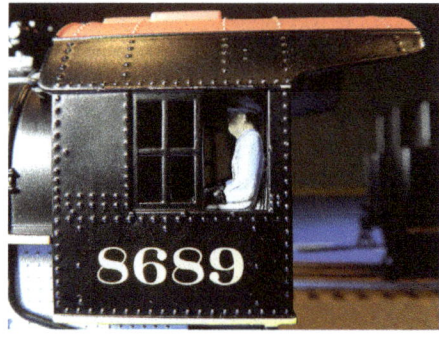

The Coolpix P500 is quite capable of shooting macro photographs, like the one above showing a model train's locomotive and its engineer. As noted earlier, activate macro focus as follows: Press the bottom direction button on the multi selector to bring up the focus menu, then press the up and down buttons or use the command dial to move to the tulip icon, indicating macro autofocus mode. You can choose macro autofocus in Auto mode or in the Program, Aperture Priority, Shutter Priority, or Manual exposure mode, but you can't choose macro (or, in most cases, other focus types) in the Scene modes, except for the Black and White Copy mode.

On the Coolpix P500, with the autofocus mode set to macro the camera is able to focus as close as four inches (10 centimeters) when the lens is zoomed out to its full wide-angle position. The camera can focus on objects as close as about 0.4 inch (one centimeter) when it is zoomed in slightly, to a focal length of 32mm. The camera doesn't provide a readout of the focal length, so you won't see any numbers to let you know when the lens is zoomed to the 32mm mark. However, you can tell by looking carefully at the zoom bar that the P500 places at the top of the screen when you are zooming.

When you select macro autofocus, the camera puts a tulip icon in the upper left corner of the screen. When the lens is zoomed to the optimum focal length for macro shooting, the tulip icon turns green. Also, when you are moving the zoom lever, the small bar that extends outward on the screen as the zoom extends turns green when the zoom is in the macro range.

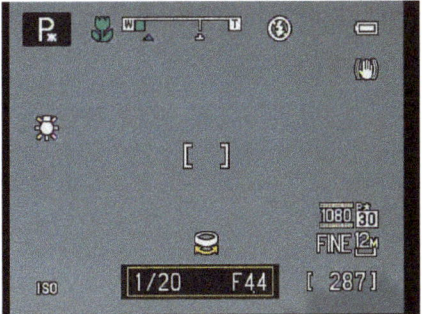

It's a bit tricky to find the exact spot in the zoom range where the lens will focus down to the one cm (0.4 in) distance. One way to find it is to start with the lens zoomed all the way out to full wide angle, and then nudge the zoom lever quickly with 3 very short nudges. If all goes well, the bar should be in the green range, slightly to the left of a green triangle. At this range, you should be getting the closest possible macro focusing.

With normal autofocus, the camera can focus only to about 1 foot 8 inches (50 cm) at the wide-angle position, and only to about 7 feet 3 inches (2.2 meters) at the full telephoto position.

If you don't want to have to fine-tune the zoom position to set macro focusing as close as possible, there are two easier methods. First, you can use the Close-up setting in Scene mode.

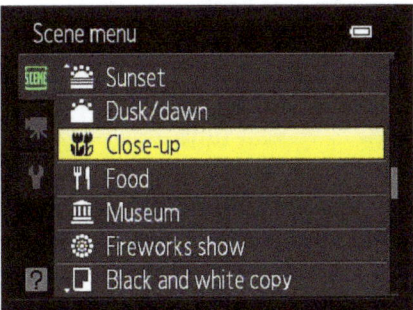

The camera will adjust for the closest possible macro shooting, setting the focus and the zoom position. It also turns on continuous autofocus and sets the AF Area Mode to manual, so you can adjust the position of the focus frame on the screen. To move the frame, press the OK button and then use the direction buttons to adjust the frame's position. Press OK to anchor it in place.

Another possibility for close-up focusing is to select the Food setting within Scene mode. This setting is similar to Close-up, except that it adds an adjustment slider so you can fine-tune the hues of the foods you are photographing.

You don't have to use either the macro autofocus setting or one of the Scene settings to take macro shots; if you set the camera to manual focus by pressing the down direction button and then selecting MF from the on-screen menu, you can also focus on objects very close to the lens. You do, however, lose the benefit of automatic focus, and it can be tricky finding the correct focus manually.

When shooting extreme close-ups, you need to use a tripod or other solid stand, because the depth of field is very narrow and you need to keep the camera steady to take a usable photograph. It's also a good idea to take advantage of the self-timer. If you take the picture using the self-timer, you will not be touching the camera when the shutter is activated, so the chance of camera shake is minimized. You should also leave the built-in flash retracted so it can't fire. Flash from the built-in unit at such a close range would be of no use.

If you need the extra lighting of a flash unit, you might want to consider using a special unit designed for close-up photography, such as a ring flash that is designed to provide even lighting surrounding the lens. There are also other creative solutions to the problem of providing even lighting for close-up photography. For an excellent discussion of this and other issues, see Closeup Shooting by Cyrill Harnischmacher (English translation published by Rocky Nook 2007).

Using Flash

As I discussed earlier, pressing the up direction button on the multi selector, the one marked with a lightning bolt, gives you access to the various settings for the built-in flash unit on the Coolpix P500. Before I discuss the details of those settings, it's important to recall one basic fact about this camera: The flash cannot fire unless you first pop it up by pressing the flash release button marked by a lightning bolt on the left side of the flash housing, near the top of the camera. If you think there's any chance the flash may be used, go ahead and press that button to have the flash ready. (If you're shooting movies, though, you should make sure the flash is down out of the way, because it can't be used and might interfere with your shooting.)

The next point to note about the built-in flash on the P500 is that a lot depends on the shooting mode you have set on the mode dial. If that dial is set to Auto, Program, Shutter priority, Aperture priority, or Manual exposure, you will generally have access to all six settings for the flash. However, other shooting modes place limits on your flash choices. For example, in Night Portrait mode, the flash is set to Auto with Red-eye Reduction—in other words, the flash will fire if necessary; if it does, it will first fire a few times at low intensity to reduce the red-eye effect, and then will fire at full intensity to take the portrait. (You can turn off the pre-flashes in the Setup menu.)

In Night Landscape mode, the flash will be forced off and cannot fire. In Backlighting mode, if you turn on the HDR option through the menu, the flash will be forced off; if you turn off HDR, the flash will be forced on. In the various modes available when the mode dial is set to SCENE, the behavior of the flash varies according to the particular characteristics of the mode. For example, the Museum setting forces the flash off, on the theory that museums generally do not permit flash.

Apart from the shooting mode, there are other factors that affect how the P500 uses flash. So, even if you have the camera set to Program mode, in which you normally would have all six flash modes available, there are some conditions that will disable the flash. For example, you cannot use the flash if you have set the focus to infinity, turned on exposure bracketing, or activated any of the continuous-shooting options other than interval shooting. So, if you believe the flash should fire but you are unable to turn it on using the flash mode button, check to see if one of the settings mentioned above has been set.

Once you have set the camera to a mode that allows choice of any of the six possible flash settings, such as Program mode, you have to decide whether to choose Auto, Auto with Red-eye Reduction, Off, Fill Flash, Slow Sync, or Rear-curtain flash.

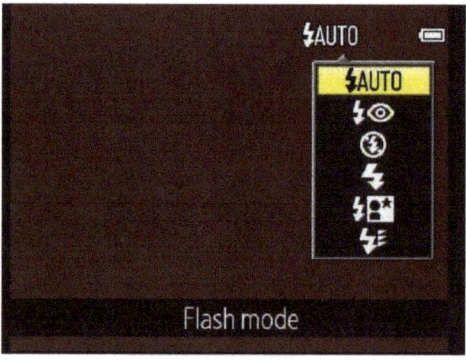

Auto and Auto with Red-eye Reduction are modes you are already familiar with—in the first, the camera's automatic exposure system will fire the flash if it's needed to achieve a good exposure. In the second, the camera adds red-eye reduction to the mix. (This option may or may not involve pre-flashes, depending on the related setting in the Setup menu.)

Let's consider the other possibilities. Why would you use the Off setting? Wouldn't it be easier to just push the flash unit back down so it won't fire? Well, yes, it might. But you may be a photographer who likes to experiment with various settings. Maybe you are taking portraits outdoors in the shade, and you want to see how they look with and without flash. If you are using Program mode and have the flash set to Auto, it may or may not fire. If you set it to Off, it definitely will not fire, and you can adjust other settings, such as exposure compensation, ISO, Active D-Lighting, and others, to achieve the effect you want without the possibly harsh appearance of flash.

On the other hand, what about the Fill Flash setting? Why would you want to force the flash to fire, when you could set it to Auto and let the camera decide whether it's needed? One case is when there is enough backlighting that the camera's exposure controls could be fooled into thinking the flash isn't needed. If, in your judgment, the subject will be too dark for that reason, you may want to force the flash to fire. Another such situation could be an outdoor portrait for which you need fill-in flash to highlight your subject's face adequately.

How about the Slow Sync setting? Normally, when the P500's built-in flash fires, the camera uses a fast shutter speed because the flash provides enough light to expose the image quickly. If you use the Slow Sync setting, the camera will attempt to take the picture with a considerably slower shutter speed so that the ambient (natural) lighting will have time to register on the image. In other words, if you're in a fairly dark environment and fire the flash normally, it will likely light up the subject (say a person), but because the exposure time is short, the surrounding scene may be black. (In Shutter Priority mode, the camera will use whatever shutter speed you set, even with Slow Sync in effect.)

If you use the Slow Sync setting, the slower shutter speed allows the surrounding scene to be visible also. For example, the two photographs on the next page were taken at the same time and in the same conditions; the only difference is that the one on the top was taken with the shutter speed set at 1/250 second, in Fill Flash mode. The one on the bottom was taken in Slow Sync flash mode with a shutter speed of 1/15 second, which allowed the ambient lighting from the farther room to light up that room and make its furniture visible in the picture.

239

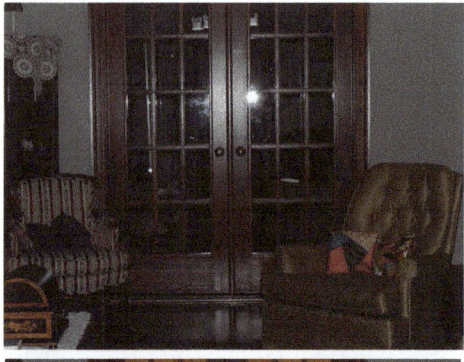

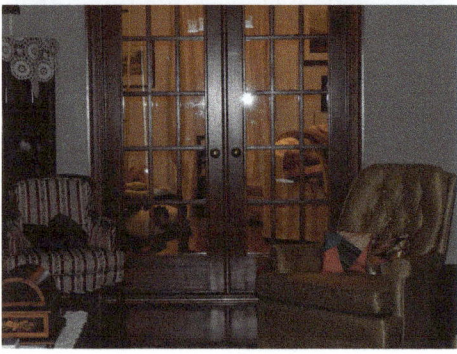

The last setting on the flash mode menu is Rear-curtain sync. This option is one you may not have a lot of use for unless you encounter the particular situation it is designed for. If you don't activate this setting, the camera uses the unnamed default setting, which could be called Front-curtain sync. In that mode, the flash fires very soon after the shutter opens to expose the image. If you choose the Rear-curtain setting instead, the flash fires later, just before the shutter closes.

The reason for using Rear-curtain sync is to help you avoid a strange-looking result in some situations. This issue arises, for example, with a relatively long exposure, say one-half second, of a subject with lights, such as a car or motorcycle at night, moving across your field of view. With normal (Front-curtain) sync, the flash will fire early in the process, freezing the vehicle in a clear image. However, as the shutter remains open while the vehicle keeps going, the camera will capture the moving

240

lights in a stream extending in front of the vehicle. If, instead, you use Rear-curtain sync, the initial part of the exposure will capture the lights in a trail that appears behind the vehicle, while the vehicle itself is not frozen by the flash until later in the exposure. With Rear-curtain sync in this particular situation, if the lights in question are taillights that look more natural behind the vehicle, the final image is likely to look more natural than with the Front-curtain (default) setting.

The images below illustrate this concept using a remote-controlled model car with headlights rather than taillights. Both pictures were shot with the P500's built-in flash, using an exposure of ½ second in Shutter Priority mode. In the top image, using the normal Front-curtain setting, the flash fired quickly, and the headlights continued on during the long exposure to make the streaks of bright light in front of the car. In the second image, using Rear-curtain sync, the flash did not fire until the car had traveled to the right, overtaking the place where the headlights had made their streaks visible.

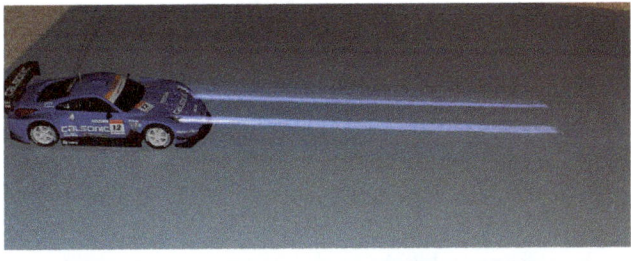

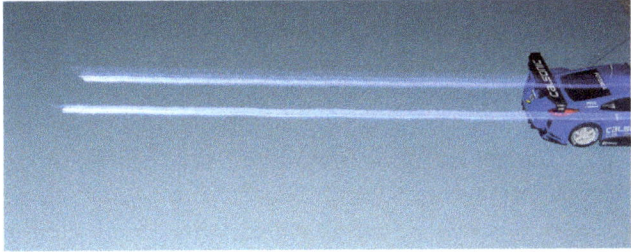

To sum up the situation with the Rear-curtain flash setting, a good general rule is not to use it unless you are sure you have a definite need for it. Using the Rear-curtain setting makes it harder to compose and set up the shot, because you have to anticipate where the main subject will be when the flash finally fires late in the exposure process.

One other flash setting that you should keep in mind is flash exposure compensation, which is available through the Shooting menu when the camera is set to the more advanced shooting modes.

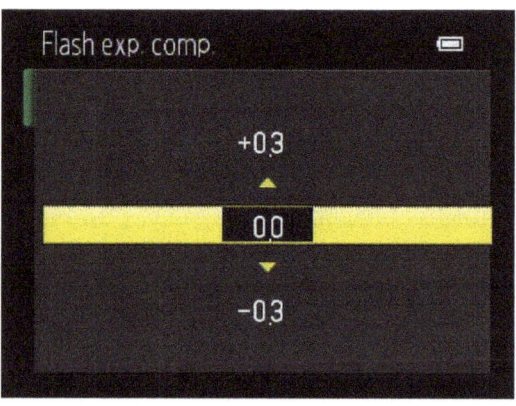

This setting allows you to reduce the intensity of the flash, even when the camera is automatically setting the exposure. Just as with normal exposure compensation, when using flash you can adjust this setting if your test shots appear too bright or too dark. Just go into this menu item and set the value to a positive number to brighten the image or to a negative number to darken it. Just remember to set it back to zero when you no longer need the adjustment, so it does not affect other shots when you don't need it.

There are a great many considerations that go into the use of flash. The best advice I can give you is to consult an expert if you want to explore the subject further. An excellent book about the use of flash is Mastering Digital Flash Photography, by Chris George (Lark Books, 2008).

Infrared Photography

In a nutshell, infrared photography involves finding a way for the camera to record images that are illuminated by infrared light, which is invisible to the human eye because it occupies a place on the spectrum of light waves that is beyond our ability to see. In some circumstances, cameras, unlike our eyes, can record images using this type of light. The resulting photographs can be quite spectacular, producing scenes in which green foliage appears white and blue skies appear eerily dark.

Shooting infrared in the times before digital photography involved selecting a particular infrared film and the appropriate filter to place on the lens. With the rise of digital imaging, you need to find a camera that is capable of "seeing" infrared light. Many cameras nowadays include internal filters that block infrared light. However, some cameras do not, or block it only to a relatively small extent. (You can do a quick test of any digital camera by aiming it at the light-emitting end of an infrared remote control and taking a photograph while pressing a button on the remote; if the remote's light shows up as bright white, the camera can "see" infrared light at least to some extent.)

The Coolpix P500 is quite capable of taking infrared photographs. In order to unleash this capability, you need to take a few steps. The most important is to get a filter that blocks most visible light, but lets infrared light reach the camera's light sensor. (If you don't, the infrared light will be overwhelmed by the visible light, and you'll get an ordinary picture based on visible light.)

As with most experimental efforts, there are many ways to accomplish this. For example, if you search on the internet, you will find discussions of how to improvise an infrared filter out of unexposed but developed (*i.e.*, black) photographic film.

A more certain, if more expensive way to make infrared photographs with the Coolpix P500 is to purchase an infrared filter along with an adapter that lets you attach the filter securely to the camera. There is an adapter available from a company called Kiwi Foto, which I found on eBay. This adapter is not ideal, because it extends fairly far out from the lens to avoid letting the filter hit the lens as it extends outward. Because of its length, the adapter causes considerable vignetting—that is, when the camera's lens is at the wide-angle end of its zoom range, your pictures will be shown in a circle, with much of the surrounding image cut off. However, you can work around this problem by zooming the lens in partway, or by cropping away the darkened corners of the image. (I discuss this adapter in more detail in Appendix A.)

The infrared filter I have seen most often recommended is the Hoya R72, and that is what I use. It is a very dark red and blocks most visible light, letting in mainly infrared light rays in the part of the spectrum that produces interesting images.

The next question is to figure out the exposure. Photographers have different approaches, and time spent looking on the internet for discussions of those approaches will be rewarding. For the image shown here, I set a custom white balance, using brightly sunlit green foliage as the base. That is, I used the camera's White Balance menu setting on the Shooting menu, and, in the screen for setting a Preset Manual white balance, I aimed the camera at the bright green foliage and pressed the OK button. The results were essentially what I expected from infrared photography; scenes with tree leaves and grass that look white, and other unusual, but pleasing effects.

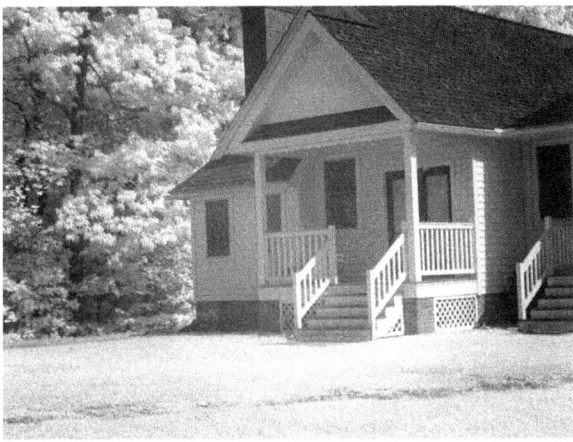

For exposure, I set the camera to shoot in Aperture Priority mode and let it select the necessary long shutter speed. (Necessary because of the dark filter.) I set the camera on a tripod and disabled Vibration Reduction, because it is not needed when the camera is stabilized by a tripod. The P500 did the rest, exposing the image for 1/4 second at f/4.7, with an ISO setting of 800. You can often get interesting results if you include a good amount of green grass and trees in the image, as well as blue sky and clouds.

Street Photography

The Coolpix P500 is not the first camera that would come to mind for what I normally think of as street photography—that is, shooting candid pictures in public settings, often without the subject's knowledge. In my opinion, cameras that are well-suited for this type of work are small, lightweight, and unobtrusive in appearance, so they can easily be held casually or hidden in the photographer's hand. The P500, of course, is somewhat bulky and not that easily concealed from view. However, it does have its good points for this type of photography. Its 22.5mm equivalent wide-angle lens is excellent for taking in a broad field of view, for times when you shoot from the hip without framing the image carefully on the screen.

In addition, I have come to appreciate the P500's swiveling LCD screen for street photography, because, if you fold it out so it is parallel to the ground, you can look down at the screen to frame your shots without drawing a lot of attention to yourself. With this system, I have found that I can even zoom in on a subject across the street and keep the framing accurate while looking down at the screen. Also, the camera shoots quickly and performs well at high ISO settings, so you can use a relatively fast shutter speed to avoid motion blur. The numerous options for continuous shooting, including the Best Shot Selector setting, give you a good chance to get a sharp image under difficult circumstances. And, you can make the camera completely silent by turning off the beeps and shutter sounds.

What are the best settings for street shooting with the Coolpix P500? If you ask that question on one of the online forums, you are, naturally, likely to get many different responses. I'm going to give you some fairly broad guidelines as a starting point. The answer depends in part on your own personal style of shooting, such as whether you will talk to your subjects and get their agreement to being photographed before you start shooting, or whether you will fire away from across the street with a zoomed-in lens and accept the risk of blurry photos from camera shake at such a long focal length.

Here are a couple of approaches you can start with and modify as you see fit. Some photographers like to shoot in color at the highest quality and image size and then use post-processing software such as Photoshop or Lightroom to convert their images to black-and-white, along with any other effects they are looking for, such as extra grain to achieve a gritty look. (Of course, you don't have to produce your street photography in black-and-white, but that is the usual practice.) I recommend you shoot in Shutter Priority mode at a fairly fast shutter speed, say, 1/100 second or faster, to stop action on the street and to avoid blur from camera movement. You can set ISO to Auto, or possibly use a high ISO setting, in the range of 800 or so, if you don't mind some visual noise. You may want to set the aspect ratio to 16:9 (by selecting an image size of 3968 x 2232 pixels) in order to take in a wide field of view for street scenes.

Another option is to set image quality and size to their highest settings and set the Optimize Image feature on the Shooting menu to the Black-and-White setting. You may use the Standard version of Black-and-White, or you may choose Custom and tweak it a bit. For example, you may want to try boosting Contrast by one notch and reducing Sharpening the same amount. To get the gritty "street" look, try setting the ISO to 1600 to include some visual grain in the image while boosting sensitivity enough to stop action with a fast shutter speed.

For the shot shown here, though, I shot at f/5.0 with a shutter speed of 1/30 second, zoomed in only slightly, to 60mm, at ISO 320. I used continuous shooting to increase my chances of getting a good, clear shot.

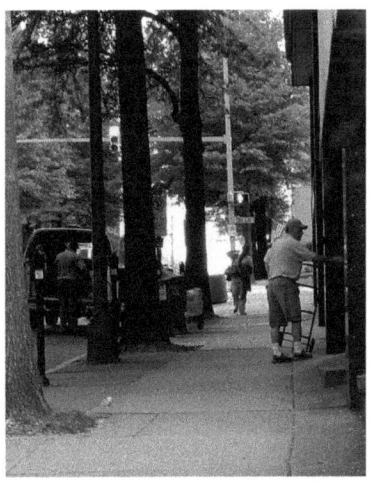

If you don't mind ignoring labels and trying something unconventional, you might consider turning the mode dial to the Scene setting and choosing the Black and White Copy option. Of course, that mode is designed for taking pictures of pages from a book and similar items, but it gives you another avenue for taking black-and-white photos without having to fiddle with menu settings. I suggest you at least try this option if you have an interest in street photography.

Also, consider turning on continuous shooting so you'll get several images to choose from for each shutter press. To get the best combination of quality and speed, choose Continuous H, though you are limited to five shots at a time. If you don't mind letting the camera choose which shot to keep out of the 10 it takes, try the Best Shot Selector feature. For any of these options, though, you have to shoot in one of the advanced shooting modes (P, A, S, or M)—you can't shoot in the Auto or Scene modes. Also, one drawback to using continuous shooting is that you'll have to wait for the camera to finish recording its sequence of rapid shots before you can start shooting again, so you could miss a photo opportunity while waiting.

I generally use normal autofocus for this type of shooting, though some photographers like to use manual focus, with the range set for the approximate distance you expect your subjects to be at. If you are shooting down at street level, fairly close to your subjects, you should leave the lens zoomed back to its full wide-angle position to maintain a broad depth of field and keep most of the image in focus.

With the P500, though, you may want to at least experiment with long-range street photography, taking advantage of the superzoom lens. This approach has the advantage of letting you stay out of sight and at a comfortable distance. It has the disadvantage of producing a narrow depth of field, so it is harder to keep all of the scene in focus. Also, you may find that the foreshortening effect of a powerful zoom lens is not the look you are seeking for street photographs. And, you may find it difficult to get really sharp images at a long focal length unless you use a tripod, which limits your options for candid shots. On a bright day, though, or at high ISO settings, you may be able to use a fast enough shutter speed to avoid blur from a shaky camera, even without a tripod.

Making 3D Images

There's been a lot of attention paid to three-dimensional (3D) movies and images lately, with the advent of 3D televisions and the renaissance in 3D movies. Some digital cameras have appeared recently with special features for creating 3D panoramas and other stereoscopic images, including the Sony NEX-3 and NEX-5, and the Fujifilm FinePix Real 3D W3. The Coolpix P500 has no such built-in capability. But why should its users feel left out of the 3D wave? It's not that hard to create 3D images using just the P500 (well, okay, or any other camera, for that matter). Anyway, for you experimental types, here is one way to get into 3D with the P500.

First, you need to take two pictures of the same scene from two different positions, separated by a short distance. What I did for the image on the next page was set up two tripods next to each other at the same height, about 8 inches (20 cm) apart, with the subject about 8 feet (2.4 m) distant. Then I took two pictures of the dolls, first one from the left tripod, then one from the right. The camera needs to be facing straight ahead each time, not angled in toward the subject.

Next, I used a Windows program called Stereo Photo Maker, which can be downloaded free at http://stereo.jpn.org/eng/stphmkr. From the program's File menu I selected Open Left/Right images. I opened my two JPEG images with this command, which lets you load multiple images at once. Then I went to the Stereo menu and, with both images appearing on the screen, I selected Color Anaglyph, and, on the sub-menu that appeared, Dubois (red/cyan). The program produced the single image shown below, which looks blurry, with red and blue lines characteristic of 3D images you may have seen in comic books or other printed materials. (If you're using a Mac, there are other programs available, though I haven't used them. One possibility is Anabuilder, at http://anabuilder.free. fr. You also can use Photoshop, but you'll need to experiment a bit, or find instructions on the web.)

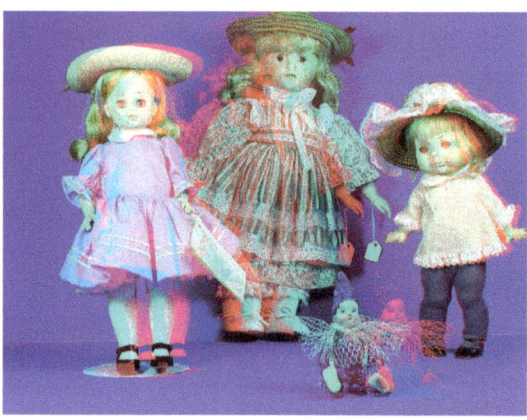

That's all there is to it! If you follow these steps with images that are properly aligned and taken from a good distance apart, the resulting image should be ready for viewing, either on screen or on paper, using old-fashioned red/blue 3D glasses. (The red side goes over the left eye.) If it doesn't pop out as a 3D image when viewed through the glasses, go to the Adjustment menu and try various adjustments, including Auto Alignment, Easy Adjustment, and others, until it looks good. (I had to use those commands to adjust the images that I worked with.)

Connecting to a Television Set

The Coolpix P500 is quite capable when it comes to playing back its still images and videos on an external television set. The camera comes with an audio-video cable as standard equipment. The cable has a mini-USB connector at one end and three composite, or RCA, connectors at the other end. The red and white RCA plugs are for stereophonic audio, left and right; the yellow plug is for composite video.

To connect the cable to the camera, you need to open the little door on the left side of the camera (when held in shooting position) and plug the small (mini-USB) connector into the upper one of the two ports inside the door.

You then need to connect the yellow, red, and white connectors on the other ends of the cable to the composite video and audio inputs of a television set. You may need to set the TV's input selector to Video 1, or AUX, or some other setting so it will switch to the input from the camera.

Once the connections are set and the TV is turned on with the correct input selected, turn on the camera in Playback mode, and you can play back any images or video you have recorded. HD video will play back with no problems on a standard television set.

You can also purchase an optional HDMI cable to connect the camera to a high-definition television set. Nikon apparently does not offer such a cable, but you can use any generic HDMI cable, as long as one end has a mini-HDMI (type C) male connector, and the other end has a standard HDMI male connector, as shown below.

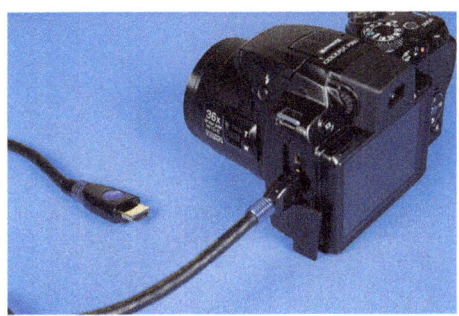

Once you have connected the camera to a TV set, the camera operates very much the same way it does on its own. Of course, depending on the size and quality of the TV set, you will likely get a much larger image, possibly better quality (on an HD set), and certainly better sound for your movies. When the camera is connected to a TV with the standard video cable, it can not only play back recorded images; it can also record.

When it is hooked up to a TV while in recording mode, you can see on the TV screen the live image being seen by the camera. So you can use the camera as a video camera of sorts, and you can use the TV screen as a large monitor to help you compose your photographs. When the camera is connected to an HDTV using an HDMI cable, though, it will only play back images and videos; it will not go into Shooting mode and cannot record.

APPENDIX A: Accessories

When people buy a new camera, especially a fairly expensive model like the Nikon Coolpix P500, they often ask what accessories they should buy to go with it. I will hit the highlights, sticking mostly with discussing items I have experience with.

Cases

There are endless types of camera cases on the market. In selecting a case for my Coolpix P500, I looked at many different types. I came to the realization that, at least for me, there is no single "perfect" case for the P500. The type of case I use with this camera depends on what activity I am involved in, and what my purpose is for carrying the camera at a given time.

Often enough, I don't use a case at all, but just place the camera in my backpack or whatever carrying bag I may have with me. When I'm going on a trip that's specifically oriented to photography, I put the camera into a case that can hold the camera along with some accessories and a few items such as a water bottle and notepad. One case I have used a good deal with the P500 is the Kata model DW-491, pictured here with the P500 in the middle compartment. It can easily hold extra batteries as well as one or two water bottles and other odds and ends.

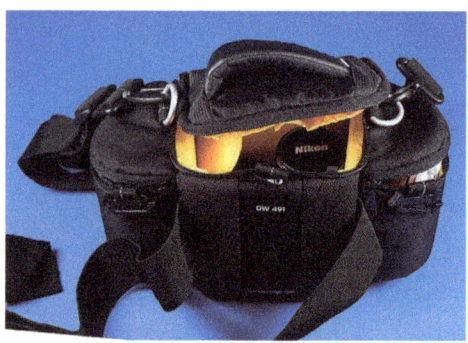

When I need to carry more items or prefer the feel of a pack that slings over my shoulder in a more comfortable way, I often use the larger Lowepro Passport Sling bag, shown below, which can hold the camera, accessories, water, and some snacks as well a guidebook for the day's hike and other items.

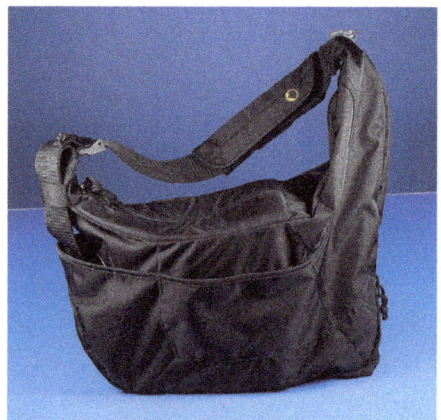

Batteries

Here's one area where you should go shopping either when you get the camera or right afterwards. I use the camera pretty heavily, and I find it runs through batteries very quickly. You can't use disposable batteries, so if you're out taking pictures and the battery dies, you're out of luck unless you have a spare battery (or an AC adapter and a place to plug it in; see below). The model number of the official Nikon battery is EN-EL5. You can get a spare Nikon battery for about $23.00 as I write this. It won't do you a great deal of good by itself, though, because the battery is designed to be charged in the camera, and you can't use the camera while the battery is charging.

There is an easy solution to this problem, though. You can find generic replacement batteries, as well as chargers to charge the batteries outside the camera, very inexpensively on Amazon. com and elsewhere. I purchased a package including two generic batteries and a charger for less than $5.00 on Amazon. com, and I later saw that package advertised for less than $3.00. Both batteries and the charger work fine. With this setup, I can have one battery charging while another is in the camera, and I have a third for backup. In this respect, the Coolpix P500 wins my vote for economy; some other cameras require the use of batteries that cost $50.00 or more.

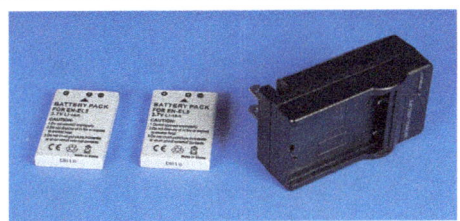

AC Adapter

The other alternative for supplying power to the P500 is the AC adapter kit, Nikon model number EH-62A. There is not too much to say about this accessory. It works well for what it does, in terms of providing a constant source of power to the camera. It consists of three parts: a standard-sized AC cord that you plug into a power brick and into an AC outlet; the fairly large power brick, which is attached to a long cable that is attached to a plastic piece the same size and shape as the camera's battery. You insert that plastic piece into the battery compartment. Before you close the battery compartment door, though, you have to pull down a small rubber flap that covers an opening where the camera's side meets the battery compartment door. You then place the cable from the AC adapter into that opening, so you can close the battery compartment door fully, as shown in the second image below.

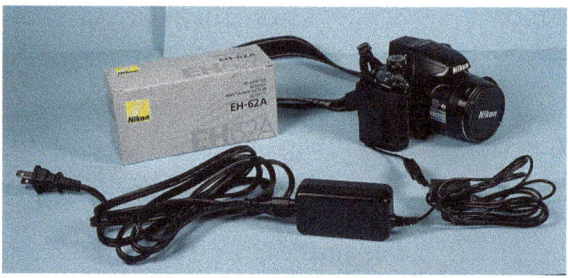

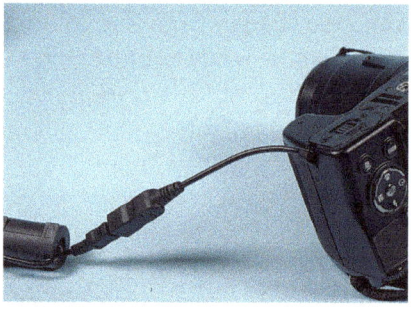

Ptroviding power to the camera is all this adapter does. It is not a charger, either for batteries outside of the camera or for batteries while they are installed in the camera. It is strictly a power source for the camera. It is useful if you are using the interval timer or doing extensive work in a studio or laboratory setting, to eliminate the trouble of constantly charging and replacing batteries. It also could be useful if you are recording many images or movie scenes in a setting where you have access to AC power. However, the AC adapter's cables and power brick are quite bulky, so using the adapter is quite inconvenient. If you don't have a real need for this setup, I recommend you invest in one or more extra batteries, and perhaps even an extra battery charger, so you can always have a couple of batteries ready for action. In short, the AC adapter should not be considered a high-priority purchase for most photographers.

Add-on Filters and Lenses

There is no way to attach a filter or other add-on item, such as a close-up lens, directly to the lens of the Coolpix P500, as you can with DSLRs and other larger cameras, whose lenses are threaded to accept filters and auxiliary lenses. The lens of the P500 is not threaded to accept such attachments, and, even if it were, that system would not work, because the zoom lens extends out from the lens barrel and would immediately bump into any filter as soon as you turned on the camera.

There is at least one solution available, though it is far from ideal. To add filters or other lens accessories to the P500, you need to get an adapter. The images below show one such adapter, which I found on eBay, made by a company called Kiwi Foto.

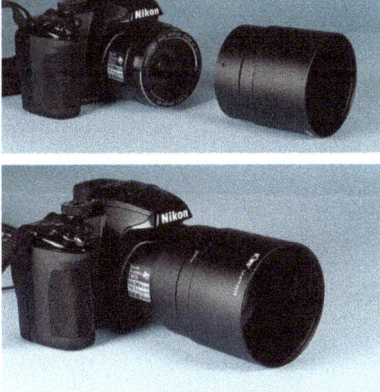

The adapter consists of a sturdy metal tube that fits snugly over the end of the P500's lens housing and is secured by tightening two screws with the included Allen wrench. With this adapter tube in place, you can screw onto its end any filter or other accessory that has a 67mm diameter. For example, as you saw in Chapter 9, I attached a Hoya R72 infrared filter using this system, to take infrared photos with the P500.

As you can see from the photo below, the major flaw of this adapter is that it causes serious vignetting because of the distance between the camera's lens and the filter, when the lens is at a wide-angle setting.

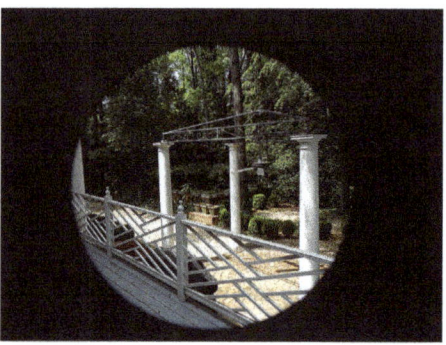

You can cure the vignetting by zooming in somewhat, or by cropping your photos in your editing software.

Just having the ability to attach filters, however, enhances the usefulness of the camera considerably. You can use a neutral density filter when you want to force the camera to use a wide aperture to blur a background, or to use a slow shutter speed to smooth out a waterfall with a long exposure. You can use infrared filters, UV (ultraviolet filters), polarizers, or any of a wide assortment of close-up lenses, as well.

Flash

Clearly, Nikon did not consider the use of external flash units to be a high priority for users of the Coolpix P500, because the camera does not have an accessory flash shoe on top, as many other advanced compact cameras do. It may well be concluded that this camera really does not need a very powerful flash, for a couple of reasons. First, it has a sensor that is capable of taking good pictures in low light, with ISO settings reaching up to 3200 and features like the Best Shot Selector that help you avoid photos that are blurred from camera shake in low light.

Second, even apart from the P500's dim-light shooting abilities, for everyday shots not taken at long distances, the built-in flash should suffice. It works automatically with the camera's light-metering controls to expose the images well, and it is even capable of illuminating bursts of continuous exposures. It is limited by its low power, though. According to Nikon, at the wide-angle focal length, the range of the built-in flash is about 26 feet (8 m), and, at the telephoto setting, about 14 feet (4.5 m), when ISO is set to Auto. This range is not very strong.

So, if you will often use the camera to take photos of groups of people in large spaces, or otherwise need additional power from your flash, you may need to supplement the built-in unit. There are some options for this purpose, though none that are practical for ordinary shooting.

If you will be shooting indoors in a space you can control (in your home studio, for example) you can set up an external flash unit with a separate optical slave trigger, as shown here.

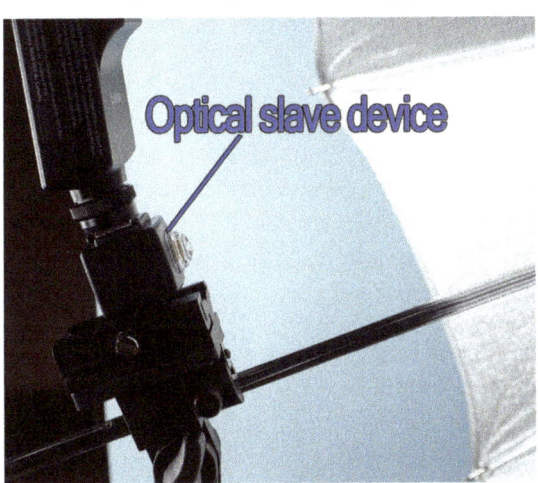

With that system, the external flash is attached to the hot shoe on the optical slave device, and aimed at your subject (or, as in the images on this page and the next, positioned to fire into a flash umbrella, which diffuses the flash out toward your subject).

When you press the shutter button on the P500, its built-in flash triggers the optical slave, which fires the external flash. With this setup, in my experience, you need to use an external flash that has a Manual setting, and leave it on that setting. You then need to set the P500 to Manual exposure mode, and experiment until you find the correct exposure.

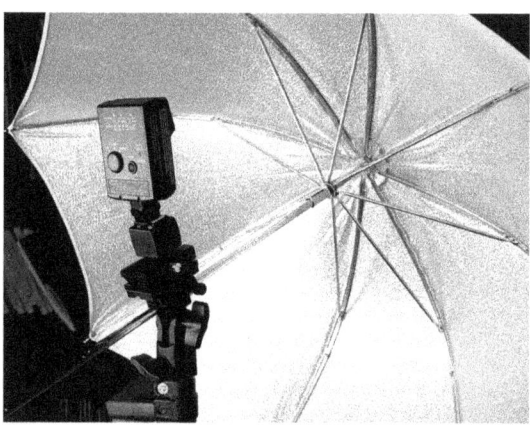

The images above and on the previous page show a setup of this type, using the SYK-3, an inexpensive optical slave unit sold by Cowboystudio, purchased from Amazon.com, attached to a Panasonic DMW-FL220 flash, which has a Manual mode. The flash umbrella is attached to an ordinary light stand using an FU SOB Umbrella Mount Bracket, sold by JJC Photography Equipment Company.

One advantage of using a generic optical slave unit is that you can use many different types and brands of flash unit, provided the unit is compatible with the optical slave and has a Manual mode. (Not all flash units are compatible, so you may want to check with Cowboystudio before deciding what flash to use.)

Also, the Vivitar SF4000 flash is a unit that is reported to have a built-in optical slave capability, and that should also work with the P500. I have not tried this unit myself.

APPENDIX B: Quick Tips

In this section, I'm going to list some tips and facts that might be useful as reminders, especially to those who are new to digital cameras like the Coolpix P500. My goal here is to give you small chunks of information that might help you in certain situations, or that might not be obvious to everyone. I have tried to put down bits of information that might be helpful, but that you might not remember from day to day, especially if you don't use the P500 constantly.

Use continuous shooting. The P500 has great continuous-shooting capabilities, which can help you capture images that other cameras might not manage. I recommend that you consider using continuous shooting as a matter of routine, unless you are running out of storage space or battery power, or have a particular reason not to use it. In the days of film, burst shooting was expensive and inconvenient because you had to keep changing film, and you had to pay for film and processing. With digital cameras like the P500, it just gives you more options. Even with stationary portraits, you may get the perfect fleeting expression on your subject's face with the fourth or fifth shot. So, press the continuous-shooting button on top of the camera, scroll down the list of options, and turn one of them on. (Remember that continuous shooting is not available in the Auto shooting mode, in most of the Scene modes, or in some other situations, such as when the flash is used.)

Take advantage of the User Setting mode. Use this feature to store your most important group of settings. For example, right now I have the U slot set up for my latest settings for street photography: Shooting mode = Program; Image Quality = Fine; Image Size = 4000 x 3000; White Balance = Daylight; Optimize Image = Black-and-White Standard; ISO = 800; Continuous shooting = Continuous H; Sound Settings = Button Sound and Shutter Sound off.

Use macro shooting for subjects other than nature. Many photographers create beautiful images using the macro capabilities of the P500, shooting insects, flowers, and other natural items. But, with its focusing down to 0.4 inch (1 cm), its super wide-angle lens, and its low-light performance, the P500 can serve you in many other ways with its macro shooting. If you need a quick copy of a shopping list, memo, driving directions, sales receipt, or cancelled check, it might make sense to set the P500's focus mode to macro, maybe boost the ISO to 800 or so, and snap a quick image of it. You also can use the Close-up setting or the Black and White Copy setting from Scene mode. When you get to your destination, you can display the image on the LCD and enlarge it using the zoom lever, then scroll around in the document with the direction buttons. The P500 becomes a portable copy machine, if you want it to.

Play your movies in iTunes, and on iPods, iPhones, and iPads. Because the P500 records its movies in the .mov format, which uses Apple's QuickTime software, the movies are compatible with iTunes. It's very easy to play these movies on your computer if you have downloaded Apple's free iTunes software. Just open a window on your computer to display the icon for a movie file (Windows Explorer or Macintosh Finder), open iTunes on the same computer, and drag the .mov file from the Explorer or Finder window to the panel for the Library in iTunes. You can then play the movie from iTunes. If you want to play it on an iPod, iPhone, or iPad, you will need to take one more step: Select the video in iTunes, then select Advanced from the iTunes menu, and, from that menu item, choose Create iPod or iPhone version, or iPad or AppleTV version, as appropriate. Then you can sync iTunes with your device, and the movie will play very nicely on that device.

Explore the P500's creative potential. The Coolpix P500 has several advanced features that give you the ability to explore experimental photographic techniques. Here are a few suggestions: Use Manual exposure mode with its shutter speeds as long as 8 seconds to take night-time shots with trails of lights from automobiles, storefronts, and other sources. Use the shutter speeds as fast as 1/1500 second to freeze moving motorcycles, track runners, and other speedy subjects in mid-motion. Try "camera tossing," in which you toss the camera in the air, set to a multi-second shutter speed, to capture trails of light and color as the camera spins around. (But be sure to catch it on the way down!) Try zooming in or out during a multi-second exposure. Use long exposures (on a tripod) to turn night into day.

Adjust the camera's color settings. The Coolpix P500 has several settings that let you make color-related adjustments: Optimize Image, White Balance, and the Food setting for the Scene mode, which lets you adjust a hue slider. Try different values for these settings until you find color and monochrome adjustments that convey what you would like to express with your images. With White Balance, you can achieve unusual effects by purposely setting a custom white balance while aiming at a colored surface, rather than a white or gray one.

Use a neutral density (ND) filter for some shots. There are some times when you want a slow shutter speed, but, in bright light, you can't achieve it, because the aperture can only go as narrow as f/8 (or somewhat narrower for movies). One solution is to get an adapter (discussed in Appendix A) that permits the use of filters, and use an ND filter to cut down on the light reaching the sensor, resulting in slower shutter speeds. You might want to do this to slow down the rush of a waterfall to a smooth, blended look, or to achieve a motion blur in a shot of a passing runner or walker. Note that you will have to zoom in the lens somewhat to avoid vignetting.

Diffuse your flash or reduce its intensity. If you find the built-in flash produces light that's too harsh for macro or other shots, try using translucent plastic pieces from milk jugs, other food containers, or broken ping-pong balls as homemade flash diffusers. Just hold the plastic up between the flash and the subject. Another approach you can try when using fill-flash outdoors is to use the flash exposure compensation setting to reduce the intensity of the flash by -2/3 EV.

Use the self-timer to avoid camera shake. The Coolpix P500 has a solid self-timer capability that is very easy to use; just press the left direction button and choose your settings. This feature is not just for group portraits; you can use it whenever you'll be using a slow shutter speed and you need to avoid camera shake. It can be useful when you're doing macro photography or using the superzoom lens, also, because those are both very sensitive to camera motion.

Set zone focusing. If you're doing street photography or are in any other situation in which you want to set the camera on manual focus for a specific zone or general distance, here is a quick way to do so. Set the focus switch to autofocus, then aim the camera at a subject that is approximately the distance you want to be able to focus on quickly. Once focus has been confirmed, press the down direction button and then select MF from the focus icons that appear on the screen, to select manual focus. Now you will have locked in the manual focus at your chosen distance, and you're ready to shoot any subject at that distance without the need to re-focus.

Keep your LCD clean. This tip is a bit more mundane than the others, but I find that it helps me to keep the LCD screen as clean and bright as possible. The best way I have found to do this is to try to keep a small micro-fiber cloth within easy reach, in my camera bag or even in a pocket. A few swipes with one of these cloths will restore the shiny surface to its pristine glory.

APPENDIX C: Resources for Further Information

Photography Books

A visit to any large general bookstore or a search on Amazon.com will reveal the vast assortment of books about digital photography that is currently available. Rather than trying to compile a long bibliography, I will list the few books that I consulted while writing this guide.

D. Pogue, Digital Photography: The Missing Manual (O'Reilly Media, Inc., 2009)

C. George, Mastering Digital Flash Photography (Lark Books, 2008)

C. Harnischmacher, Closeup Shooting (Rocky Nook, 2007)

J. Paduano, The Art of Infrared Photography (4th ed., Amherst Media, 1998)

Web Sites

Since web sites come and go and change their addresses, it's impossible to compile a list of sites that discuss the Coolpix P500 that will be accurate far into the future. One way to find the latest sites is to use a good search engine such as Google or Bing and type in "Nikon Coolpix P500." I recently did so in Google and got more than 4 million results.

Another approach can be to go to Amazon.com, search for the product, and read the users' reviews, though you have to be careful to weed out the reviews by people who are disgruntled for reasons that don't have anything to do with the product itself. You can also visit a reputable dealer's site, such as that of B&H Photo Video, and read the users' reviews of the camera there. I will include below a list of some of the sites or links I have found useful, with the caveat that some of them may not be accessible by the time you read this.

Digital Photography Review

http://forums.dpreview.com/forums/forum.asp?forum=1007

This is the current web address for the "Nikon Talk" forum within the dpreview.com site. Dpreview.com is one of the most established and authoritative sites for reviews, discussion forums, technical information, and other resources concerning digital cameras.

Reviews of the Coolpix P500

The links below lead to reviews of the Coolpix P500 by Photographyblog.com, CNET.com, PC World magazine, imagingresource.com, dcresource.com, bhphotovideo.com, and other sites.

http://www.photographyblog.com/reviews/nikon_coolpix_p500_review/

http://reviews.cnet.com/digital-cameras/nikon-coolpix-p500-black/4505-6501_7-34497849.html

http://www.imaging-resource.com/PRODS/CP500/CP500A.HTM

http://www.pcworld.com/article/229981/nikon_coolpix_p500_review_36x_superzoom_has_farreaching_features.html

http://www.dcresource.com/reviews/nikon/coolpix_p500-review

http://www.bhphotovideo.com/indepth/photography/hands-reviews/hands-review-nikon-coolpix-p500

http://www.pcmag.com/article2/0,2817,2383757,00.asp

http://www.digitalcamerareview.com/default.asp?newsID=47
16&review=nikon+coolpix+p500

http://www.ephotozine.com/article/nikon-coolpix-p500-digi-
tal-camera-review-15993

http://review.techworld.com/compact-cameras/3286429/
nikon-coolpix-p500-review/

http://www.whatdigitalcamera.com/equipment/reviews/com-
pactcameras/129083/1/nikon-coolpix-p500-review.html

http://www.expertreviews.co.uk/digital-cameras/1283851/
nikon-coolpix-p500

The Official Nikon Site

The United States arm of the Nikon company provides resources on its web site, including the downloadable version
of the user's manual for the Coolpix P500 and other technical
information.

http://www.nikonusa.com/Nikon-Products/Product/Com-
pact-Digital-Cameras/26256/COOLPIX-P500.html

Flickr Discussion Group

This site hosts a discussion forum about the Coolpix P500;
there also are photos taken by the camera posted in other parts
of the site.

http://www.flickr.com/groups/1625845@N24/

Infrared Photography

This site provides some helpful information about infrared
photography with digital cameras.

http://www.wrotniak.net/photo/infrared/

Index

F

W

Z

www.ingramcontent.com/pod-product-compliance
Lightning Source LLC
Chambersburg PA
CBHW040951170526
45159CB00013B/3101